# THE FIRST DISSIDENT

# THE FIRST DISSIDENT

## THE BOOK OF JOB
## IN TODAY'S POLITICS

# WILLIAM
# SAFIRE

RANDOM HOUSE

NEW YORK

Grateful acknowledgment is made to the following for permission to reprint
previously published material: HENRY HOLT AND COMPANY, INC., AND
JONATHAN CAPE LTD: Excerpts from "A Masque of Reason" from *The Poetry
of Robert Frost* edited by Edward Connery Lathem. Copyright 1945 by Robert
Frost. Copyright © 1969 by Holt, Rinehart and Winston. Copyright © 1973
by Lesley Frost Ballantine. Rights throughout the British Commonwealth are
controlled by Jonathan Cape Ltd. Reprinted by permission of Henry Holt and
Company, Inc., and Jonathan Cape Ltd. OXFORD UNIVERSITY PRESS: The Book
of Job in its entirety from *The New English Bible.* Copyright © 1961, 1970,
1989 by the Delegates of Oxford University Press and the Syndics of the
Cambridge University Press. Reprinted by permission of Oxford University
Press.

Library of Congress Cataloging-in-Publication Data
Safire, William
The first dissident : the book of Job in today's politics /
William Safire.
p. cm.
ISBN 0-679-41755-9
1. Bible. O.T. Job—Criticism, interpretation, etc.
2. Dissenters. 3. Political participation. I. Title.
BS1415.2.S18 1992
223'.106—dc20       92-50167

Manufactured in the United States of America on acid-free paper
using partially recycled fibers
24689753
First Edition

*Designed by Oksana Kushnir*

*To Mulla Mustapha al-Barzani*

# CONTENTS

# BLAKE'S ILLUSTRATIONS

WILLIAM BLAKE, the mystic poet, artist, printer, and engraver, created a set of twenty-one watercolors illustrating the Book of Job in 1820. Five years later, he reproduced these as engravings, adding detail and commentary.

Blake's engravings are more interpretations than illustrations of the biblical book. "Not a line is drawn without intention", he cautioned, inviting the reader into his world of symbols. In the artist's conception, the story is played out inside Job's mind. The sufferer's affliction is not physical, but a disease of his own soul; the pain humbling his pride is not punishment for sin but a stimulus to reject tradition and assert his individual spirit.

Sixteen of Blake's engravings are printed in two sections herein, slightly reduced in scale; illustrations 9, 18, and 19 are left out. Two of the most symbolically complex and artistically striking appear as endpapers; these are 14, the divine imagination at the creation of the universe when "all the Sons of God shouted for joy", and 15, the depiction of the monster Behemoth and serpent Leviathan, icons of disorder.

# INTRODUCTION:
# THE JOB OF THE BIBLE AND
# THE NEWS OF THE DAY

WHEN JOHN F. KENNEDY was asked in a 1962 news conference about army reservists demonstrating over the unfairness of being recalled to active duty, he offered a philosophical aside: "There is always inequity in life. Some men are killed in a war and some men are wounded, and some men never leave the country." The President then jarred many of his constituents by putting forward a painfully realistic judgment: "Life is unfair."

That reminded me of Job, one of the most towering figures of the Bible, daring to question God's fairness: "Why do the wicked enjoy long life, hale in old age, and great and powerful?"[1]

Again, in 1990, I was reminded of Job when a Kurdish friend smuggled out of Iraq a film showing Saddam Hussein's poison gas attack on the village of Halabja two years before. On the film, a Kurdish man, his eyes glaring in anguished accusation, was carrying a corpse toward the camera, the body of his dead child. That brought to mind Job, who angrily accused God of moral unconcern: "When a sudden flood brings death, he mocks the plight of the innocent. The land is given over to the power of the wicked . . ."[2]

Another example: China's paramount leader, Deng Xiaoping,

pointed out how indifferent the world was to the long ordeal of Wei Jingsheng, China's leading pleader for political freedom. Deng boasted: "We put Wei Jingsheng behind bars, didn't we? Did that damage China's reputation?" A decade before the massacre at Tiananmen Square, the isolated dissenter Wei was apparently forgotten by many around the world who claimed to share his cause at Democracy Wall. His dissident voice, though suppressed, was echoed in Job's despair at having been abandoned by the power he believed in: "I call for thy help, but thou dost not answer; I stand up to plead, but thou sittest aloof . . ."[3]

I began collecting books about Job as a Syracuse University sophomore (just before I dropped out). Over the years I have been struck by Job's influence in art, literature, and especially in politics. I see Job's ancient challenge to the highest authority as a political metaphor for the modern dissident's principled resistance to authoritarian rule, as well as for his refusal to accept abuses of democratic power. That's a political subject; this is a political book.

And I'm a political person. Although I was attracted to (and will grapple with) the moral theme in the Book of Job because it is the specific fight being fought, my underlying interest is in what Job has to teach us about confronting an adversary in the arena. When Job takes issue with God's injustice, the disputants debate and resolve the issue in a play of power.

Job reaches across the millennia to express modern Man's outrage at today's inequities. The Book of Job's tone is not a weary resignation to life's unfairness. Rather, it is a sustained note of defiance. The book's message is not that we should accept the dictates of Fate, but rather that we should object to Authority's injustice or unconcern, and assert our morality as best we can.

The Book of Job is, in short, a daring manifesto. Revolutionary ideas always upset people: Ancients were troubled by its thesis that suffering is no proof of sin, just as moderns are discomfited by its corollary, that victory is no proof of virtue. Challenging religion on moral grounds was shocking to established authority because it dared assert that tradition may not be rightly expressing God's design; in the same way, challenging authoritarian political leadership today on human-rights grounds is troubling to some powers that be because the challenge itself strikes at the basis of the regime's legitimacy.

My book is about that kind of dissidence, the kind of challenge to Authority exemplified by Job. Driving it is the innate need for the individual to confront and resist the unfair reality of happenstance, and to submit only to the dictates of conscience. That is the dissidence that leads to dignity, and is a force that has transformed our world.

Just as the articulate dissidence of a man like Andrei Sakharov helped to bring down the Soviet tyranny; just as the silent witness of Wei Jingsheng will one day lead to the political redemption of a billion Chinese; so the biblical Job's refusal to resign himself to the seeming caprice of Fate forced God out of hiding and called him to account for moral mismanagement of the universe.

In our time, the triumph of the political dissident has led to an explosion of freedom, reaching to almost half the population of the world. I will argue that in ancient times, the obligation of Man to hold even the highest authority accountable for injustice was first set forth in the most controversial, irreverent, and daringly subversive pages of the Bible—the Book of Job. In those pages can be found the blueprint for modern dissidence.

Studying the play of power is a political writer's preserve. Analyzing the use of irony, rhetoric, and arcane wordplay to destroy an opposing argument is a language maven's dish of tea. Examining the use and abuse of power—after having danced around it for a lifetime—is just my meat. In sum, the Book of Job, along with the language of the times and the news of the day, offers the enthusiasms that have informed my life.

As a speechwriter associated with Richard Nixon from 1959 to 1973—through most of his soaring ups and plunging downs—I took some instruction in a modern political variation on Job's shuttle between dungheap and pinnacle. Postgraduate White House studies in the use and abuse of power followed. Shortly thereafter, in my first novel, I took the name of one of Job's blowhard visitors and gave it to a character who is a pompous political columnist, "Sam Zophar". Still later, when I was researching *Freedom*, an historical novel about Abraham Lincoln's central mission in the Civil War—and how that mission changed from preserving the

Union to emancipating the slaves—I was struck by how similar a fragment of President Lincoln's writing was to an out-of-place meditation in the Book of Job.

For the past couple of decades, as an op-ed page *New York Times* columnist, I have been drawn to the dissent of the refusenik and the suffering of the abusenik. Because I am a contrarian by inclination and a libertarian conservative by political choice, I delight in the dissection of hypocrisy. Frankly, a book about the play of political power in Job was something I had to get out of my system. This puzzling and infuriating biblical character has haunted my life.

Never has a book received such blurbs:

> "There is nothing written, I think, in the Bible or out of it, of equal literary merit." —THOMAS CARLYLE

> "The greatest poem of ancient and modern times."
> —ALFRED LORD TENNYSON

> "If you want a story of your own soul, it is perfectly done in the book of Job—much better than in [Dostoyevsky's] *Letters from the Underground.*" —D. H. LAWRENCE

> "The most tragic, sublime and beautiful expression of loneliness which I have ever read is the Book of Job."
> —THOMAS WOLFE

An American political imprimatur comes from the Union's Daniel Webster, one and inseparable: "The most wonderful poem of any age and language."

The beauty of the book's form is emphasized, not the cogency of its message. "Nowhere in the world has the passion of anguish found such expression," Søren Kierkegaard, father of existentialism, has a character say. "In the whole Old Testament there is no other figure one approaches with so much human confidence and boldness and trust as Job, simply because he is so human in every way."

This part of the Holy Scriptures is almost always called a poem. Not an epic story ("outdoes *Beowulf*!") or a drama ("tops Sophocles at his bloodiest!") or an extended parable ("presages the Gospels!"), all of which it is and does; nor is the Book of Job labeled a history, which part of it may also be; and especially not a masterpiece of controversy, a quality that does not always sell in what H. L. Mencken derided as the Bible Belt. Calling it a poem is safe; we allow poets imaginative leeway that we deny to prophets, philosophers, and even storytellers. Because poets cloak their most outrageous statements in amusing tropes or obscure images, they are rarely held fully responsible for their messages; on the contrary, they hold a license for obscurity and are notorious for double meanings.

In this book, I will explore the poetry, and prose, in the Book of Job, written by the most courageous poetic genius of his time, in order to show how leaders and free people can learn from Job about effective dissent.

I begin by rejecting the view of Job as a man who was rewarded for patient suffering. That is directly counter to the point of the poet. One of my main points will be to demonstrate how the author of Job reveals something crucial about the play of power between master and subject, the interchange and constant tension that we call politics. And I will suggest how the political guidance in a book written two and a half millennia ago can have direct bearing on the way we express dissent, as well as the way we govern ourselves, today.

The moral excitement in the Book of Job is the sufferer's outrage at God's refusal to do justice. It centers on a search for the roots of unfairness in the real world, despite the promises elsewhere in the Bible of God's punishment to the evildoer and reward to the good. Even the most devout believers have asked themselves: If life is unfair; if the good often die young and the wicked prosper; if Man cannot depend on God for a fair shake in the end—then what is the purpose of ethical behavior, of faith, of worship? The author of the book (identity unknown, called poet-Job to distinguish him from his character) broke with the pious illusion of divine retribution and came to grips with the mysterious disorder of real life. He tried to answer the hardest question: How do believers cope with the fickleness of Fate?

All of us deal with that unfairness issue at all levels and throughout our lives. Every parent is familiar with the acute sense of fairness in the minds of children, especially those with older siblings: My daughter, at age four, used to drive us up the wall—for example, on the subject of comparative bedtimes—with the repeated challenge "That's unfair!" (I taught Annabel to say "that's inequitable", an offbeat locution which, coming from a child, puzzled her playmates but made her complaining more tolerable at home.) Later in life, the perception of unfairness leads to deeper questioning: When the system does not produce promised results, where do you go to complain? Who's accountable for moral mismanagement? When God appears to be uninterested in mankind or to be loafing on the job of moral law enforcement, can there be such a thing as devout defiance?

Those questions reveal a second theme in the Book of Job, less frequently explored. It is the struggle for power between master and subject; the tempestuous relationship between a distant, almighty God and his puny, ignorant, but probing and demanding creation, Man.

This political theme—the conflict between a governing God and governed Man, between responsible lord and consenting or dissenting vassal—is the genesis of much modern interest in Job.

We are fascinated with Job because, now more than ever, we admire stand-up guys. People today are attracted to heroes who get into trouble by defying the powers that be. We identify with the gutsy little guy defying distant Authority, shaking a fist at Establishment fiats, getting on the case of ukases, and demanding a hearing or even a share of Authority's power. Drawn to the principle of orderly dissent, we root for the underdog.

When individual dissenters or underdogs are so mangy that they turn us off, we join Voltaire and stand up for the principle of dissent. Upholding the right to be wrong by supporting a dislikable candidate is called "casting a clothespin vote", as if holding the nose with a clothespin (a locution that is dying in the era of automatic dryers). For many of us, that contrarian highmindedness mixes with an admiring underdoggery to concoct a value that protects dissent.

In politics, the exploitation of this natural resentment at being bossed around by distant bigshots and domineering fatcats is called populism. In religion, the mild form of this human inclination is called irreverence, the outrageous form blasphemy, the systematic form heresy.

The Book of Job delights the irreverent, satisfies the blasphemous, and offers at least some comfort to the heretical.

Meek acceptance of the presence of wrong in the real world is not the style of the original dissident. To win a bet with the Satan about the unselfishness of believers, the deity puts his servant Job—certifiably "blameless and upright"—through the worst agonies imaginable.

How does Job react? With an explosion of blasphemy: "Damn the day that I was born!"[4] (Some translations soften that to "Perish the day", but the ancient letters stand for either "damn" or "bless", and in context this verb is surely not "bless".) This keening curse shocks his friends, wears out his wife, shakes the portals of heaven, and allows poet-Job to presume to write the Bible's longest and most profound speech attributed directly to God.

Not content with denouncing God's injustice, the man from Uz goes on to criticize divine management of the universe and even predicts accurately that God will be a bully if and when confronted. Best of all, we are assured that Job's display of disaffection has the stamp of canonical approval, because the complaining is all right there in the Bible, respectable as could be. He creates a fellowship of the infuriated, a congregation of the cantankerous (not to mention an assembly of the alliterative).

The Book of Job is more than an early expression of anguish in beautiful literary form. It is a provocative, even inflammatory body of radical writing produced by a mind determined to change his world; that is why, even today, it is the only biblical book held in reverence like a hot potato. The fact that it was written approximately twenty-five hundred years ago suggests that the complexity of the human mind has not increased much in the five millennia since the early Sumerians invented writing. If proof is needed that understanding has been plodding along while knowledge has exploded, the Book of Job stands as that proof.

But what about "the patience of Job"? That misleading phrase cannot be fairly applied to the Job portrayed in the Book of Job. "Ye have heard of the patience of Job," wrote Jesus' Apostle James, "and you have seen the end of the Lord, how the Lord is very pitiful and of tender mercy" (5:11). That was in the King James Version of 1611, but anyone who reads the book today, especially in modern translations truer to the original text, knows that "end" is better expressed as "purpose", and "patient" is hardly the word to associate with Job's denunciation of God's injustice.

In fairness to the Apostle James, we should note that all translators agree he wrote in the New Testament that we have "heard of" the patience of Job; this may refer to the oral tradition's ancient hero, a legendary or mythic figure who predated by a thousand years the character re-created by the mysterious poet who wrote this book. The apostle of the recently crucified Jesus may have interpreted the Bible's Job as the patient sufferer of antiquity for a necessary evangelical purpose: to show early Christians, anguished by the crucifixion of Jesus, that this ancient Gentile had been chosen by God to enable humans to endure a loss even as great as that of a messiah. A familiar example of undismayed steadfastness was needed by the faithful, and the legendary Job—not the biblical Job—met that need.

Whatever the purpose of James's reading of Job as piously resigned under great provocation, this selection of a word most widely translated as "patience" stuck—and helped to change the meaning of the Book of Job, in the minds of millions, for millennia afterward.

But the uncomplainingly enduring Job of the "heard-of" legend is not the combative, dissident Job who damns the day he was born in the Old Testament. In the hoary tale, this legendary proto-Job persevered through God's painful test with no objection, and was rewarded handsomely in the end. The simple point of the original story was that unwavering faith in God's justice paid off.

This may have been the Job whom the prophet Ezekiel grouped with two others, an early Dan'l and Noah, as a trio of men who were able to save themselves from destruction by their rare righteousness.[5] In the Bible's Book of Job, however—despite what some think is an incongruous, tacked-on happy ending—the point of the poet was a far cry from any material reward for patience.

Adding to the confusion between the legendary Job and the character in the Bible is our mental picture of Job. In our mind's eye, we see a patriarch wearing a long beard and a beatific expression. William Blake's illustrations to the Book of Job, especially the one numbered thirteenth, have affected how we envision Job: a bearded man standing awestruck before a bearded God who appears out of a whirlwind. On Job's face is a long-suffering look reminiscent of drawings of Hebrew prophets.

Yet that comforting picture in Blake's vision does not portray the man as he is written about in the Bible. That Job is a man in the prime of life, with children too young to be married, and at the peak of his mental and physical powers. And far from being, like Abraham, a patriarch of his people, the wealthy chieftain from the land of Uz wasn't even Jewish.

Nor is the God of this argumentative work merciful or compassionate. On the contrary, at the start he seems all too ready to inflict unjust suffering; toward the end, his voice rings out of the whirlwind environed in wrath—sarcastic, capricious, intimidating. At first reading, the version of God set forth by the author of the Book of Job is one who instills fear and demands worship, but derides understanding, and does not appear to care to elicit love.

The seeming unconcern of God with life's unfairness is a central theological puzzle that was avoided by most early theologians. The author of the Book of Job was a notable exception: poet-Job took on the forbidden subject of divine injustice frontally, by creating a character who can fairly be described as the first dissident.

Poet-Job's sustained boldness in challenging God's injustice and isolation must have been a terrible burden to the reverent compilers and blue-quilled redactors of the early versions of the Bible. They found his blasphemy too shocking to transmit in the raw; as a result, poet-Job was edited to remove irreverence. His editors may have tacked on the upbeat epilogue to contradict the main political point of the book: that God could be contradicted, argued with, and even summoned to account for his actions by mistreated Man. Scribes down the centuries mistranslated him to tone down his borderline heresy. The textual "helpers" of poet-Job sensed, perhaps, that the obvious blasphemy would be quoted out of context by opponents of their religion, and that the Joban rebellion early in the book would be exalted over what they believed to be the main point of the work: its final message of acceptance and reconciliation.

Despite their tampering with the text, and despite all the softening interpretations, it was to the credit of early sages that they found a place in the canon for poet-Job's troublesome point of view. It could not have been easy: The inclusion in the Holy Scriptures of the work by a daring dissenter must have involved some fierce negotiation among the guardians of religion, many of whom must have bitterly resented poet-Job's attack on the misguided orthodoxy of the time. Perhaps a crisis in the faith caused a new open-mindedness; at any rate, such acceptance of radical realism by the early religious leaders, later called rabbis, prevented the ossification of what today's politicians like to call the Judeo-Christian tradition.

A religion need not provide all the answers to satisfy its followers—that's where blind faith sees the way—but it cannot ignore the questions that grow out of its members' life experience without risking wholesale defections. Modern political platform-writers face the same pressure; that's why we see such debate about controversial planks in party platforms, as institutions painfully adjust to changing voter demands while television pundits dismiss it all as unworthy of airtime.

In secular politics, the adage is "The candidate who takes the credit for the rain gets the blame for the drought." In spiritual politics, after thanking God for our blessings, whom do we blame for inequity? Whose job is it, anyway, to straighten out the world?

To those interested in both worlds of governance, the secular and the spiritual, the Book of Job teaches the body politic how one upright human being can challenge any authority's abuse of power; it teaches the spiritual in us how unsuppressed dissent can strengthen the relationship between God and Man.

Take, for instance, the example of the Russian refusenik Anatoly Shcharansky. He was offered his release in return for a confession and the names of other Jews crusading for freedom.

At his trial, Shcharansky denounced this offer in a ringing speech to reporters in the courtroom. Then, when one of his Communist inquisitors asked, "What do you have to say to this tribunal?" he expressed his scorn to his judges in these words: "To you I have nothing to say." Such contempt for concession to falsity echoed, for me, Job's answer to pious friends trying to get him to submit to the apparent will of the Almighty by confessing to sins he had not committed: "I swear by God, who has denied me justice . . . I will not abandon my claim to innocence. I will maintain the rightness of my cause, I will never give up."[6]

A bureaucracy, a book of the Bible, and a political constitution have this in common: They not only are what they started out to be, but are what succeeding generations have made them to be. Everyone who writes about the mysterious character named Job adds his barnacle to the hull: My interest is in the symbiosis of master and subject, the needs and limitations of Authority, the balance of power plays, the special interest of this age in the rights and obligations of a dissenter.

Political scientists have begun to apply their discipline to the Bible; one example, from 1984, is Aaron Wildavsky's "Moses As a Political Leader". The judgments herein are based on my life in the trenches of profitable contrarianism, and a lifelong interest in the challenge to power, by one whose journalistic motto has been "Kick 'em when they're up."

I believe the only power that endures is the kind that takes its chances. That's what poet-Job requires his powerful God to do, and he proceeds to level the power-playing field by making it dramatically possible for God to lose his bet with Satan.

I believe that poet-Job's message to modern activists is that the defiance of Job was divinely induced to lead him to a newly enlightened devotion. I will argue that in the exercise of any kind of power, the best way to create a constituency of the devout is to stimulate the creativity of the defiant.

This is neither a how-to book about enduring inexplicable suffering nor a guide to good grief. It deals primarily with the *politics* of Job—the struggle for the right balance to be struck between creator and created, and, by extension, between political authority and consenting public. But before there can be a power struggle, each side has to have enough power to make the contest interesting. As the title of Vinette Carroll's play put it, *Your Arm's Too Short to Box with God.* What can puny Man do to get any footing for a conflict with his creator? How can one human being use the power given him to challenge the power of the all-powerful?

The lone individual has two weapons. One is the power to withhold his allegiance, and allegiance is something that people in power cannot long do without. Right from the roots of our civilization, then, from one of our civilization's first books, came this message: Power flows from the bottom up.

The source of all authority—whether the spiritual power of God or the temporal power of kings and modern rulers—ultimately resides in the individual person's willingness to convey fidelity. When a subject feels oppressed or unfairly treated or poorly defended by a higher power, that subject has the power to challenge even the God who gave him life by suspending worship.

The second power granted to humanity—a shield given to Job to protect him from even the most omnipotent adversary—is moral authority. Job gets that in Genesis, when God is about to demolish Sodom and Gomorrah because of the alternative life-style of most of its residents. Abraham intercedes, saying, "Wilt thou really sweep away good and bad together? . . . Shall not the judge of all the earth do what is just?"[7] The Lord goes along with sparing Lot and his family, thereby entrapping himself into Man's expectation of God's doing what is just—and submitting to a moral authority of Man's own making.

That was the beginning of what we now call power-sharing. It set up in the mind of Man the firm anticipation of divine justice. He came to see this as an entitlement; in his eyes, the moral authority vested in him could not be ignored by the highest authority. Humanity thus assumed the right to subject God to moral discipline; the original power imbalance righted itself; and the possibility of a real political contest emerged.

The evolving confrontation between God and Man in the Book of Job—as each strong nature tests the integrity, the persuasive power, and, finally, the endurance of the other—can be usefully looked at as the prime example of such a mutual testing of power. Consider the book in a nutshell: At the start, the almost-Almighty lets himself be goaded by the Satan into proving the selflessness of human worship. Then, in an extended legal metaphor, humanity challenges Authority on the rational ground of simple justice. In a tumultuous nonresponse, Authority reacts in its voice from the whirlwind, revealing a hint of truth while repressing dissent. Finally, the challenger—letting down the side of Man—sheepishly expresses satisfaction with Authority's puzzling nonresponse, and in so accepting, Job loses the power struggle.

Or does he? Perhaps the silenced subject can claim a victory of sorts in forcing Authority to reveal itself—even though Authority then bombastically refused to account for its governance.

Poet-Job is teaching us something both supportive and subversive about the ruling and the ruled. These are a few of the questions raised in Job that I will deal with in this book:

Does Man have a right to challenge God, and thus a divinely inspired right to confront any authority? Or should Man accept spiritual authority when it is revealed in all its majesty?

To what extent does any political authority need challenge from below to exercise, strengthen, and legitimate its powers? Is it weakened by tolerating a subject's presumption?

Does right make might, as Job insisted, or—to put the issue in bumper-sticker terms—does Almightiness make Alrightiness?

Heroic questions, worth the trouble of loin-girding. But this is a book about politics; to bring that power struggle down to earth, where humanity is creator and government its creation, we will deal with the rules of Joban resistance as they apply to dissidents today:

How much help can a citizen demand from his government when he opposes his government? Can moral outrage compete successfully with absolute power? Does Job's example of defiance and ultimate acceptance under fire teach us anything useful about how to take heat from secular power centers?

In the depths of his despair, Job's friends let him down; how much loyalty can a politician in hot water legitimately demand from his friends?

A familiar cop-out for a politician caught belonging to a restricted club is "I'm working from within." Should dissidents in any field associate themselves with a system containing unfairness in return for a look inside the workings of power, to see those grand designs with their own eyes?

"If only there were one to arbitrate between man and God,"

muses Job.[8] Does a dissenter need a lobbyist, ombudsman, or redeemer to intercede in an argument with Authority?

My plan is to (1) review the baffling story of Job, with a running punditorial; (2) examine why we get a sinking feeling at the way Job caves in at the end; and (3) look at the Book of Job's birth, growth, suppression, and release. Then (4) to consider the spiritual lessons drawn by students of Job, leading to a look at the way such literary geniuses as William Blake and Herman Melville have used him. Finally, to examine the lessons Job has for (5) today's leaders and (6) today's readers and voters, especially those defiantly devoted to the idea that all Authority can and should be held accountable.

Now, an aside about style:

No biblical text is as vexing as the language of the Book of Job. For two and a half millennia, give or take a few centuries, translators and texcavators have been breaking their heads over what they call hapax legomena—words that occur once only, which makes their meaning especially hard to figure out. More rare or unique words are used in Job than in any other book of the Bible; on top of that, puns and wordplay trip the unwary, and emendations by pious early editors and censorious scribes made murky what had been the poet's intent to show outright rebellion.

The text of the Book of Job used here, unless otherwise specified, is the New English Bible, published in 1970 by Oxford University Press and Cambridge University Press. This is usually truer to the original than the sonorous, deliciously archaic 1611 King James Version, but when the KJV has greater impact and is as accurate, I'll use it: "Does Job fear God for nought?" is a more memorable translation of the Satan's sly question than "Has not Job good reason to be God-fearing?"[9]

For the convenience of the reader who is not in a hotel room with Gideon Bible handy, the entire Book of Job—only about twelve thousand words—can be found in the back of this book. Whenever the Bible is quoted in my prose, an unobtrusive number appears after the quotation, which directs the reader to notes in the back citing chapter and verse, which can then be examined in context. Because translators sometimes disagree about the sequence of lines in Job, not every citation will match up; when the 1611 King James verse conflicts with the modern translation, I go with the NEB.

The noun *dissident,* based on the Latin "to disagree", is used here as synonymous with *dissenter,* from the Latin for "to think apart", though the modern connotation of a dissenter is "one who expresses disagreement in writing; a thoughtful withholder of approval". *Dissident,* from "to sit apart", has a different connotation: "one who demonstrates his disagreement by action; a damned troublemaker". They are used interchangeably here because my premise is that thoughtful troublemaking is good, and I need more than one word to describe the book's hero. *Heretic* is too specific, *agitator* too shallow, *malcontent* not thoughtful enough; *iconoclast,* rooted in the Greek "breaker of images", is in the ballpark.

Some readers will wince at my stick-in-the-mud acceptance of the word *Man* as a synecdoche for *mankind.* I have often been put on notice, usually with some acerbity, that *mankind* is being driven out of the language by the sexless *humankind.* Sexism in language is plain rude and should be avoided when possible—*firefighter* is an improvement in several ways over *fireman*—but straining mightily to avoid seeming to favor the male is an insult to everyone's intelligence. Thus, I will choose *person* or *human being* instead of *man* when writing of an individual who may be either male or female, because that is more precisely imprecise; and as a sop to sensitivity, I will choose *humanity* over *mankind* at times, stopping short of the enforced correctness of *humankind.* However, when dealing with the individual who stands for the species, I will not shy from *Man,* capitalized when standing for every man and every woman. If he were alive today, the poet Milton, who sought to "justify God's ways to men", would probably not resist changing that to "men and women" or "people" (if it scanned); but neither he nor I would strain to avoid the dread M-word in describing Job's posture as "Man challenging God". We're talking in this instance about one individual representative of a species, and "Individual challenging Deity" lacks the necessary zip: Read capitalized *Man* to mean individual challenger who stands as symbol for us all—and whose sex is irrelevant. Thus, when I refer herein to "puny, miserable Man", that includes women. (I'll have a beer on that with the poet

Housman: "And malt does more than Milton can / To justify God's ways to Man.")

The same logic causes me to refer to God as *he*. God has no sex, of course, and it would be just as inaccurate to refer to God as *she;* some modern exegetes do that from time to time, to drive home that point of fairness with a pronoun, just as many judges alternate the use of *he* and *she* in legal opinions. (The genderless *it* substituting for God would verge on metaphoric error, if you accept the satisfying notion that we are made in God's image.) I'll stick with *he* and *him,* partly for consistency's sake and partly because—outdatedly, I know—I think of him as a paternal figure dominating our spiritual lives. (The *dom* in *dominate* is from the Latin for "lord".) Hebrew makes unconscious amends for treating God as "the Father" by assigning feminine gender to the word for God's presence that permeates the here and now, as well as to the word for *wisdom;* as we acquire her—especially in the acceptance of sex equality and difference—we may relax in the use of *him*.

If I use *he,* why not capitalize *His* pronoun? That mark of reverence was undermined in a parenthesis a century ago by the novelist Herman Melville, who wrote to his mentor Nathaniel Hawthorne: "The reason the mass of men fear God, and at bottom dislike Him, is because they rather distrust His heart, and fancy Him all brain like a watch. (You perceive I employ a capital initial in the pronoun referring to the Deity; don't you think there is a slight dash of flunkeyism in the usage?)"

No stylistic flunkeyism is suitable when examining the argument of the character who has turned out to be the world's longest-lived dissident.

What got me started on this book was an episode in an antiquarian bookstore in Washington's Georgetown.

The bookseller had advertised the selling of a collection of the works of William Blake, which drew a fair-sized crowd of lookers as well as a few serious buyers. The highest-priced item was the Pierpont Morgan Library edition of *Blake's Illustrations of the Book of Job.* This set of four volumes of color prints, beautifully reproduced, was out of my price range, but I asked to look at it anyway.

The bookseller plopped a boxed set down on the counter and said bitterly: "The set isn't complete anymore. Couple hours ago, a punk ran in here, grabbed the two books on top, and ran out. I couldn't catch him. The two books he has mean nothing to him, and he won't be able to sell them for much. And I'm left with a broken set, not worth a quarter of what the complete set of *Blake's Illustrations of Job* were worth. Here, take 'em for two hundred bucks—I've lost all I was going to make on this collection. And that little bastard goes scot-free. There's no justice."

The voice was the voice of the bookseller, but the words were the words of Job. Through that bookman's lament, the original dissident seemed to be saying to me: Buy what's left of Blake's prints, write what you can of your book.

Both the bookseller and poet-Job were right: There's no justice on earth guaranteed from on high. But there is a morality that we work out, as best we can, for ourselves and each other. That morality begins with the obligation to hold fast to our integrity—in Job's phrase, "to maintain my ways"—by protesting injustice against all the odds, no matter how distant and remote its source may seem.

# PART 1

### THE BOOK
### AND ITS IMPACT

# 1

## THE STORY OF JOB

"THERE LIVED IN the land of Uz a man of blameless and upright life named Job, who feared God and set his face against wrongdoing."[1]

At the beginning of the book, Job is living the good life, in both senses of that phrase: The powerful chieftain is not only painstakingly pious, but also blessed with ten party-throwing children and he has three thousand camels in his stable. We are told he is "the greatest man in all the East".[2]

Among the angels presenting themselves to God at his heavenly court is the Satan, or the accusing angel. (In many translations, the definite article precedes the word *Satan* in the Old Testament, suggesting a title like Special Prosecutor, or Inspector General, rather than a person's name. He's not the same as the Devil in later biblical references; the linguistic roots of *Satan* include "roaming" and "accusing".)

God asks the Satan where he has been. That's a curious way to begin a biblical book; God is shown to be, or shown pretending to be, not omniscient. Unless God is making idle conversation, which he does nowhere else in this book or in the rest of the Bible, God is admitting ignorance, or feigning it—he does not seem to know one of his angels' recent whereabouts.

The Satan dutifully gives an account of his absence from the celestial court: "Ranging over the earth from end to end."[3] God asks, "Have you considered my servant Job? You will find no one like him on earth, a man of blameless and upright life, who fears God and sets his face against wrongdoing."[4]

By selecting for consideration a man so morally pure and worshipful as to be unlike any other on earth, God seems to be taunting the member of his court whose assignment it is to be skeptical of man's goodness.

Provoked, the Satan sneers, "Has not Job good reason to be God-fearing?" (The King James Version is more memorable: "Does Job fear God for nought?")[5] The Satan implies that God's favorite human has good material reason for his piety—that it has brought him great wealth and respect. Having stated the issue of motive boldly, the Satan proposes a test: "stretch out your hand and touch all that he has, and then he will curse you to your face."[6] (In Edwin Good's recent translation, the Satan says, literally, "If he doesn't curse you to your face—" leaving unsaid but implicit the rest of an oath, which would be "may I be cursed". Such an "oath of clearance" by the swearer would force God's hand, a technique Job later uses to provoke God into doing his duty.)

God, who perhaps stimulated this trial to satisfy his own doubts about the reason for the best man's obedience, takes up the challenge. He makes what amounts to a bet with the accuser: Take everything away from Job and let's see if you're right.

An innocent man is thereby consigned to suffering, and it strikes the modern reader as wrong—the good end of discovery is put before the cruel means of torture. But poet-Job assumes it is not unreasonable for God to wonder if man worships him only for what he can get. It is not an idle bet, not even the "celestial wager" that it has been termed to be for centuries. Neither the folktale nor poet-Job's version suggests that God and the Satan were making book on Man's motives just to pass the time of a long day. For this test of Job's motive to be fair and instructive, Job had to be kept ignorant of the fact that he was being tested.

With God's permission, the Satan then proceeds to cause disasters to rain down on Job. All of Job's ten children are killed; his vast herds of sheep, asses, and camels are stolen or slaughtered; his home is destroyed by a great wind; but "Throughout all this Job did not sin; he did not charge God with unreason."[7]

Then the Satan gets God's permission to go after Job's person, stopping short only of taking the man's life. He afflicts the hapless Job with loathsome sores from the top of his head to the soles of his feet.

Although Job's wife is not shown to be suffering, she too has lost ten children and her comfortable way of life; and she must now care for an outcast and afflicted husband. The strain on her can be inferred from her agonized advice to Job: "Curse God and die!" But her husband, the human ulcer, scratches his body with a broken piece of pottery and resolutely asks, "If we accept good from God, shall we not accept evil?" The chapter concludes in many translations with "In spite of all this Job did not sin with his lips."[8]

Talmudic scholars as well as modern exegetes have taken the last three words to mean that the apparently patient Job might have begun to formulate sinful thoughts about God's justice, in his heart. You have to watch out for those concluding modifiers in Job; when the Satan predicted that Job would curse God "to your face", that might have implied that people were already cursing God behind his back. Is this reading too much into the text? The subtle text of Job invites such minute examination.

Here we have literary irony in its most striking form: The reader knows something that vitally affects the central character in the story, but the character himself has no way of knowing it. The author has told the audience why Job has been egregiously afflicted, but the hero himself is in ignorance; he does not know that he is the one chosen for the great test.

The reader wants to tell the man from Uz: "Hey, it's all right, your suffering only seems unjust, but you are part of a grand design. You are not suffering for no reason, or for some sin you don't know about; instead, you are the subject of the greatest wager ever made on the reason for Man's devotion. It's up to you to show the Satan that Man does not worship God only for power or fame or a big family or the modern equivalent of three thousand camels. Stick with it, Job—by maintaining your faith in God's wisdom, you justify God's faith in the purity of mankind's motives for worshiping him."

This, of course, is the straightforward message that many have found in the book: Take comfort in times of inexplicably unjust pain or senseless stress by seeing it as part of a greater pattern, known to God but not vouchsafed to mortals. The Lord gives, the Lord takes away; our blessings may not be permanent, and it is not for us to ask why. But there is much more to this story and its message.

Job rejects as wickedly foolish his wife's embittered advice to curse God; the Satan appears to be losing his bet. Three eminent Eastern chieftains who are friends of Job, and who have evidently heard from afar of his misfortune, come to console him. As envoys from the world's elite, they sit beside him for a week in silence; the right word for their sympathetic presence is *commiserate,* to share his misery actively. So ends the seemingly simple prose prologue to the book.

Studied closely, this opening tale reveals the poet-Job's view of what Carl Jung, one of the founders of psychiatry, called God's self-doubt, or at least God's apparent need to test the motives of his worshipers. The story is presented in the childlike style of a folktale.

Then poet-Job moves from plain prose to potent poetry. With the switch in style, the nature of the book changes abruptly. It is as if poet-Job drew on the popular legend to hook us with an easy-to-follow two-dimensional opening pageant, and then suddenly wiped the cardboard storybook characters away, to confront us with human beings of different mettle facing a wrenching reality. The prosaic, legendary Job's piety is dissolved by the pain being experienced by the poetic, human Job.

"Damn the day that I was born!"[9] this outraged Job cries out, as much to himself as to the three colleagues who have come to comfort him. ("Perish the day" in the NEB and even "Curse the day" are to me timid translations.) "Why was I not still-born, why did I not die when I came out of the womb?"[10] Longing for the darkness of death, Job dares to derogate God's gift of light and to question God's mercy: "Why should the sufferer be born to see the light? Why is life given to men who find it so bitter?"[11]

This surely goes beyond lamentation to outright blasphemy. For centuries, scribes and translators have softened God's refusal to end unbearable pain with the relief of death by using the passive voice. The device is familiar to modern bureaucrats: "I made a mistake" is fudged to the passive "mistakes were made", which evades direct responsibility. In Job's case, the passive "Why is life given" softens the direct accusation that is the plain meaning of this line: "Why does God keep the sufferer alive?"

In cursing the day of his creation, Job is implicitly cursing his creator—the one who brought the order and the light of day to the chaos of night. Damning God's day damns God. To drive that shocking point home, Job also mocks God's first words in Genesis, "Let there be light," when he says of his own birthday, "May that day turn to darkness."[12]

This unexpected blast gives heart to those readers taking a piece of the Satan's bet: As the accuser predicted, when Job was stripped of his wealth and health, he implicitly cursed God to his face.

Stunned, Eliphaz the Temanite, senior member of the trio of visitors, tries to soothe Job. He casts no blame but rebukes him gently for not accepting his fate. Eliphaz asks rhetorically: Can an innocent man be punished for no reason? Of course not; relying on the doctrine we now call retribution, or distributive justice, Eliphaz argues that we all get what we deserve in the end.

Although he is usually described as representing the orthodox religion of his time, Eliphaz ascribes his view of the world not to the tradition of sages, but to a vision of a spirit that came to him one night: Only God is pure; the rest of his creations, even including the angels, are not, which means that human beings must accept some punishment for their inescapable impurity. Such discipline is said to be good for us: "Happy the man whom God rebukes!"[13] Job must have sinned, not because he was evil but because he was human. "Man is born to trouble,"[14] Eliphaz holds, as surely as sparks fly upward, an ancient version of our not-too-comforting "things are tough all over," or "nobody's perfect"; but it subtly offers Job an escape from his dilemma: If some sin is in every person, then there is justice in the punishment being wreaked on the seemingly blameless man.

Job brushes all this aside: "show me where I have erred."[15] In a speech that makes up in passion for what it lacks in coherence, the sorehead on the dungheap accuses God of attacking him for no good reason. "I have not denied the words of the Holy One,"[16] Job insists, despite his curse. Job turns on Eliphaz as disloyal: "Devotion is due from his friends to one who despairs and loses faith in the Almighty."[17]

Such a stunning demand for loyalty despite loss of faith is worth a second opinion from translator Marvin Pope, who upholds that meaning: "A sick man should have loyalty from his friend, though he forsake fear of Shaddai." Job is insisting that his friends remain loyal even if, as Eliphaz has intimated, Job in his unbearable pain has begun to turn away from fear of, or faith in, Shaddai, the Almighty. Job accuses his friends of treachery for siding with God against him: "Would you hurl yourselves on a friend?"[18]

"Let me have no more injustice,"[19] Job tells them, and he refuses to shut up: "I will not hold my peace; I will speak out in the distress of my mind and complain in the bitterness of my soul."[20]

Bildad the Shuhite, unlike the gentle Eliphaz, shows no pity for Job's pain and denounces his "long-winded ramblings". "Does the Almighty pervert justice?"[21] Of course not: "Your sons sinned against him,"[22] and thus invited destruction. And so a new way out of the bind of the apparent miscarriage of God's justice is proposed: The sins of the sons are to be used as the reason for the father's punishment. The brusque Bildad insists on the promises in the covenant: "God will not spurn the blameless man, nor will he grasp the hand of the wrongdoer."[23] That belief, of course, is the essence of traditional religion; surely no one would argue with that?

"Indeed this I know for the truth, that no man can win his case against God,"[24] replies Job, calming down. But he does not abandon the idea that God has indeed perverted justice in his case.

Then a certain shrewd originality manifests itself. Job comes up with a notion that nobody has ever dared to express, the idea of defying God's judgment by bringing him before a court. He toys with the idea of suing God (a daring notion presaging today's litigious society) but concludes prophetically that the contest would not be fair because God would overwhelm him: "If the appeal is to force, see how strong he is; if to justice, who can compel him to give me a hearing?"[25] This prospect of power triumphing over justice depresses Job, who bitterly accuses God of moral mismanagement: "The land is given over to the power of the wicked."[26] Although the friends are infuriated, the reader knows from the prologue that Job's charge is true: God has given Job's affairs over to the hands of the Satan, who was not in poet-Job's time considered wicked but was surely not seen to be on the side of Man.

Job has hold of a great idea: imposing a judicial discipine on the executive Authority. Given that God has the political power to pervert justice by intimidating the plaintiff, how could a fair trial be ensured? A second original thought pops into his mind: "If only there were one to arbitrate between us and impose his authority on us both."[27] With an attorney or some other interceder or intermediary between the presumptuous mortal and the easily offended God, Job might be able to speak up: "I would then speak without fear of him."[28]

This speculation about arguing with God in court—the indictment theme—is a dramatic augury. (Introduce a gun onstage in the first act, and it will surely go off in the last.) The theme is reprised as the sufferer turns his testing into a testing of God's morality, and again at the end of Job's speeches to his friends, when he calls for an indictment, a specific set of charges, from God—in the King James translation, wishing "that mine adversary had written a book".[29] With this dramatic device, within an extended legal metaphor, poet-Job sets up an explanation for Job's surprising conduct in the story's denouement.

Zophar the Naamathite, the blustering third friend, weighs in: "Should this spate of words not be answered?"[30] He offers no escape hatches, as did Eliphaz with we're-all-impure, or Bildad with your-sons'-sinning-brought-it-on-you. Zophar rebukes Job directly, by charging that Job's punishment is the result of Job's own secret and substantial guilt, which he must be hiding even from himself, and that he is getting off lightly: "Know then that God exacts from you less than your sin deserves."[31]

This accusation that his suffering must be the result of some terrible, hidden sin gets Job's dander up again. He lashes at his friends with sarcasm: "No doubt you are perfect men and absolute wisdom is yours!"[32] God knows everything, does he? Then why does he run the universe so ham-handedly? Look around at all the violence and destruction: "If he holds up the waters, there is drought; if he lets them go, they turn the land upside down."[33]

Drought and flood affect the wicked and the good alike; the divine power that we see exercised with our own eyes, through our own experience, appears to be random, senseless, devoid of moral meaning. In politics, "He makes counsellors behave like idiots and drives judges mad; . . . He leads peoples astray and destroys them . . . and leaves them wandering in a pathless wilderness."[34] In a daring translation of an obscure passage, the New Revised Standard Version offers: "The tents of the robbers are at peace, and those who provoke God are secure, who bring their god in their hands"[35]— that last phrase meaning that "they make power their god."

Poet-Job has now enabled his protagonist to escalate the struggle from a divine test of Job's faith to a human test of God's morality.

Never in the history of gambling has an ante been so upped. The sufferer shows his contempt for friends who are trying to salvage morality out of rank injustice: "I wish you would keep strictly silent. That would be wisdom for you." Then Job, expressing his willingness to die for his dissent, pronounces the most courageous statement made up to that time: "I will put my neck in the noose and take my life in my hands. If he would slay me, I should not hesitate; I should still argue my cause to his face."[36] The Pope translation: "He may slay me, I'll not quaver. I will defend my conduct to his face."

Most of us remember the central part of that ringing assertion from the King James Version as conveying a startlingly different meaning: "Though he slay me, yet will I trust in him." Thousands of sermons have been preached on that serene expression of faith, but the King James text on which the sermons were based was a twisting of Job's meaning—from blasphemy to piety—too severe to be attributed to error. The point of this key line, modern translators agree, is not faith, but courage; not submission, but defiance.

After all, why should Job quaver? What did he have to lose— his life? That's what he wanted to lose, though suicide was not an option. The friends become repetitive and querulous while Job's disputations grow in strength. The visitors—by this time they are neither friends nor consolers—have put forward a doctrine of retribution that is dramatically shown to be merely a long-repeated theory, not rooted in practicality; real life demonstrates God's patent unfairness. Job dares to argue that wisdom is not necessarily found in sages, and that pious fraud is inherently impious.

In the two cycles of argument that ensue, Eliphaz—now thoroughly incensed by Job's personal baiting and evident impiety—clings to the idea of distributive justice—God treats Man as he justly deserves. He claims that Job is being punished for good and moral cause, and that Job's stiff-necked and irreligious attitude obviously proves him to be wicked. The fault is the victim's, the visitors agree; if Job had not done wrong, he would not be a victim.

At one point, Job envisions himself as dead, but instead of being thankful for the final rest he sought earlier, he cries, "O earth, cover not my blood." In ancient cultures, blood spilled cried out for vengeance by a kinsman or vindicator, and Job did not want his blood "covered"—to be dead and buried—until the injustice was somehow undone or avenged. "For look! my witness is in heaven; there is one on high ready to answer for me."[37] (What does Job mean? We don't know if the witness, the redeemer, or the vindicator that the distracted Job had in mind was someone who would contest with God, or, as more reverent interpreters suggest, was God himself or a God having second thoughts.)

Although his pain is personal, Job's brief on inequity is universal: "Why do the wicked enjoy long life,"[38] he demands to know, while "The poor . . . though they work till nightfall, their children go hungry. . . . like wounded men they cry out; but God pays no heed to their prayer."[39]

The bickering about who is the pious fraud winds down; the argument about distributive justice versus divine amorality and aloofness concludes. Job is apparently left with the last word, and—like a defense counsel summing up before a jury—he changes the mood from bitter frustration to sad recollection. He recalls the days "when God was watching over me, when his lamp shone above my head, and by its light I walked through the darkness!"[40] Those were the days of power: "If I went through the gate out of the town to take my seat in the public square . . . men in authority broke off their talk and put their hands to their lips . . . and waited in silence for my opinion."[41] He recollects the respect he was given: "I presided over them, planning their course, like a king encamped with his troops."[42] Those bygone times were days of charity and ethical conduct, too: "I was eyes to the blind and feet to the lame; I was a father to the needy, and I took up the stranger's cause."[43]

(William Blake, the poet-artist whose illustrations illuminate this book, challenged Job's motive in giving to the poor. In Illustration 5, Job is shown sharing his last loaf with a lame beggar, but handing it to him with his left hand. In Blake's code, that meant that the decision to be charitable came from Job's calculating mind, because charity was seen to be correct by society, and did not come from the heart.)

All power and prestige taken away. "But now I am laughed to scorn by men of a younger generation . . . Now I have become the target of their taunts . . . They run wild and savage me."[44] God has become his torturer: "Days of misery stretch out before me. . . . The wolf is now my brother."[45] Such grumbling does no good; rational discourse leads nowhere; hope has been worn out; not even blasphemy brings a response. Job's boils burn his skin, his shattered esteem roils his brain, and his sense of injustice sears his soul.

Where is God when Job needs him most? "I call for thy help, but thou dost not answer."[46] How can the great complainer break through the line of God's visiting spokesmen and send his message directly to the remote creator? How can he force an isolated and indifferent God to react?

The last resort of ancient man was the oath of clearance. This solemn feature of Jewish criminal procedure enabled the accused to clear himself by making an unbreakable contract with God. He swore to accept real punishment if the promise given was not performed, and God, in the oath-taker's mind, was inexorably obligated to mete out that punishment for perjury.

Because the concluding apodosis, or call for punishment, was so fearsome a conclusion to the oath's bargain, ancient Man usually shied away from saying the terrible words aloud. The method to be used by God in his inescapable punishment was left understood, unspoken, in ellipsis. But Job for the most part becomes explicit, nailing God's punishment down to specifics—what God is to do if what the oath-taker says is untrue. Job digs within his despair to produce the most terrible oath sworn in the Bible—forty verses of the most serious swearing in recorded history.

Job swears he has trod the ethical path. Not for him the easy swearing of not having committed monstrous acts; Job specifies under oath how he has lived up to the moral requirements of everyday life. In general, "If my steps have wandered from the way", then let God inflict punishment in this way: "May another eat what I sow, and may my crops be pulled up by the roots!" Another: "If I have raised my hand against the innocent . . . then may my shoulder-blade be torn from my shoulder, my arm be wrenched out of its socket!" If he had not respected the land of his farm or repaid his debts, he demands ruination: "May thistles spring up instead of wheat, and weeds instead of barley!"[47] Adultery? "If my heart has been enticed by a woman . . . may my wife be another man's slave, and may other men enjoy her."[48] Job was denying he had ever even allowed himself to be tempted by a woman, and if this denial were a lie, he was calling on God to cause his wife to be raped and thus forced into what was then considered counteradultery, the most degrading form of retribution known to ancient man.

This oath of clearance put the challenge to God in the most unmistakable terms. If Job were lying about having lived an ethical life; if he had committed any of the violations or sins he had denied—then God was duty-bound by the oaths to carry out the punishments specified. However, if Job was telling the truth, and had indeed lived a blameless and upright life, then God would stand revealed as unjust, unconcerned, and a betrayer of the covenant he had made with Man. Now let God answer with these specific, horrible punishments (which Job knew he did not risk, because he was telling the truth); or let God answer by ending the inexplicable punishment; or let him answer with a direct and personal explanation of why the innocent should suffer while the wicked prosper.

The oath is Job's gauntlet thrown at God's feet, the most irreverent moment in Scripture. Job concludes his speeches with these lines, demanding a written list of charges against him and promising a ringing defense in any fair adjudication:

> *Let me but call a witness in my defence!*
> *Let the Almighty state his case against me!*
> *If my accuser had written out his indictment,*
> *I would not keep silence and remain indoors.*

*No! I would flaunt it on my shoulder*
*and wear it like a crown on my head;*
*I would plead the whole record of my life*
*and present that in court as my defence.*[49]

At this point, all eyes look heavenward for the Lord's answer. God has been told, in essence, to fish or cut bait: either punish Job by pulling his arm from his socket, enslaving his wife, etc., as the man has demanded if guilty in his oath of clearance—or admit him to be innocent and unjustly punished. Job leaves God one other choice: to come forward with some explanation, which the reader already knows but Job and his visitors do not. God is trapped, unable to turn away: If he does not carry out the punishment in the curses, he would tacitly be admitting that Job is in the right. But if he explains the unjust punishment with the truth—that it is a test of Job's motive in worshiping God—then the test would be spoiled. God has no other logical move; Job appears to have checkmated him.

But wait: The earthly prosecution has a last-minute entry.

Three men of power and experience have failed to sway Job with their arguments that if he is being punished, he must have sinned. A young man enters—Elihu the Buzite—with a fresh argument. He is the only speaker with a Jewish name; he may be a later interpolation by a different hand than poet-Job. Usually, Elihu is dismissed as a brash windbag ("windbag" is an epithet that poet-Job frequently uses), and the young man actually boasts that his belly is full of wind that must be expelled. But his scorn at the other visitors' arguments is shocking, because it is a thumb in the eye of tradition, which called for a youth to respect his elders.

Elihu makes an important new point, reshaping the doctrine of retribution: that suffering can be the discipline of the virtuous, not necessarily a punishment for sin. The good man's goodness can be reinforced through suffering, as he is reminded what lies in store for the evildoer. Thus, Elihu finds God faultless without condemning Job. This version of God's justice, however, is unaffected by the actions of human beings; on this theory, God would be under no pressure to answer Job's demand for a hearing.

Elihu is angry with Job for daring to challenge God's justice, and angry with the friends for failing to state God's case convincingly. In this section, the friends are called "men", which can be taken as evidence either that Elihu is not yet a man, or that this part was written by someone else and added to poet-Job's drama.

Ironically, the reader knows that the upstart Elihu happens to be right about Job, who was chosen for this test because he is the most virtuous of all men. The reader will soon see that Elihu was right, too, about the older consolers, because God himself later agrees that their arguments were wrong. The young interloper holds that "God is so great that we cannot know him,"[50] suggesting that God's judgments are "beyond comprehension", introducing the idea that God cannot be held accountable on the basis of the little that people know because "his power is beyond our ken".[51]

Elihu also serves the purpose of unwittingly setting the scene for the theophany—the awesome appearance of the deity. "He charges the thunderbolts with flame and launches them straight at the mark; . . . Listen, listen to the thunder of God's voice and the rumbling of his utterance. Under the vault of heaven he lets it roll . . . as he thunders with the voice of majesty."[52]

Then the young man who assumed the role of God's spokesman because he was sure God was unaccountable, and would never respond to the summons of Man, is thrust aside to make way for the thunderous voice of God.

The Lord, apparently fed up with unending complaints about his misfeasance in office, and probably roused to wrath by the return receipt demanded by the plaintiff's oath of clearance, comes roaring out of a whirlwind to jolt Job with the most intimidating series of sarcastic questions ever posed, beginning with: "Who is this that darkeneth knowledge by words without counsel?" That is a sound bite of the sonorous King James Version; the NEB has it: "Who is this whose ignorant words cloud my design in darkness? . . . Where were you when I laid the earth's foundations? Tell me, if you know . . ."[53]

This is the scathing voice of a blustering God infuriated by Job's presumption. The doggedly questioning human, with his fierce courage and his inescapable oaths, has forced the divine hand; God, not Man, is now on trial and must defend his cosmic management. But God, as Job had feared, blows away the courtroom, resists the plea to explain his purpose in torturing Job. Instead, using lofty poetic images, God flexes his muscles and mocks the man's effrontery by showing the chasm between creator and created: "Have you descended to the springs of the sea or walked in the unfathomable deep? Have the gates of death been revealed to you? Have you ever seen the door-keepers of the place of darkness? Have you comprehended the vast expanse of the world? Come, tell me all this, if you know."[54]

God pointedly does not answer Job's legitimate questions about the suffering of the innocent. Instead, he rages at him, flaying the startled man with sarcasm, trying to frighten him with rhetorical questions that all make the indisputable point that God is God and Job is not. He makes the man look puny, ignorant, meaningless, weaker than the animals—a far cry from the vision presented elsewhere in the Bible of the human being as special, the only being in the universe created in God's image.

Job cannot claim to be surprised. God's raging reaction is exactly what Job had predicted when he expressed the wish for some intermediary who would be a buffer between the accusing man and the insulted deity. We were forewarned by Job's prediction: "If I summoned him to court and he responded, I do not believe that he would listen to my plea."[55] Most modern readers, however, instinctively take the side of the underdog. Here is powerless Man being beaten down by the God who is declaring his omnipotence—a fact never in dispute—and not even mentioning his justice, which is what concerns Man. Perhaps angry at himself for not being able to reveal the celestial wager that was at the root of Job's suffering, God tries to overpower his challenger. But by failing to respond to the charge of not caring if the wicked prosper or the good suffer, God is booming out *nolo contendere*—he is refusing to make a rational defense, to lay out the requested indictment, to reveal his purpose. Instead, he seems to try to scare Job into submission.

Which he does. What is the reaction of our hero? To be decidedly unheroic. "What reply can I give thee, I who carry no weight? I put my finger to my lips."[56] Less than brave, but not cowardly; Job does not admit at this point that he has been wrong, nor does he apologize for dissenting; he simply asserts that he is no match for God and decides not to cross-examine.

Job's qualified submission is apparently not enough for God, who in his second speech becomes angrier: "Dare you deny that I am just or put me in the wrong that you may be right?"[57] Pope translates the end of that line in a way that puts the issue personally and baldly: ". . . condemn me that you may be justified?" Which one is the criminal, the God who imposed suffering on the innocent, or the man who dared to say that this was unjust? Poet-Job's God fully comprehends the zero-sum game that Job is playing: If one is right, the other must be wrong. And God refuses to join the man's game.

"Behold now behemoth, which I made with thee,"[58] goes the King James version of this evocation of powerful forces of nature. ". . . his strength is in his loins, and his force is in the navel of his belly." Fishing for a sea serpent: "Canst thou draw out leviathan with a hook?"[59]

Behemoth and Leviathan are not merely names for the hippopotamus and the crocodile; these are ancient Man's mythic monsters, living fortresses of malevolent power. Managing the universe, bringing stable government to the fearsome forces of chaos, involves God in matters more urgent than moral bookkeeping for one of his creatures which he made along with Behemoth and others. The introduction of these symbols of darkness and chaos seems intended to show that God's work to bring light and order cannot be judged by human standards. With this account of the epic difficulties that God confronts, the poetry ends.

In the prosaic epilogue, the browbeaten and awestruck Job caves in. Not only does he assure God that "no purpose is beyond thee"—Job had never disputed that—but he admits, "I have spoken of great things which I have not understood, things too wonderful for me to know," which had been Elihu's final point. As the prologue demonstrated, the epilogue confirms: God's ways are inscrutable to Man. Inquiries will not be answered, at least not directly. "I knew of thee then only by report," Job confesses, "but now I see thee with my own eyes. Therefore I melt away; I repent in dust and ashes."[60]

What made Job stop questioning and end his rebellion? That's left up in the air; the only motivation given by poet-Job for his character Job's total turnabout is the stunning impact of the personal encounter with God. The reason he submits is the power of personal revelation: "now I see thee with my own eyes."

Now it is God's turn to turn about. He says to Eliphaz the Temanite, "I am angry with you and your two friends". (The third, young Elihu, is not mentioned, which again suggests he may have been a subsequent insert—or could suggest that God did not disagree with Elihu's arguments of sinless suffering as discipline, or the young man's insistence that God's works were beyond human comprehension.) Why was God angry at the consolers? "Because you have not spoken as you ought about me, as my servant Job has done." He tells them to ask Job to ask forgiveness on their behalf, and repeats for emphasis, "you have not spoken as you ought about me, as he has done."[61]

Having been thunderously rebuked for speaking in ignorance, Job is now twice commended for having spoken "as he ought"— presumably by telling the truth or being religiously right at least part of the time. It is no news that Job was not being punished for sins; we were informed right from the start that the visiting power elite was wrong about that. But was God saying that the old arguments put forward by that day's organized religion were untrue? If so, then Job did not lose his argument with God; the repeated divine condemnation of the friends would be evidence that Job's position was vindicated.

The ending is unrelievedly upbeat. God not only restores but redoubles Job's fortunes: That makes six thousand camels, a thousand yoke of oxen, etc. His wife bore fourteen sons to replace the seven lost, and the three dead daughters were replaced by the three most beautiful women in the land. (In ancient times, double the number of daughters would not have been considered a blessing, but poet-Job showed a curious modernity by giving the three women shares of Job's inheritance, unprecedented equal treatment.) His wife did not need replacement, having been spared by the Satan in the prologue's general slaughter, presumably so she could urge her afflicted husband to "curse God and die", at least half of which he did not do. Job's submission was rewarded handsomely; although the Satan does not reappear in the story, the echo of his sly question returns to the reader's mind: "Does Job fear God for nought?"

"Thereafter Job lived another hundred and forty years, he saw his sons and his grandsons to four generations, and died at a very great age."[62] In the older translation, he died "full of days", perhaps more sated than satisfied with his time on earth.

So the story of the Book of Job ends, leaving readers for thousands of years uplifted, puzzled, comforted, dissatisfied, provoked, or scandalized. With the words of the voice evoked out of the whirlwind—and with the hero's sudden surrender—poet-Job opened more lines of questioning about suffering and sin, injustice and outrage, authority and dissent, and about stability and freedom, than his story answered—which might have been what the author intended.

# 2

## THE DISMAYING COMPROMISE

"I READ THE Book of Job last night," the author Virginia Woolf wrote a friend, "—I don't think God comes well out of it."

There's no denying that for disciples of dissidence, the end of the Book of Job, starring a bombastic and sarcastic God and a crumbling Job, is an abrupt letdown. At the end of the poetry, the previously defiant Job—who had "maintained his ways" and held fast to his challenge through the terrible testing—changed those ways and set an example for the Italian astronomer Galileo, who saw truth about the universe through his telescope and then, when called before the Inquisition, piteously recanted his observations.

There was our hero Job, face-to-face with his divine tormentor at last. The trial was on; the key witness—almighty God himself, in person—had been forced out of hiding and called to account; Job had succeeded in turning that witness, who doubled as the supreme judge, into the defendant. At that crucial point, the jury of world opinion had more than a few members leaning strongly toward convicting God on four counts: mercilessness, mismanagement, isolation, and amorality.

And what happened? God the accused shouted down the prosecutor-plaintiff, who then panicked and gave up the case. In return, as the prosaic epilogue recounts, the awed and intimidated accuser was corruptly paid off with six thousand camels, a thousand oxen and as many she-asses, a fresh family, and only God knows what other material rewards.

Up to the terrible moment of truth, Job maintained his integrity—an English word rooted in the Latin for "untouched, pure, whole". His suffering had gone beyond a sense of loss of his children and property, beyond the physical pain of being covered by sores, to reach the mental agony caused by the rupture of the unity of righteousness and God.

At no time, we should note, did the plaintiff cease to believe in God: It would make no sense to be angry at a nullity or annoyed with the nonexistent. Nor at any time did Job doubt God's omnipotence: In fact, only because he was certain God could do anything could Job fault him for not doing the right thing. "He is no longer able to have a single faith in God and in justice," wrote the theologian Martin Buber of Job. "He believes now in justice in spite of believing in God, and he believes in God in spite of believing in justice."

This unstable equation leads to a jangling in the head that modern behaviorists call cognitive dissonance; the human mind, uneasy at having to hold contradictory beliefs, forces out one or the other by rejecting or ignoring information reinforcing the weaker. (If you just bought a Chevrolet, you don't read Ford ads; if you just voted, you don't read editorials excoriating your candidate; our brains are bandwagons that want to go in the direction of our parade.) Job cannot conceive of righteousness without God, and the contradiction has been agonizing his soul, but he grimly rejects the false comfort of his human disputants, demanding a straight answer from God in a proper legal setting. Not even God could be above God's law.

By Job's courageous refusal to bow to tradition; by his ethical outrage at injustice for himself and his species; by his insistence, against all the argument of established religion represented by the consolers, that the unjust punishment inflicted on him was proof that suffering was arbitrary and not proportionate to sin; by his heresy in charging "If I cry 'Murder!' no one answers; if I appeal for help, I get no justice"[1] and thereby accusing God of moral unconcern—one tough-minded fellow representing all of us had succeeded in forcing our creator to justify the great flaw in our theology, thereby establishing the previously unimagined challengeability of God.

And what happens? It is as if God appears in a tie-dyed T-shirt emblazoned with the words "Because I'm God, That's Why". The gist of the stormy answer he blew at Job was fairly summed up by hellfire-and-brimstone preacher John Calvin in five words: "Who are you to ask?" After a brief show of reluctance to admit error in the face of this bombast, Job suddenly—and at first reading, inexplicably—gives up the case. How come? After having heard the afflicted innocent ask, "Why, God?" for the length of the poetry, shortchanged readers are entitled to ask, "Why, Job?"

Granted that a theophany, or appearance of God, accompanied by burning bushes, thunder, lightning, and other effects, is an emotional grabber to any human witness. But it is a mistake to assume that Job was scared out of his wits: Fear is too primitive a motive for the astonishing reversal of the most blameless man in the world. Awe? That must be part of the answer, but it had to be more than fireworks that got to him. To be able to speculate rationally, we must first consider the tone and content of the answer God gives Job.

God the accused turns out to be not only unresponsive to the serious charge of breach of covenant but downright sarcastic about the plaintiff's legal standing. *Arrogant* is not a word one easily associates with the creator—who, after all, has much to be proud of after six strenuous days—but arrogant is the way the poet portrays him in this scene. It is as if the Lord is irritated about having to take time from his major duties in the universe to appear as a defendant in this trivial class-action suit on earth.

We know from the prologue that the opposite is true—that this case is far from minor, that God's doubt about the motive of human worship drove him to this cruel testing of the world's best man. Again the Joban irony is in the fire: We know that the matter of the innocent suffering and the subsequent challenge to his injustice cannot be trivial in God's eyes. As a result, throughout the answer out of the whirlwind, the probing reader is forced by poet-

Job to ask: "Why is God acting like such a bully? Why did he come all this way to berate instead of answer Job?" His answer out of the whirlwind—Chapter 38, which includes the most glorious poetry in the Bible—seems at first reading to be no answer at all. To Job's challenging oath of clearance on the issue of justice, God replies with a tirade about the need for order.

"Who is this whose ignorant words cloud my design in darkness?"[2] The bringer or giver of light, as God is sometimes called, accuses his accuser of being a giver of darkness—but he was the one who put Job in the dark. He then asks a series of impossible-to-answer rhetorical questions—for example, "Has the rain a father?"[3]—that are designed to belittle and intimidate the human source of his irritation.

The literary critic I. A. Richards, who felt that the attentive reader could get to know Job intimately, was repelled by the message from the whirlwind, holding that its tone and content prepared the world for political dictatorship: "In the course of chapters 38–41 (edit them as we may)," he wrote after Hitler's defeat, "what sort of mind do we feel is vociferating? Is it not well to reflect whether more than two thousand years' adoration of this utterance (however magnificent its phrases) might not have something to do with the sad state of the world and with the mad and abominable tyrannies which have so mercilessly infested it?"

The tone of Job's brief reply to God's apparently irrelevant tirade is submissive, though he does not overtly submit. His opening word in Hebrew is *hen,* usually translated "Lo" or "Behold" but also meaning "If". "Lo [or *if*] I am small, how can I answer you? My hand I lay on my mouth . . . I will say no more."[4] This could mean "Okay, if you're intent on showing you are bigger than me, what can I say? I have to shut up, but I still think what I think." At the least, it means Job is being practical: "I am too small to contend with you in person, so I will shut up." No recanting or retracting, certainly no repenting, is necessarily implied in Job's verbalized gulp.

This weakening of the knees at God's show of power is exactly what Job predicted would happen if he had no witness/umpire/protector/advocate/vindicator/redeemer before a heavenly tribunal. Indeed, Job's prediction of such fearsome fireworks sets a trap that God steps into, causing the reader to think "You see, Job was right, God doesn't play fair in court."

Having his accuser fall silent is not enough; exasperated at Job's respectful intractability, God gets even tougher. In his second speech, God again begins by telling Job to pull up his socks—"Gird up thy loins" in the KJV—a way of saying he should adjust his dress for combat. In rhetorical ridicule, God asks if Job proposes to make God out to be evil just to prove his own innocence. This seems to impugn the motive of Job, in an unworthy substitute for argument, but perhaps the meaning of God's mocking questioning is: You can assert your innocence, Job, without making me out to be evil. (Political authorities under reformist fire have been taking that moderating position ever since.) God, as poet-Job portrays him in this scene, appears uncomfortable with the charge of being the source of wickedness. In this case, that's indisputably what he is, by giving the power of unfair punishment to his accusatory agent; the Satan, not yet a fallen angel, is here getting started in the mischief-and-temptation business.

To refute or make moot that annoying charge of being unjust, God suggests Job step into his shoes and see how well he would do if he were all-powerful. "Deck yourself out, if you can, in pride and dignity, array yourself in pomp and splendour." In other words— go ahead, puny Man, here's your chance to play God for a day. "Unleash the fury of your wrath, look upon the proud man and humble him; . . . throw down the wicked where they stand."[5] Go ahead and crack down on injustice in the same efficient, totalitarian way you expect from me. "Then I in my turn will acknowledge that your own right hand can save you."[6] If Job-as-God could then do what he accuses God of failing to do, God says he would take off his hat to him.

To the political eye, that's a fascinating passage. God seems to be saying "Look, nobody's perfect; I haven't struck down all the proud and the wicked, and, yes, I've been soft on Leviathan. But if you had my limitless power, could you do better?" By straining a little, civil libertarians may detect a tantalizing hint in this context that the use of unlimited power without restraint, even in the pursuit of justice, may not be the best way to govern. Leaving a little evil in helps the good stand out; we'll focus on this God-for-a-day section in a later political chapter.

To interpret God's meaning as "nobody's perfect" is to give irreverence a bad name. Am I reading into this more than is there? Are hermeneutics (the art of interpretation) and semiotics (the study of signs and symbols) being used here to see and sell a point of view more in the mind of the beholder than the beheld?

Of course I am and they are; I am abandoning the pretense of objective analysis of what the author meant, and am joining in the editing and updating of the ancient book to fit my circumstances. That's what most students of Job do. Poet-Job's genius, beyond his ability to conjure striking images, is to write with open spaces between the lines, tempting honest interpreters into conclusions they cannot prove and their disputants cannot fairly dismiss. Written on stretch papyrus, the Book of Job can be fitted to the times and to the changing limits of dissent.

As I write this, I'm rooting for God to do what I believe to be all the right things—to permit dissent, to account for unfairness, to refrain from abusing power (no more tests, entrapments, or sting operations)—just as scribes and exegetes in previous times were either pulling for him to maintain tradition and justify retribution, or wishing that Job would be more respectful and less heretical in his style. This kind of interpretation is seasoning to taste, not cooking the Good Book. To do that is to give God the benefit of his self-doubt.

And what about the parade of animals from ravens to ostriches to show how insignificant Man is in the great scheme of things? God boasts of handling Behemoth and Leviathan, the ancient mythic symbols of chaos, fearsome brutes who would knock back a mere human being in a gulp. Tough guy, this God; but Job never questioned his power, only his fairness.

Let's not take that long animal analogy in God's second speech as a put-down or an evasion or a scary chamber of horrors. Instead, we can accept the zoo parade in the theophany as a symbol of the answer we are looking for, taking Robert Gordis's explanation that "Just as there is order and harmony in the natural world, though imperfectly grasped by man, so there is order and meaning in the moral sphere, though often incomprehensible to man."

Even so, the pro-Job reader's feeling of letdown is undeniable. In refusing to be the celestial cop, God cops out; the accused deity fails to answer Job's indictment with reasons we can put to use in our own lives.

Job's final reaction to this apparent failure is to flinch and then roll over, to abandon his legal challenge, to take the camels and run. His final words after God's second harangue are: "I repent in dust and ashes."[7] The recanting is unequivocal; the literal meaning is "I loathe my previous words." This is a full retraction, no fingers crossed, and his repentence is genuine. The Job scholar J. Gerald Janzen suggests that the phrase "in dust and ashes" need not mean "in finitude and mortality" as an expression of self-abasement, but is an evocation of the dignity of Man, who was created from dust by God. Some other interpreters accept the shred-of-dignity notion, but that hopeful spark won't fly upward; dust is sprinkled over the head in mourning, as a sign of repentance for sins. Job caves in all the way.

Why? And why so hastily, without adequate explanation?

We will examine the reasons theology offers for this sudden submission in a chapter to come, but first let's take up a lower-level betrayal: the author's abdication of literary responsibility. Why did poet-Job, after bringing onstage his most charismatic character, endow God with the most Godlike eloquence in the Bible only to huff and puff and change the subject? Even worse, why did he tack on a happy ending, giving Job back his huge herd of camels twice over, replacing his children with more sons and daughters (one, apparently adept with cosmetics, is named "Eyeshadow"), and blessing him with a long life? That cornball conclusion makes tradition's point that there is indeed divine justice in this world, which is not at all the point of the dialogues; in fact, the pot of soothing syrup at the end of the suffering negates the book's courageous and controversial point—that when it comes to just deserts, God says that's not his table.

Why didn't Job the questioner, having shamed or wheedled or annoyed his maker to come before him, stand up and follow up? No character in literature held a stronger hand. Instead of meekly repenting in dust and ashes, he might well have reserved that for use after a mind-opening and soul-satisfying answer, and gone after that answer with a line of questioning on this order: "Never mind the sarcasm—why did you pick on blameless me for punishment?

Didn't you and Abraham make a covenant in which you promised to be just? You know I never challenged your power, only your justice—why are you telling me how powerful you are and how weak I am? Don't you realize that's what I predicted you would do—to shut me up by scaring the wits out of me? Why did you give me this inquiring mind if you didn't expect me to demand to know why you're being so inconsistent? Why won't you appoint a special prosecutor, an umpire between us, so that this can be a fair contest? Come on, now—why do you, under covenantal contract to be merciful and just, let the good die young and the wicked prosper?"

That would have been consistent with the character of Job, and would have required a third divine speech from the whirlwind, offering a responsive reply or inspirational statement (a draft of which not even this former speechwriter has the presumption to offer). Poet-Job did not suddenly lose his courage or forget his point, nor was he forced to a premature and mystifying ending by reasons of space. We know only this: Job was unpersuaded by pietistic but specious arguments before the voice came out of the whirlwind, but was convinced beyond any doubt after the voice spoke. If we are to play by the rules of Herman Utix—that is, to deal with the book we have as it is, and not to avoid the issue by assuming the end was tacked on by somebody out to vitiate poet-Job's point—then we have to ask what it was in the text or in the action described in the text that turned Job around in his tracks.

To figure out what happened on the way to the whirlwind, let's review the historic or textual possibilities.

*1. The fix was put in by orthodox scribes.* Instead of "What reply can I give thee, I who carry no weight?"[8] the opening remark can be read as conditional, making the meaning "Suppose, as you say, I am small—then how can you expect me to argue with you?" That's not nearly so roundheeled, and could be the irritant that causes God to blaze away again in his second discourse. This would not be the first time scribes preferred a meaning that did not make waves; in Genesis 18:22, God was originally depicted as standing before Abraham; according to Janzen, this notion of the judge of all the earth coming before that pile of dust and ashes that is Man to negotiate justice for the few good people in Sodom was unthinkable. As a result, the Genesis text was fixed, deliberatedly altered to have Abraham sidle up to God. Here in Job, too, possible stiff-neckedness in Man may have been downplayed in translation.

**2. Poet-Job, in order to publish without being punished for heresy, had to make compromises.** One may have been the insertion of Elihu, the intrusive youth who suggested that suffering was a discipline bracing for the soul, expressed by political figures today as "a character-building experience". (Perhaps Elihu was inserted afterward because his argument was sound, or maybe poet-Job forgot a character and didn't want to waste the work, which happens to all of us.)

The greatest of all emendations may have been the ending itself, as if the author or his editor said, "There, there, I didn't mean it." Matitiahu Tsevat, writing in 1966, held that "the very radicalism of the book's answer, shattering a central biblical doctrine and a belief cherished in ancient Israel, would itself demand the protection of a veil." God's answer—that his natural order was not connected to Man's moral order, and that if humans wanted to do good, they should do it only because it was good—"may never have been tolerated or preserved for us," speculates Tsevat, "but for the protection of its form." In other words, the sugarcoating was needed to help the pill go down.

**3. The author was genius enough to come up with the question but not enough to work out a satisfactory answer.** This sometimes happens to those blessed with inspiration but afflicted with a lack of stamina; when it comes to disparities in the distribution of creative brainpower, life is not always unfair. Maybe poet-Job painted himself into a corner, and the ambiguity we find so tantalizing was less what the author had in mind than what the author failed to work out in his head. He bit off more than any human of his millennium; perhaps he needed the help in chewing it that has been so eagerly offered ever since, including help from the author and the reader of this book. If not even God's work can be finished, as the testing of Job's motive shows, why must a text be finished, perfect, unalterable, dead?

**4. Job's sudden surrender is too abject to be true; he didn't mean it, and the frequently tricky and subtle poet-Job is signaling us to read it backward, or in a mirror, or between the lines.** Antiques dealers, on the back of price tags, often put down numbers that, read backward, indicate the bottom-line selling price. Antique poets may have done something similar.

Elie Wiesel, the concentration-camp survivor who serves as a conscience-haunting witness to the Holocaust, taught a course on the Book of Job on French television. He does not accept Job's sudden cave-in or the book's happy ending: "Much as I admired Job's passionate rebellion," he writes, "I am deeply troubled by his hasty abdication. . . . I prefer to think that the book's true ending was lost. That Job died without having repented, without having humiliated himself. . . . I was offended by his surrender in the text. . . . He should have said to God: Very well, I forgive you . . . but what about my dead children, do they forgive you? . . . By accepting your inequities, do I not become your accomplice?" Wiesel searches for the reason for Job's surrender and finds a clue in the suddenness of his acceptance: "By repenting sins he did not commit, by justifying a sorrow he did not deserve, he communicates to us that he did not believe in his own confessions; they were nothing but decoys." Through that coded Joban message, "we know that it is given to man to transform divine injustice into human justice and compassion."

The suddenness of the collapse of Job's defiance, especially in light of God's refusal to deal with his charges directly, is dramatically inconsistent and philosophically jarring. The use of such irony to get past the censors is possible, but I hate to judge meaning on a trick. It is too much to say that poet-Job had his fingers crossed when he wrote the end; we'll have to find more nourishment in Yahweh's speeches from the whirlwind.

**5. Job knew he would win his case, and let God cop a plea on Job's accusations of him in return for acquittal of all charges against Job.** Sounds farfetched, but we can find, in the epilogue's final scene, a clear signal from the poet that appears to direct us to read much of the book differently. After Job's recantation, Yahweh turns to Eliphaz, who represented the thinking of traditional religion about sin and suffering, and twice tells him angrily that he and his two friends had not spoken the truth as Job had.

What's going on here? It's easy to see that God would refute the speeches of the three friends: They held that suffering was evidence of sin, an old position that the experience of life had shown to be in error. But for God to stress that Job was the one who had spoken the truth in the dialogues is a puzzlement. Was this a blanket statement, including Job's heresies in charging God with being aloof and unjust? Or was this divine approval of Job's extended fulmination a limited one, supposed to discredit only the mistaken notion that suffering had to be taken as evidence of sin?

Well, um, you see, said some exegetes, the epilogue was tacked on by another hand; it fails to mention Elihu or the Satan; and we cannot therefore use the two endorsements by God in the prose ending to apply to horrendous statements made by Job in the poetic middle.

Sorry, that evasion does not wash; my ground rules are to deal with the book as it stands, permitting only corrections of mistranslations that most modern scholars agree on. Besides, God is telling the truth about Job having been right during the dialogues: Job in his suffering insisted that he was not being afflicted as punishment for sin, and we know that to be true from the story of the bet with the Satan in the prologue.

That leaves the disciples of dissent dissatisfied with what seems to be God's abuse of power, discomforted by his evasion of pointed charges with a repressive "Who are you to talk?" Reading the book for the first time, the inquisitive modern reader—burdened neither with a need to justify religion nor a predisposition to declare it absurd—is left with the feeling that he or she has been led into a stone wall. The temptation is to root for the hero right up until his moment of sudden submission, and then to say: What a moment for poet-Job, as the first celebrator of dissidence, to flinch.

Did the author flinch? Before accepting Job's unexplained submission to Authority as a sellout by the dramatist, we should consider how the text before us came to be. The book comes to us with both religion's halo and skepticism's baggage; we should examine the interpretation that has shaped its reception, softened or weakened its message, and in some cases may have covered up poet-Job's intent.

Poet-Job's work was emended and watered down in the days of the ancients and misinterpreted through two millennia. Let's take a closer look at how the rebellious message in Job was watered down by the guardians of the temple, and smothered in reverence for its literary beauty. After that, we will see how Job's message of outrage at injustice was recaptured and reshaped to fit the new orthodoxies and mystic visions of modern theologians, artists, and politicians.

# 3

# SILENCING THE REBEL

WHO WAS THE real Job? Where and when did he live, if at all? Who wrote the book about him? How and why was poet-Job's outrage at the world's unfairness calmed, suppressed, or adulterated?

Let me come at the question of the "real", original, legendary Job obliquely. Ancient storytellers on the island of Majorca, aware of the winding mythic path to truth, liked to begin their folktales with a more subtle notion than our own "once upon a time". They had a way of linking the real and the symbolic: Their favorite opening was *it was and it was not*. Such forthright ambivalence is helpful in understanding the history of Job.

Was there such a man as Job in the land of Uz? There was and there was not. Because so much biblical legend is rooted in history, perhaps a man named Job did exist, to shock the ancient world by arguing with God. Perhaps the original Job lived and died a pious man, losing and regaining his wealth, and the story of his life was taken up and used for the purposes of a religious teaching. Perhaps he never existed at all. Whether he was real when civilization was young is unimportant; what counts is that the legend about a greatly pious man named Job existed, and was useful to a poet writing a story that deals with reality.

The character used by poet-Job was and was not that legend-ary Job. In the prologue and epilogue of the book, the hoary, legendary, patient Job is the focus. But in the middle poetry, the Job who appears is not the same man, and Joban students do well to keep the two characters separate.

The character of Job in the poetic section of the biblical book about him is a man in the prime of life (with children too young to be married) and at the peak of his mental and physical powers. The words that typify his personality are not the prologue's resigned "The Lord gives and the Lord takes away; blessed be the name of the Lord,"[1] recited to comfort the grieving at funerals, but the outraged "Damn the day that I was born!"[2] at the opening of the poetry, signaling his rebellion.

Why did the author select a character famed for piety as the framework for his disputatious, vigorous Job? For the same rea-sons he chose a story that rewarded a sufferer for patient belief as the setting for his book attacking that notion: Not only did it let poet-Job advance his argument against a contrasting backdrop of irony, but it provided a cover for radical thought.

The respectability of that Joban cover was unassailable. The prophet Ezekiel, cited earlier, spoke of a trio of respected ancients: Job, Noah (the blameless man whose integrity enabled humanity to survive), and Daniel (not of the lion's den, but a legendary good Canaanite king whose name is usually written as Dan'l).[3] All were Gentiles, all renowned for uprightness. Of these three, Job was probably a seminomadic chieftain from the land of Edom, later called Uz, probably located in what is now Iraq. If the legendary Job lived, this paragon might have been a contemporary of the patriarch Abraham, but the original, or "real", Job is lost in what are helplessly called the mists of antiquity.

A folktale transmitted orally down through the centuries re-counted the adventures of that Job, a great and respected leader in the Gentile world, who was tested by God to discover the purpose of his worship. Despite terrible and undeserved suffering, the inno-cent man, unaware of the sublime use to which his life was being put, refused to abandon his faith in God. In the end, his patience and virtue were rewarded with the return of his wealth, a fresh set of descendants, and a patriarch-length happy life.

This ancient Judaic tale of Job had been used to help propagate the idea of monotheism—a single, all-powerful God who dispensed justice tempered with mercy to those who selflessly worshiped him. Such a God was deemed necessary for Israel's survival in war.

Then there appeared a school of thought in Judaism that broke with this comforting tradition. It was led by the author of the Book of Job, a philosopher capable of creating a dramatic document that reflected the experience of real life. All the assurances of religion that God would dispense justice evenhandedly ran smack into the way the world really worked. The truth was that some evildoers prospered, some good people got hurt. The faith of the fathers was being endangered by the facts of life, and since the facts could not be changed to fit the faith, the most skillful propagandist among the radical sages (five centuries before the emergence of rabbis) wisely adapted the faith to fit the facts.

To disguise his radicalism, poet-Job set his story in a time a thousand years before his own era. He selected a folk figure as his hero, and used a richer and more elite language than any other writer whose work was destined for the canon. Poet-Job muddied the time and setting of his story. He made his characters Gentiles, unaware of Hebrew history. In these ways, the characters and their author were less likely to be accused of blasphemy or of undermining the Hebrew religion.

The author's language and feel for irony suggest that he was a well-read scholar with an original intellect, who was familiar with the customs and history of the nations of his world. His refusal to be pinned down to a time or a people not only provided a cover from disapproval but also enabled poet-Job to reach beyond standard Hebrew theology and politics to deal with universal matters. In taking cover in the tradition he intended to modernize, poet-Job remained loyal to monotheism, but ignored or set aside Judaism's laws of conduct.

He presumed—in as stunning a presumption as any religious thinker has ever undertaken—to disconnect earthly morality from God's plan for the universe. He adopted a new approach to the proper conduct of human beings in the face of universal injustice or cosmic unconcern. He emitted a roar of poetic outrage about the dark side of the bringer of light and struck a new and less unequal power balance between God and Man. Not just in literary power, but in political moxie—at least until the puzzling end—this book's heretical objection to amorality in heaven stands like Everest in the range of Scripture.

What sort of man would dare to do this? During a period of priestly obfuscation of the Book of Job's radical thesis, the poet who wrote Job was thought by many to be Moses, who lived twelve centuries before the birth of Jesus. Most modern scholarship doubts that guess of date and authorship, and places the time of the writing of the Book of Job at least a half-millennium after Moses led his people out of slavery in Egypt. Informed speculation places poet-Job's work between the sixth and second centuries B.C., with most around the fifth. Some scholars picture a teacher presenting an answer to the suffering of Jews in exile in Mesopotamia after the destruction of the Temple; others hold that the author of Job worked in the ferment of the Second Commonwealth, after the return from the Babylonian exile, when prophets gave way to sages whose "wisdom literature", with its universal themes, flourished.

A word to that wisdom: First came the Torah, or law, to say "this is what to do"; then came the prophetic books to add an ominous "or else"; finally came the wisdom literature, written by the second-thoughted sages and poets of Ecclesiastes, Proverbs, Psalms, and Job, to add a realistic "but if you are having difficulty with the foregoing, this is the way to adjust".

Scholars try to date the authorship of Job by tracing the book's relationship to other Scripture. Poet-Job seems to have been influenced by the prophet Jeremiah (who lived, scholars are fairly certain, from 626 to 582 B.C.) and to have made a great impression on the prophet labeled Deutero-Isaiah (not the first Isaiah, but a lesser-known prophet—deutero means "second"—who lived nearly a century closer to our time). For example, the curse so often cited here, "Damn the day that I was born!"—defined as a defining moment by political jargonauts—is a coinage of Jeremiah, part of one of those ringing denunciations we have come to call jeremiads.[4] Poet-Job reused those words in Job 3:3. Jeremiah took up the legal metaphor, so central in Job, with "O Lord, I will dispute with thee, for thou art just; yes, I will plead my case before thee. Why do the wicked prosper and traitors live at ease?"[5]

Job, who unlike Jeremiah knows God to be unjust in his case, seeks a court trial throughout his affliction, demanding to know, in his own jeremiad, why the wicked do so well while good men like him suffer. Comparing poet-Job's work with the equally anonymous Deutero-Isaiah, however, we find it hard to tell who preceded whom. That prophet of the Hebrew exile came up with the daring suggestion that the suffering of Israel was not punishment for any known national sin, but a painful contribution to the moral education of the human race.

That pain-can-be-good-for-you rationalization of the unfair suffering of the innocent is also introduced in the Book of Job by Elihu, the young intruder who joins the three friends who argue with Job. But the character of Elihu, some say, was not written by poet-Job at all. His name is Hebrew, unlike all other names in the Book of Job, and his speaking style is disconcertingly verbose. Samuel Terrien, writing in 1957, was certain that Elihu's speeches are a later interpolation by a different writer, and that the book before us is the product of a school of sages, scribes, and storytellers who worked on it for a few centuries—and who tacked on a happy ending to assuage the scandalized.

Robert Gordis, in 1965, differed completely with this committee theory. Although he conceded that the Elihu speeches, along with a discordant but fascinating meditative hymn, could have been written later in life by poet-Job, Gordis held that the book's intrinsic unity, poetic style, and line-by-line ironic techniques demonstrate the work of one genius working alone. Marvin Pope in 1966 leaned toward that single-author theory because he felt the book bears the literary imprint of a single personality, and he added an intriguing suggestion that poet-Job as well as his hero might not have been an Israelite. Edwin Good in 1990 concluded that nobody has the slightest idea who the author or authors might have been, and since the text is what counts, it doesn't matter.

Who's right, and does it matter? When experts clash, laymen can apply common sense in reaching their own judgment. I think context does matter in illuminating a text; and it would help us clear a path to the political meanings of the book if we could reach tentative conclusions about the author, his circumstances, and his likely intent.

Logic suggests that this book of the Bible was not produced by a group of anonymous theologians, operating the way newsmagazines did before those publications permitted bylines. The work is one of blinding insight, and such a work is started and permeated by, if not completed by, one inspired person. Groupthink is rarely inspired, never ingenious, usually safe.

At the same time, common sense suggests that the first draft of anything, even the five books of Moses that tradition holds were dictated by God, was unlikely to have made it through the hands of a priesthood into the Bible pristine and unemended.

On that hypothesis, we can further assume that poet-Job—who sensed the faith-shaking issue in the air at the time, understood what had to be done, and wrote an entire iconoclastic work himself—then had to deal with the practical problem of getting it accepted by a consensus of his colleagues. To get it passed along, he needed approval of at least a respectable minority of the sages of his day. This reasoning of ecclesiastical politics suggests that poet-Job made such compromises in his copy as he thought necessary to bring along enough religious leaders to ensure canonical status for his book.

Now take a Mel Brooks leap: Lift the flap of a tent in Palestine just after the creation of the Book of Job. Two men, a writer and an editor, are hunched over a pile of scrolls.

"You really want to say 'Damn the day that I was born'? You know who made the day—that comes as close as you can to cursing Shaddai."

"Jeremiah got away with it—leave it in."

"How about this supposedly happy ending, then, where you have Job dying wealthy but childless—what's the use of dying with money, if you have nobody to leave it to? That will depress everybody."

"If you want, we can change it to have God give him a new set of children, but none of my serious readers will believe it."

"Look—Job has to get everything back double, or it's not going into the canon. Instead, because you did a lot of work on it, we'll dump it into the Apocrypha in the back."

"Okay, Job gets back everything as his reward—my readers, who are inclined to irony, will take it as my way of poking fun at retributive justice."

End of playing around. After poet-Job's time, editors surely nibbled away at his copy. As it was laboriously copied by hand, one scribe added one bit, another took a bit out, but no master copy—no "original"—existed to act as a point of reference. This rounding of the hard edge of meaning by early copyists was redoubled in later translation: We know, for example, that seventy rabbis gathered in Alexandria in the third century B.C. to transcribe the various pieces of the canon into Greek, for the benefit of Jews in Egypt who were untutored in Hebrew. This committee produced the Septuagint—"the work of seventy"—in which the Book of Job is considerably shortened and its defiance of Authority softened. No other book in the Bible took such a condensing at the hands of the seventy "publishers". The Book of Job comes into our ken, then, encrusted with translation error, horrified cuts, and worshipful interpolation—along with some creative interpretation. This refreshing hermeneutic shower prepares us for a quick survey of the vast, two-millennia euphemization and concerted concealment.

Early Christian scholars studied the Septuagint's expurgated Greek version, not the near-scandalous book in its original Hebrew. Christians and Jews in the Middle Ages turned away from the troubling poetry in the biblical canon to the "Testament of Job" in the Apocrypha, a repository of ancient writings of doubtful authority, not included in authorized versions of the Scriptures. Most believers preferred the unsanctified version of the folktale of Job; it recounts the oral tradition about his family connections (his wife was supposedly named Dinah, who may have been a daughter of Esau), but makes Job to be a king of Egypt and—most important—no rebel. This apocryphal Job, suffering in silence, an example of the inexplicably outcast, became the patron of the victims of leprosy and syphilis. That folktale Job of patience was glorified while the rebellious, poetic Job of the Bible was ignored or explained away.

Didn't the early sages, who could read Job in the unexpurgated Hebrew, know better? Some did and some did not. The influential eleventh-century Talmudist Solomon bar-Isaac ("Rashi"), along with the invaluable scribes called Masoretes (from the Hebrew word for "tradition"), led the cover-up: Rashi toned down what we now read to mean the defiant "He may slay me, I'll not quaver"[6] passage to a much different "Let him kill me, I will not separate from him, and I will always hope for him," adding with reverent certitude in his commentary, "Therefore, there is no rebellion or transgression in my words." One modern translator, Marvin Pope, comments drily: "Both the consonantal text and the context support the opposite sense."

The 1611 King James Version put the piety in the lead: "Though he slay me, yet will I trust in him", adding the subordinated "but I will maintain mine own ways before him." In the 1985 Jewish Publication Society translation, the weasel-wording is rejected and the rebellious and stouthearted meaning is asserted: "He may well slay me; I may have no hope; Yet I will argue my case before him." Even the 1989 translation of the Judaica Press, which features the Rashi commentary and was sent to me by an aide to the orthodox Lubavitcher Rebbe, has a version straightening out Rashi partially: "Behold, let Him kill me, I will hope for Him; but I will prove my ways to His face." But for the past thousand years, Rashi's pious misinterpretation stretched the plain meaning of the Hebrew words beyond the author's intent, smothering the rebel's voice.

Moses Maimonides, the Aristotle of the twelfth century, did better in addressing the issue of innocent suffering raised in poet-Job's book. In his *Guide for the Perplexed,* Maimonides read Job as a man of uprightness who could find no meaning in his suffering because he lacked the cosmic knowledge denied mankind. Job learned from the Lord's speeches not to measure God in a human scale, not to make "the error that His knowledge is like our knowledge or that His purpose is like our purpose". This was an early expression of the "big picture", or "grand design", explanation of the book's meaning, which we will examine later in both its theological and political contexts. The idea that any suffering could be borne by one who had a profound "knowledge of the deity" also gave a philosophical underpinning to the traditional value of humility, or at least resignation in the face of seeming injustice. Maimonides believed that the theoretical apprehension of God's intellect, and not the practical virtue of a person living the ethical life, was the path to wisdom; and that Job's attainment in the end of this "certain knowledge of God" was why he could be happy accepting whatever seeming injustice God willed for him. Even the most respected of the early commentators dwelt on the instructive error, not the disquieting rebellion, in Job.

Meanwhile, Christianity created its own version of the patient Job. Late in the fourth century, the ascetic John Chrysostom of Antioch viewed Job as "a wrestler of self denial" ready for "bodily mutilation and indignity" whose life "displayed an endurance firmer than any adamant". (An "adamant" was an unbreakable stone, and has become an adjective meaning "stubborn".) Chrysostom was the first to use Job as a political pacifier. When riots broke out in Antioch in the year 387 after the imposition of heavy taxes, the fiery ascetic exhorted the people to consider the impending wrath of Emperor Theodosius. "When Job lost all . . . he bore away an illustrious victory from the devil" in his endurance of suffering. He took Job's lesson to be that material wealth meant nothing, that subjugation to God's will was all; and the people of Antioch should follow that Joban example and stop rioting about taxation. They did, and the emperor pardoned the rioters; the paradigm of Job the patient sufferer did the soothing trick.

The author of many Latin texts used in the Vulgate translation of the Bible, Jerome of Bethlehem, used Job as the forerunner of the resurrection of Jesus. To him, "I know that my Redeemer liveth" in the KJV, expressed as "I know that my vindicator lives" in the NEB,[7] was evidence that Job "knew and saw that Christ, his Redeemer, was alive, and at the last day would rise again from the earth." Jerome used this to inveigh against competing doctrines that denied the resurrection of Christ's body. Since Jesus had not been born when Job lived, Job's imputed testimony was treated by Jerome as part of a vision: "The Lord has not yet died, and the athlete of the Church [Job] saw his Redeemer rising from the grave." Although poet-Job had argued against the notion of divine retribution, the brilliant translator and propagator who became Saint Jerome read that as only a delay of God's justice, with a promise of retribution in an afterlife. Not surprisingly, in the Roman catacombs, the legendary Job can be seen portrayed as a prototype of Jesus, an innocent whose terrible punishment redeemed human sin.

The *Exposition of the Book of Job,* written at the turn of the seventh century by Pope Gregory I, took up Jerome's thesis and fixed Job as the prefigurer of Jesus. The Pope set aside the troubling problem of innocent suffering and wicked prosperity, choosing instead to focus on the way "the Lord blessed the end of Job's life more than the beginning", as the epilogue put it.[8] To Pope Gregory, determined to establish the spiritual power of the Church, that spelled the absorption of the Jews into the Church of Christ, as "the Lord consoles the pain of Holy Church by a manifold ingathering of souls".

Islam went along with this sustained pacification of the rebellious Job: A thirteenth-century commentary on the Koran held that those who serve Allah "should be patient as Job was patient, then they would be rewarded as he was rewarded".

As most Jews, Catholics, and Muslims sought to ameliorate or ignore Job's rambunctiousness, Protestantism came along to shift the focus and to use Job's ire in its cause. Martin Luther, who studied the learned rabbi Rashi's work and who translated the Book of Job into German in 1524, did not see Job as a precursor to Jesus. Nor did he ignore the book's hard-to-avoid theme, which he put plainly as "whether misfortune can come to the righteous from God". But he saw the book's purpose as teaching "that God allows even his saints to stumble". Job's stumble was in assuming God to be "only a judge and wrathful tyrant, who applies force and cares nothing about the good life". Luther in effect embraced a Maimonidean reading of Job: Man cannot know God's purpose, and can best endure apparent injustice by accepting that such divine purpose exists. Thus did theology's first protester get short shrift from the first Protestant.

John Calvin, the French preacher of the sixteenth century, seized on Job's presumption, however, and drove it home in his fierce sermons as a nail in the coffin of human contemptibility. Of his 700 sermons, 159 were on Job, for good reason: In his view, God showed himself in terror in a voice out of the storm because the questioning Job needed to be beaten into obedience. Calvin's interpretation of God's angry opening line, "Who is this that darkeneth counsel?" was "And who are you, man?" The hot-eyed, hard-edged preacher, who set up a harsh theocratic government in Geneva and founded an "ism" that swept England, used the Lord's speeches out of the whirlwind to show the depravity of mankind, the vanity of the vessel of villainy. The Calvinist message: God told Job to shut up and stop asking foolish questions, and if an otherwise blameless man like Job is to be corrected so harshly, far worse portends for sinners like thee.

A variety of religions and sects have twisted the Book of Job to their own purposes. The character of Job has been regularly co-opted. Instead of the first dissident shaking his fist, we have had the patient saint folding his hands. Rather than a stubborn believer on a moral quest, we have had a cardboard character in hopeless error. Where poet-Job evoked a man whose God-given free will enabled him to strike a power balance with his creator, we have had the spectacle of fire-and-brimstone preachers making him the object of God's cruel chastisement of the stiff-necked. The interpretive declension of Job among too many religionists through two millennia went from exemplar of profitable piousness to irritable ignoramus to symbol of foolish pride.

In modern political parlance, this sort of purposeful obfuscation is called a cover-up. Has the obstruction of the outcry against God's injustice been unfair to the spirit of the Book of Job? The temptation is to reply with the classic "Life is unfair," but one of Job's lessons is to look inward rather than heavenward for moral redress.

Fortunately, it is in the nature of cover-ups to be uncovered. As the world turned from a concentration on the need for order to a realization of the importance of freedom, the smothering of poet-Job's political and moral protest in pillows of earnest piety could not continue.

In recent centuries, artists of genius and dissidents of talent have drawn on the central, poetic portion of this book—the "good" part about the "bad" Job—to ennoble and justify their own protest at Fate's unfairness or malevolence. Along with some theologians and political philosphers, they have used the Book of Job to criticize what they believed to be the rigidity of organized religion. They have sometimes exploited the presence of Job's blasphemy in the biblical canon to help them express their own sense of despair at life's "absurdity" and God's seeming moral unconcern.

Even in his compromise—in allowing his human protagonist

to embrace the ambiguous answer and mysterious hint from his divine antagonist—poet-Job has given a framework and a forum to other poets, novelists, and playwrights in their less-inhibited quests. Let's see how some of the best of them handled the angry question raised by the creator of the first dissident.

# 4

## PROTOTYPE
## OF THE DISSIDENT

WHY, AFTER CENTURIES of misinterpretation and prayerful cover-up, has the Book of Job excited so much fresh discussion and original exegesis? Something in its mysterious message speaks to our time and rushes into the vacuum of nail-nibbling anxiety as no other book in the Bible.

I think Job has attracted artists and thinkers because it demonstrates the power of dissent to wear down the resistance of Authority. Not to overthrow it, necessarily; only to wear down the center of command to the point of compromise.

The verb for that inexorable erosion is *subvert*—a disreputable word, like *corrupt* and *pervert*—because it is rooted in the frightening notion of overthrowing established order. But subversion, the tool of the dissident, has its saving graces. It is a way of doing combat with Authority without openly fomenting revolution; it is a way of gradually leveling the playing field of power. Artists and writers particularly, empowered only by their ideas and genius of expression, are natural subverters of order. (In modern times, the paradox of their need to break constraints and their need to reach audiences is why Federal support of the arts is steeped in controversy. Orthodoxy does not like to encourage the unorthodox.)

Job, the first dissident (along with his presumed contemporary, Prometheus), turned out to be a paradigm for those artists and poets who followed. Consider the way the Book of Job—confined and cosseted by reverent interpreters, as we have seen, for thousands of years—has in the last couple of centuries been taken up by the artistic disturbers of the status quo.

Disbelievers could make a case that Job is not only blasphemous in his words but cunningly heretical in his ideas; that he undermines blind faith with a dose of hard-eyed realism, right up to that I-was-only-foolin' conventional ending. We have seen how even that suddenly submissive fade-out can be read as ironic—written, like the sanctimonious counsel of the friends, to be disbelieved.

Irony, which is so central to modern criticism, also permeates the study of Job. Irony lets an author get away with literary murder: He is saying, "Let the bumpkins be misled with what I have spread out on the surface—you and I know that on a deeper level, I mean something else."

To most native speakers of English, *ironic* is an adjective synonymous with "mocking, humorously or sarcastically inverted"; when Stephen Sondheim's lyric of "Send in the Clowns" begins "Isn't it rich?" the meaning is "Isn't my mental lapse, late in life, rich in irony?" Instances of that mocking tone, crossing into savage sarcasm, are found throughout the book: Job lashes back at the pompous consoler Zophar with "No doubt you are perfect men and absolute wisdom is yours!"[1] God uses the same contemptuous tone when he taunts know-it-all Job with "Doubtless you know all this . . . so long is the span of your life!"[2] The intended meaning of both statements is, obviously, the opposite of the words: Wisdom will not die with the death of the pompous Zophar, and the sum of Job's days is a ripple in the long current of time.

Irony also reverberates in the modern mind because it goes beyond quirky coincidence to define an event of special incongruity or unfairness—for example, the holdup of a police station or a riot in a place of worship. The basis of God's choice of Job for testing was that he was God's favorite, the only blameless man on earth, one whose innocence made his suffering seem especially inappropriate or meaningless. Job's damnation of the day he was born was based on the irony in this unfairness.

One ancient form of irony is feigned ignorance. It is often called Socratic irony, after the method used by the philosopher, in Plato's dialogues, when he wanted to use an innocent untruth in order to get at a truth. Modern journalists call the technique "fishing". ("I guess you felt you had to mislead Congress that way, Director Casey, because you were protecting the President from guilty knowledge.")

The playwright Arthur Miller calls its use in the theater "acting against the words": an actor contradicts the words he is speaking by the way he uses his body. When Richard Nixon, in the throes of Watergate, told a news conference, "I am not a crook," a television critic wrote that it was as if Shakespeare's deformed Richard III had announced, "I am not a crookback": Body language seemed to speak against the words.

Using a similar irony, poet-Job sets the stage for the testing of Job in the prologue by having God pretend not to know where the Satan has been roaming. In fact, the reader knows that God knows everything. Irony—which can also mean the truth spoken as if untrue—is based on words playing against each other.

That sends us down into the etymology of the word. The Greek *eiron* is "one who dissembles, who speaks untruths"; that is based on *eirein,* "to say", in turn linked, along with the Latin *verbum,* to the earlier Indo-European *wer,* "to speak", which is also the source of the word *word.* That, as speechwriter Bryce Harlow liked to say, "peels the onion right down to where the tears are".

Poet-Job plays ironic word-tricks. Job asks God, "Why dost thou hide thy face and treat me as thy enemy?"[3] The Hebrew word for "enemy" is transliterated *oyeb,* which poet-Job may have been playing against the Hebrew name for Job, *Iyyob.* Could God's favorite also have been in some way God's enemy? Irony—it makes you ponder.

Apply this interplay of truth and falsity to what playwrights in the beginning of the twentieth century labeled "dramatic irony": the situation in which the characters on a stage are ignorant of what the audience knows. Not only does this give the viewer or reader a sense of Godlike superiority, it instills a sense of helplessness: The reader understands but cannot intercede. Yet this very helplessness wrenches the audience back up to an identification with God, who gave Man free will and must not intervene as he makes the most terrible mistakes.

Nowhere is this sense of dramatic irony more vivid than in the Book of Job. The prologue lets the reader in on the celestial bet: The purpose of the infliction of suffering on a man who deserves no punishment is to test the disinterestedness of Man's piety. Job is never told this central purpose; he protests injustice when the point is not God's justice but the motive behind Man's worship. We know Job does not understand; we do. We know the consolers are wrong when they assume all suffering must be the result of sin; they cannot know, but we know. The tension in this dramatic irony is what has gripped the reader for more than two millennia, but the modern reader finds it especially gripping: We like contradictions and revel in cross-purposes, getting a charge out of a combination of involvement and detachment. In Job, we find ourselves working both ends of our double-handled whipsaw: The passionate poetry involves us while the cool irony detaches us.

That slices open the text: We are permitted to disbelieve any words we see in Job on the grounds that they may be ironic, intended to mean the opposite. The Hollywood ending? A device to provide a sop to the sanctimonious. Job's self-predicted cave-in at the blast from the whirlwind? A technique of saying submissive words while remaining one of the "children of pride". Of course, this recourse to irony when it suits us to deny what is in plain sight leads to an anything-goes interpretation, the celebration of alienation, and the reduction of meaning to absurdity. That is not my own thing; it shows why, however, poet-Job's fondness for irony has been catnip to many of the artists and critics of the recent century.

Is Job's challenge unique? Job's sustained rebelliousness sticks out of the Bible like an angry index finger, but his supreme effrontery has company in Western tradition. The same tingling challenge to political and religious systems that fail to deal with real-life anguish reverberates (I try to avoid "resonates") in our most ancient myths and texts.

Prometheus is Job's ancient soul mate. Like Job, the Greek god is a favorite of those who enjoy the high life of the mind. A gilded statue of Prometheus bound to a rock inspires the ice skaters at the rink in New York's Rockefeller Center, or at least those few who recognize him, to dizzying whirls; he was chosen by the builders of Radio City to crouch there, a burst of bronze flame in his hand, because he is the patron god of communication and the arts. (Hermes, the messenger of the gods, pictured like his Roman counterpart Mercury with the silly wings on his feet, is disdained by high-domed media types; that's because communicators now presume to be gods shaping events, not merely messengers for the gods of politics, finance, or culture. Prometheus puts media biggies in the center of action, at the decision-making level.)

We remember Prometheus as the member of the society of immortals who infuriated Zeus by giving fire to Man. You know the myth: The chief god, realizing that this gift of power made men godlike, chained Man's benefactor to a rock and inflicted unending punishment. But our hero refused to beg Zeus for mercy, and unflinchingly cried out against his injustice. We like that.

There was more to the pattern of Hesiodic folktales than that mythical thought-bite. Prometheus was a minor immortal who gained some notoriety among the gods because he created Man; Zeus was a tyrant toying with the idea of destroying this troublesome creation. When Prometheus got wind of Zeus's intent to snuff out mankind, he stole some of the fire from Olympus and gave it to Man, which opened the way to art and science—a bridge to immortality. Zeus, furious at the insubordination and worried about no longer being able to treat humanity as mortal—thus, killable—chained the communicative friend of Man to a rock and prepared to force Prometheus to do away with the upstart god's human creation. (Not even the chief god could make a certified immortal die, but he could try to break his resolution.)

Now the myth picks up speed. The mother of Prometheus, a prophetess, slipped her suffering but defiant son a secret on which the future of Zeus depended. The secret—which the audience knows, but Zeus does not, the same dramatic irony used in Job—was that Zeus was about to marry a bride "whose son would be greater than his father". Zeus discovered that the god chained to a rock knew something important that could affect the Olympian future, but could not sweat the secret out of gutsy Prometheus. Zeus began to suffer anxiety about the loss of his primacy among the gods, so a deal was struck: Prometheus was released along with all his Titan family, and mankind was allowed to survive, in return for the information that was so valuable to Zeus—that he should not marry that girl.

Aeschylus, the Greek dramatist who lived in the fifth century B.C.—possibly a contemporary of poet-Job—took this mythic miniseries and wrote a trilogy, only parts of which survive. His allegory had a political purpose: The Greek city-state was experimenting with democracy, having just thrown off the power of tyrants, and the playwright wanted to show how nascent democrats could teach those in authority a lesson in humility. Putting fragments of the trilogy together with the other plays of Aeschylus, the critic Gilbert Murray posited that the dramatist's point was that suffering taught Zeus understanding, and that "aching with remembered pain", he freed Prometheus and did all those other reconciling things. Thus, the tyrannical Zeus was both softened and strengthened by the suffering he endured from having to tolerate the dissident Prometheus. The message was that gods are not complete, but are perfectable; challenge from below is good for them.

Did poet-Job read Aeschylus, or vice versa? We don't know. But both of these original thinkers dealt with the need to reconcile godly omnipotence and human dignity, and both writers used a myth or legend as the device to give them cover in undertaking what otherwise might have been condemned as heresies.

They came at it in different ways. Prometheus was undeniably guilty of fire-stealing; humanity is empowered by his stolen goods, another form of original sin. Job, on the contrary, was stipulated to be blame-free. Prometheus hated the despotic Zeus; although Job was angry at an unjust God, and was disappointed in God's apparent inattention to his obligations, the man from Uz was determined to "maintain his ways"—hold fast to his personal integrity—despite God's disfavor. Unlike Prometheus, Job never hated his master; on the contrary, he kept trying to engage him in personal disputation to achieve justice and shake a depressing sense of isolation.

The two myths differ in the feeling of persecuted for persecutor, but they contain these common strands: dissent from dogma, defiance of supreme authority. Both Job and Prometheus insist on individual integrity despite great pain. This insistence on the purity of principle, even against the high and mighty, is not wrong but right—and divine certification of that righteousness can ultimately be wrung from Zeus or elicted from God.

Bring that myth into the nineteenth century. With a poet-painter-printer-prophet in 1818 named William Blake came a wholly new look at Job, breaking with artistic and religious tradition. Blake was a one-man band of communication, the multimedia pioneer: He could envision, write, illustrate, engrave, print, and bind a book, and then serve as its literary agent. In his watercolor illustrations and engravings, this paragon of versatility took as many liberties with the biblical Job as poet-Job did with the original, apocryphal Job; indeed, Blake put the whole book and all its characters inside Job's mind, with the search for God one man's search for his own soul. But Blake's Job served the purpose of associating this book of the Bible with Man's freedom against the repression of civilization and the strictures of organized religion.

Some of Blake's illustrations of the Book of Job adorn, illuminate, and deepen this book. He first painted the illustrations in watercolor, and years later made engravings of them, framing the pictures in artistic and verbal commentary.

In Blake the artist's first illustration, facing page 82, which shows the prosperous Job with his doomed family as night draws near, Blake the poet asserts "The Letter Killeth/The Spirit giveth Life." Symbolic forms count heavily in Blake—"not a line is drawn without intention," he wrote a friend—and this admonishes the reader to look beyond the literal, or the book in Job's lap, to find reality in the spiritual world.

The action, remember, is not literal, but takes place within Job's mind. That's why Job's face so closely resembles God's. Blake's Job creates the Satan and his own version of God; the left hand or foot represents the bad, the material, while the right signifies the good, the spiritual.

The scholar Joseph Wicksteed broke Blake's symbolic code a century after the poet-painter-printer's death, helping mightily to discern his mystical system and give shape to the Blakean universe. In that system, legality, the law's campaign against sin and guilt, culminating in forgiveness or punishment, was on the left, the sinis-

ter side; inspiration and desire were on the right, the side of goodness. Blake saw his Job's tragic error in admitting the presence of
the proud Satan to his mind, where an accuser or censor should
have no place—Man's imagination should be untrammeled, his
secret desires no business of society's. The biblical Job fought injustice; the Blakean version of Job fought the rigid and unforgiving
justice that Blake believed smothered Christian love and creativity.

That notion of organized religion stultifying God's inspiration
shocked Blake's contemporaries and remains troubling to many
people today; most artists, contrariwise, go with Blake, free imagination and desire against the suppressive forces of law, which is
why both Blake and Job did not come into their own until the
modern era.

A long generation after Blake, across the Atlantic, another
work of art was written that was also to be a late bloomer: Herman
Melville launched his symbol-laden novel *Moby-Dick*.

Melville used a variety of myths and epics to define his vision
of God's harsh and often sinister relationship to Man: Prometheus,
Faust, Milton's Satan, Job, and Jonah. He strewed his fictional
landscape with biblical associations and mythic allusions. At age
thirty-two—debt-ridden, ill, unhappily married, fearful of blindness—Melville could have easily identified his fate with Job's: "the
truest of all men was the Man of Sorrows", he wrote in *Moby-Dick*.
Like Job, who was long identified in sermons as the Man of Sorrows, Melville struck out at his unjust tormentor in his artistic rage.

Students in freshman English at college regularly go overboard
fishing for symbols from the *Pequod*'s whaleboat. The great American novel is the great repository of biblical symbolism, and its
bones have been picked over by every critic. Still, I think the Joban
slant deserves another look.

In the Bible, Ishmael is the son of Abraham's rejected concu-
bine, and—in an early hint of God's unconcern for justice—is
driven with his mother from his father's house, condemned to
wander abroad. In *Moby-Dick,* the character named Ishmael is
Melville's outcast, the eternal wanderer, the lonely survivor.

Although he is at the compositional center of the novel, the
narrating Ishmael is not the protagonist. That heroic role belongs
to Captain Ahab, named for the biblical king who defied God and

worshiped idols ("Ahab did more to provoke the Lord God of Israel to anger than all the kings of Israel that were before him"[4]). The biblical author recounts that at the irreligious King Ahab's death, dogs licked up his blood, in an extreme example of God's retribution in the part of the Bible that demonstrates distributive justice.

Captain Ahab's antagonist is the white whale, symbolizing—you name it—a tyrannical God, the uncaring universe, the reflecting self. "Be the White Whale agent or be the White Whale principal," says the driven captain, alluding to the Satan or God himself, "I will wreak that hate upon him." Ahab has been previously afflicted by the whale—he has lost his leg to it in a previous encounter—and burns with the need to wreak vengeance at injustice by killing his nemesis or himself. Blasphemy? All caution is rejected: "Talk to me not of blasphemy, man; I'd strike the sun if it insulted me." The critic Edward Said calls the work "a book about going too far, pressing too hard, overstepping limits"—as Prometheus did with Zeus, and as Job did with God.

Ahab is Joban in his determination to confront God as an equal. When Melville wallows in whale lore and uses the sea as a symbol of chaos, he follows the analogy to tumultuous nature that poet-Job employs in the Lord's second speech out of the whirlwind. Hostile nature or the forces of disorder are epitomized in Leviathan, cited as "king over all the children of pride".[5] The anti-humility symbol is now generally assumed to be the crocodile, but was considered by Melville and most others of his time to be the whale. But both poet-Job and Melville had in mind no natural beast. Leviathan—the name rooted in the surrounding or coiling action of a snake—is a mythical monster of the chaotic sea, the eternal rebel, a permanent threat to God's order and Man's life. Poet-Job was undoubtedly familiar with the Ugaritic myths of his time. He has Job close out his curse of the day he was born with "Cursed be it by those whose magic binds even the monster of the deep, who are ready to tame Leviathan himself with spells."[6] Refusing to "hold my peace", Job asks God: "Am I the monster of the deep, am I the sea-serpent, that thou settest a watch over me?"[7]

Leviathan was pictured by William Blake in illustration 15 (in the endpapers of this book) as a twisting serpent fighting God's global constraints. Like the "Tyger! Tyger! burning bright" in his most famous poem, Blake's Leviathan is a mythic beast, created by or tolerated by God, that stands for the tyranny of nature (or sanctified repression) over Man. Yet God made all creatures, including the forces that threaten his order. This assertion of the universal fatherhood of God—of even the children of pride—is in Blake's question about the fearsome tiger: "Did he who made the Lamb make thee?" Job, in his summation of his defense before the thunderous theophany, points to his fair treatment of slaves and breaks through to the concept of universal human brotherhood by linking powerful and humble: "Did not he who made me in the womb make them? Did not the same God create us in the belly?"[8]

Blake was not plagiarizing any more than Melville; both were writing their variations on the Joban theme. "Melville's Moby Dick is another Tyger," wrote the critic Harold Bloom in 1963, in one sentence linking Melville, Blake, and Aeschylus in Joban rebellion, "but Ahab strikes through the mask, and asserts the Promethian defiance . . ."

Now, hold on: If Leviathan represents chaos, and Ahab is fighting Leviathan, doesn't that place Ahab—albeit a little too singlemindedly—on the side of God and the good? No. To Ahab, and perhaps to Melville, God equals chaos and a malevolent fate and the deathly-white whale. That's my interpretation, and if it was not the author's symbolic intent, deconstructionists would call it a fruitful misunderstanding.

Other Joban allusions abound in *Moby-Dick,* the work of the nineteenth century that this century rightly treats as "the great American novel". Before the voyage begins, Ishmael meets one of the owners, Captain Bildad, "the pious Bildad", a hard-hearted Quaker pictured thumbing his Bible, "mumbling to himself out of his book", not very subtly representing petrified religion, much as Bildad the Shuhite in Job. On the voyage, Ishmael marvels at how Ahab goes "chasing with curses a Job's whale around the world". Ahab's final words, as he hurls the harpoon at the sea-monster destroying him, are "Thus I give up the spear!"; the selection of the synonym "spear" rather than "harpoon" may be an allusion to God's description of Leviathan's invincibility by Man: "he laugheth at the shaking of a spear".[9]

The whaler *Pequod*'s voyage ends as Ishmael, the only member of the crew who had not sworn an irreligious oath to kill the whale, stays afloat by clinging to a coffin after Moby-Dick sinks the ship, using an image of death to save his life. He is picked up by the devious cruising ship named the *Rachel,* searching for one of her lost crew—as in both the biblical books of Jeremiah and Matthew, Jacob's wife, Rachel, was described as "weeping for her children".

The epilogue to *Moby-Dick* is begun with the words of the Job prologue: "And I only am escaped alone to tell thee." These are the repeated words of messengers to Job telling of his catastrophes. (One of them, from a Blake illustration, adorns the jacket of this book, prefiguring the journalists who bring the news of new suffering to dissenters.) The others on Ahab's ship cursed God and died, as Job's wife suggested that Job do; Ishmael, the only one who did not challenge God, is the only one to survive the wreck. That allows him to be the bearer of the novel's bad news to the world.

And what is that bad news? Like poet-Job, Melville lets the reader figure that out for himself, but the message is surely not that God—or Nature, or Destiny—is merciful or just. As I get the message, Melville, like poet-Job, sees the universe run badly, even malevolently, and that heroic Man must seek his destiny in defiance of this injustice. "I have written a wicked book," Melville wrote to his friend Nathaniel Hawthorne, "and feel spotless as the lamb"— much as poet-Job may have felt. Melville evidently considered his work, like poet-Job's, blasphemous but not really wicked. (Unfortunately, we have no correspondence between poet-Job and Aeschylus.)

Let's follow Melville's Joban inspiration into his use of the prophet Jonah, who also offers an argument about justice and power. Jonah is almost a parody of a prophet. He did not want the job; commanded by God to go east, he headed west, running away over the sea even to the point where, in Ira Gershwin's rhyme, "he made his home in dat fish's abdomen," only to be upchucked by that great fish onto the shores of his assigned prophetic city. Then he trudged into Nineveh, a heathen city, to announce loudly that it would be all over for its sinful citizenry in forty days. Instead of being ignored or hooted at, as is usually the lot of prophets, Jonah is believed. The local king penitently puts on a garb of sackcloth and, Joblike, sits on a pile of garbage; as a result, God spares the city.

Because his dire prophecy does not self-fulfill, the reluctant prophet goes out into the desert and makes himself a hut in which to brood. God provides for a leafy plant to shoot up and provide shade, which Jonah appreciates. Then God kills the plant, infuriating his newly hot-headed prophet, who tells God, "I should be better dead than alive."[10] At that point, the biblical author springs his trap. God says in effect: You're making a big deal out of my killing one miserable plant, and yet you want me to destroy a city of more than a hundred thousand people, plus animals? Where's your justice in that?

Here is Jonah's God asking his prophet the same question that Job asks of his God: How can you be so wantonly cruel? In Jonah, God is merciful and just, while the prophet is not; in Job, just the opposite. The reason that our century brushes off Jonah and embraces Job is not merely that Jonah is a petulant fumbler and Job a suffering genius. The reason is that the source of injustice is not poignant and infuriating when it comes from supposedly perfect God, not from fallible Man. Even the prophets have their human failings; God has no such easy excuse for the inexplicable misery rained on the human beings who did no wrong.

Now we are at the threshold of the modern fascination with Job. The simple answer suggested at the start of this book—that we admire stand-up guys—is not enough of an explanation for the phenomenon of Joban popularity today. We especially like stand-up guys who take on the battles we wish we had the guts to take on ourselves—who express our innermost doubts about the way the world is run and demand not so much spiritual solace as emotional satisfaction.

Great waves take a long run before slamming down on a modern beach. Several currents of thought and art began to run in the first half of the nineteenth century that became waves of influence in the second half of the twentieth. We've glanced at the Joban influence in Blake and Melville; consider now Søren Kierkegaard, a Danish philosopher who disentangled himself from the prevailing view about a God of ethics requiring universal obligations of Man.

Kierkegaard, whose notions of a subjective, inward religious passion did not make much of a splash in a time dominated by the rational, cool-headed philosophy of Hegel, argued that God was more concerned with faith than with ethics, and that the individual human being was often closest to him in suffering. Best known as the author of *Fear and Trembling,* the title of one his books (now a modern cliché not to be confused with Whitelipt & Trembling, S. J. Perelman's accountants), Kierkegaard held that man could be certain of nothing, could "know" little of the design of the universe, and this very lack of knowledge was the basis of faith.

To the comfortably devout, Kierkegaard directed this shaft of anxiety, rooted in the experience of Job: "Perhaps you believe that such a thing cannot happen to you. . . . Are you powerful, is this your assurance of immunity? Job was reverenced by the people. Are riches your security? Job possessed the blessing of lands. Are your friends your guarantors? Job was loved by everyone. Do you put your confidence in God? Job was the Lord's confidant . . . there is no hiding place in the wide world where troubles may not find you." He picked up the shuddering thought that also afflicted and stimulated Blake and Melville: "No man knows the time and the hour when the messengers will come to him, each one more terrifying than the last."

I am not the only one escaped alone to tell you that a useful fear and trembling blossomed and withered in our time in the philosophy of existentialism. It held that it was not reason but existence—living with the intimation of danger—that was the basis of the relationship between Job and his God. "There was a Promethean excitement in Job's coming face to face with his creator and demanding justification," wrote William Barrett, foremost American exponent of this philosophy, in 1958. He saw the resolution of the confrontation not in Job getting the answer about injustice, but in reaffirming his blind faith. That sort of elemental and personal trust comes before belief in organized religion, and what seems blasphemous is actually a desirable directness of dealing: "When faith is full, it dares to express its anger," wrote Barrett, "for faith is the openness of the whole man toward his God . . ."

This discomfiting path led some into nihilism, which proudly marches off to nowhere; yet the existentialists were groping for a need in today's humanity to fill a void in human consciousness first recognized by poet-Job. That hole in the soul is a sense of isolation, of unexpected and unwanted detachment from God, of David Reisman's lonely-crowdedness. By the 1960s, the trendiest politico-philosophical term had become *alienation*. We all remember the superficial expressions of that stampede to estrangement: the publicized anguish of the misunderstood, the self-rejecting glorification of the dropped-out, the regimentation of noncomformity. The vogue word that followed *alienation* was *absurd*—the absurdity of life, the theater of the absurd—and grotesqueness and boredom were elevated to art forms.

Other artists and thinkers found a more lasting Joban message in Kierkegaard, from the letters of his fictional young man in *Repetition:* that being in the minority does not mean being in the wrong. "The secret in Job, the vital force, the nerve, the idea, is that Job, despite everything, is in the right." All Job's friends, all the experts, berate him, press him to admit his error, but they are all wrong; only Job is right when he insists that his suffering has nothing to do with sin. What greater example can be found to justify defiance of received wisdom? Thoreau's "different drummer" may be the one to have the rhythm right, a reading of Job suggests, and the rest of the world may be out of step. Iconoclasts everywhere found in Job a champion of cutting against the grain, of swimming against the current: The man vilified for being sinfully wrong was right all along, and even God admits it twice in the end.

That's why a sign in pseudo-Latin is hung on the iconoclast's wall: *Illegitimi Non Carborundum* ("Don't let the bastards grind you down"). Today's experts are tomorrow's ignoramuses. As the Danish philosopher wrote, "Passion is often smothered in a person when faintheartedness and petty anxiety have allowed him to think he is suffering because of his sins, when that was not at all the case." Kierkegaard condemned the fainthearted whose "soul lacked the perseverance to carry through an idea when the world incessantly disagreed with him".

No wonder, then, we see this new generational interest in the insight of poet-Job. He recognizes, as we do, that the universe is not organized to deliver justice or even fair play to our eyes, and that God isn't even going to apologize. We are given some assurance, however, that all is not absurd—because human beings may have been created to give moral meaning to life. Job's fear and trembling does not stop him from insisting on his ways, from complaining mightily and often rightly, or from demanding that the impersonal universe be more orderly and more personal. Job does not win, unless you fall for the point-killer ending, but winning is not all. His struggle for purpose against his mortal-friendly adversary in heaven is what keeps him going and what makes the twenty-five-hundred-year-old work relevant to the point of immediacy.

The most memorable opening sentence in a twentieth-century novel, comparable to Melville's "Call me Ishmael" in the nineteenth, begins Franz Kafka's *The Trial:* "Someone must have slandered Joseph K., for without having done anything wrong he was arrested one fine morning." The rest of the novel about inexplicable star-chamber persecution, which resulted in the word *Kafkaesque* being added to the language, never refers to the Book of Job but was described by the theologian Martin Buber as the best Job commentary of that generation.

To the question, Why does this work keep exciting fresh interpretation among creative artists, philosophers, and political soreheads? my answer is: The Book of Job is not perfect, and was left unfinished by the original author for good reason. The troubling text comes to us as a "work in progress", inviting each of us to fix it our way or otherwise move its progress along. Job's open-endedness ropes us in.

# PART II

# THE VERDICTS IN JOB V. GOD

# 1

## WHAT BELIEVERS
## TAKE FROM JOB

PEOPLE WHO BELIEVE in God have drawn some of the following lessons from the Book of Job:

### 1. Don't ask God to do you a favor.

Suggesting that a do-gooder is motivated by a sinister or unworthy purpose is a familiar political slur. When candidates tell us they want only to be "public servants", when they go on about how much they respect us and promise to do all we want, even the most charitable voter is tempted to wonder: What are they really after? What's in it for them? Power, glory, and a lucrative book contract afterward?

When God taunts the Satan about the uprightness of the world's most blame-free man, the skeptical angel puts the question of motive forward with a sneer that can be felt through the ages: "Does Job fear God for nought?" Is Job, God's favorite, really being religious out of the goodness of his heart, or is this wealthy and powerful chieftain merely seeking a continuance of his good fortune?

Communist propagandists were fond of beginning derogations of capitalists with a cliché that was translated as "Not for nothing . . ." Not for nothing does Job eschew evil, suggests the Satan. Not for nothing does Job worship God. On the contrary, a keen sense of self-interest is involved. The crux of the issue is stated in the lead of the story: What does Job worship God *for*?

One of the Book of Job's central lessons is that we should not worship God for what we can get out of him. Obviously this rules out praying for Job's herd of she-asses and pack of camels, but it also goes for things that many unselfish people pray for—a worthy spouse, health for our children, peace for the world. We may not even pray to him to get what we are sure we deserve, like peace of mind; that comfort often comes out of the process of worship, and—let's face it—may be an unspoken purpose of worship, but it should not be the goal of religious devotion.

Worship should have no goal at all. Devotion should be about giving and not about getting, so forget about a quid pro quo. Praying to get something good or to avoid something bad is not worship; Job teaches that a worthy worshiper (two words with the same root) is neither a mendicant nor a negotiator. Worthy worship is wholly impractical.

We tend to burden political idealism with a load of practicality, too. Democracy is sold as the necessary precursor to free enterprise, the economic system that raises everyone's standard of living. The argument is true enough, but is unworthy of the ideal: The human spirit yearns for freedom, and democracy is the best way we have found to secure a free society. The economic growth that free enterprise brings is a bonus to the free, just as the sense of congregation is an extra reward believers get from praying with others. But freedom and worship are ends, not means. Our motive in seeking freedom, like our motive in worshiping God, is not what freedom or God can do for us. Our motive in each case should be to stretch and fulfill the human spirit.

## 2. God is not a just God or an unjust God; he is just God.

To moralists who wonder why the innocent must suffer, the answer that poet-Job offers is disappointing but unequivocal. To those seeking strict moral guidance in the books of Moses, God provides commandments, but to those seeking moral law enforcement in the Book of Job, the deity shrugs: not my department.

Because no celestial cop walks a beat enforcing individual morality, humanity has worked out its own system to define and discourage sin, and to offer incentives for an ethical life. To believers, poet-Job teaches sternly that we have to work out the best justice we can here on earth. God does not mete out reward or penalty according to what each of us deserves as a result of our actions.

But if that bleak and lonely path is the way of the world, why did God give Moses those ten hard-to-follow commandments? Why is worship so intertwined with morality, with directions from on high chiseled on tablets of stone about right and wrong? What about all those dire warnings elsewhere in the Bible about keeping the covenants God made with Man?

These paramount issues are addressed by poet-Job. Judaism's traditions began with the idea of retribution: In the felicitous phrase of the Book of Micah, the believers in a single God were enjoined "to do justly, love mercy and walk humbly" with him. Implicit was a promise that they would get something valuable for that behavior, as well as a threat that wickedness would bring God's abandonment and suffering. In the sterner Leviticus 26, God says, "If you conform to my statutes . . . I will give you rain at the proper time. . . . If you reject my statutes . . . I will bring upon you sudden terror, wasting disease . . ."[1] In a passage of Isaiah that was often quoted by President Lyndon Johnson, Yahweh says, "Come now and let us reason together"; a closer interpretation of the last two words is "dispute together as if in court". God's invitation to dispute contains a hard edge, for Isaiah's passage goes on: "If you are willing and obedient, you will eat the good of the land; But if you refuse and rebel, you will be devoured by the sword."[2]

This is often what a tough-minded litigant offers his opponent at law. Deuteronomists and modern litigators know that the carrot of reward was never as great as the stick of punishment: A tribute is a payment, and *retribution* means "to pay back".

There was more to the contract described in Genesis than a mere "worship only me and I'll protect only you." Along with a reverential requirement laid on Israel went moral strictures in the form of commandments. In return, ancient humanity came to place an ethical obligation on its one God—to do justly, or at least to govern mercifully. Retribution is the way of most of the biblical world: Worship God, as Joshua did, and win the wars; ignore God, as King Ahab did, and die with your blood being licked up by dogs. Ally yourself with God, as the duly fearful Noah did, and survive; oppose him and his moral commandments, as did fun-loving residents of Sodom and Gomorrah, and face annihilation. The people of the Torah voluntarily recognized a higher power out of gratitude (for all God has done so far) and fear (for the consequences of wrongdoing) and awe (for the wonderment and mystery of life).

This theory of just retribution, expounded throughout the early books of the Bible, worked for a few centuries because the moral dos and don'ts of the commandments had the muscle of reward or punishment behind them. But that retribution theory kept running aground on the rocks of reality: We, the good people, often suffered for no apparent reason, and they, the demonstrably wicked set having a fine old time up on the hill, showed no sign of ending their orgy. This obvious inequity in the frequent triumph of iniquity must have seeded the clouds of doubt; some Joban scholars think it precipitated an early crisis of the Jewish faith.

It could be argued that the five books of Moses dealt with paying back not to the individual, but to the tribe of Israel as a whole, and, by extension, to all humanity. People were to get what they deserved only on average, goes this modified form of retribution theology. But human lives are not lived in the aggregate, and one of the features of Judaism was the intensely personal relationship between God and each of his people. The religion had to recognize and counter this logical doubt about individual retribution in the minds of believers or lose its moral authority. A new religious theory had to be advanced to take the place of divine retribution, to take account of the reality of everyday injustice, of the obvious unfairness of life.

Enter poet-Job, somewhere between the fourth and sixth centuries before the birth of Christ. He knew that the promise of retribution in this life was no longer working; the promise of retribution in a life after death had not yet been advanced. The covenantal tie was too tight; after a few centuries of trial, the contract showed its strain and needed reinterpretation.

At that crucial time, poet-Job had an idea to restructure religious belief in a radical way: to reject the whole fear-inspiring, greed-inducing notion of divine retribution. He rerooted religion in real life by taking God entirely out of moral law enforcement. Poet-Job's plan was to realign the lord-vassal relationship by lessening the earthly requirements of the lord and increasing the spiritual freedom of the vassal. God was no longer to be held responsible for enforcement of the moral law, as promised so specifically in Leviticus; his worshipers were to be given the right to complain mightily and to challenge the interpretations of the orthodox leaders.

This denial of any obligation by God to distribute justice with an even hand required a wrenching change in what had been the relationship between God and Man. No longer could the human being be God's central creature, created in his own image, destined to lord it over all others. Instead, his human creation had to be diminished until he was a speck in the universe, an incident in the great conquest of instability and darkness by the bringer of order and light. This is the part of the Job-message many moderns find unacceptable; when we come to political lessons, we will find interpretations that rebuild human significance.

In poet-Job's revision of the world, God could make commandments available to humanity that would help him bring the order of goodness to the anarchy of the jungle. However, his human creations could not impose that same order on God, or demand that God act as moral policeman or Court of Claims. In Robert Frost's *A Masque of Reason,* the modern poet has a much-relieved God tell Job:

> *You realize by now the part you played*
> *To stultify the Deuteronomist*
> *And change the nature of religious thought.*

*My thanks to you for releasing me*
*From moral bondage to the human race.*

Poet-Job removed from God responsibility to be the world's moral policeman—but what could he substitute for the fear of punishment and hope of reward to people secure in their faith? He hit on this positive idea: Prayer has a value in itself. That's the flip side of the negative, don't-look-for-a-material-payoff lesson. The truly religious person, in Joban theology, not only worships God with no payoff in mind but is uplifted by that unselfish love. Goodness is self-edifying; ethical living satisfies the conscience; virtue is, as proverbially advertised, its own reward, and don't look to God for a bonus.

In political terms, this idea represented an extraordinary devolution of power. The people in the boondocks, who had looked to the capital in heaven for supreme authority on the administration of justice, were now told: You have the laws, work out the enforcement yourselves on a local level. Don't keep running to God for reward or punishment; in modern jargon, a person's fate is not behavior-driven. Federalize moral authority: Determine your own justice, beat your own swords into plowshares, manage the affairs of fairness, and on those occasions when the injustice is overwhelming—the city shattered by earthquake, the baby born with a drug addiction—call these "acts of God" and consider lesson three, about the inscrutability of God's ways:

### 3. God's ways are not Man's ways.

The voice from the whirlwind informs Job that there are vast areas of human ignorance—things "beyond his ken" that humans may never learn. The universality of the puzzle should give comfort to the puzzled individual. To resolve his dilemma of injustice under an all-powerful God, Job's Man had to view God's ways as inscrutable. Not only did Man not know, he could not be privy to the knowledge and power that order the universe.

Man's need for justice for himself was far less important, Job seemed to teach, than the needs of a commander of the cosmos who sometimes had to compromise with chaos's floods and earthquakes. Earthly injustice was part of cosmic justice. What seemed to Job to be innocent suffering was part of a vast design, unknown to mankind, that would—if any eye could see it—demonstrate God's ultimate evenhandedness. What seems to the earthly reader to be a cruel bet between God and the Satan about Job's motive in the prologue is a necessary cosmic exercise to reaffirm the purity of Man's love of God. It's as if we could see only one of the two scales that the goddess of justice holds aloft. Somewhere forever out of our sight there is another scale, making what seems like injustice fall into some kind of balance.

The assumption that the injustice we see would all be made right if we could only see the big picture has long been taken to be a central message of Job. In this Job was answering the doubters who knew that the old theory of retribution wasn't working. Faced with the fact of injustice, poet-Job could say only that God's ways were not Man's ways, and that we must satisfy ourselves with the prospect of eternal inscrutability.

To the philosopher Friedrich Nietzsche, this placed God "beyond good and evil". The scientist and educator James B. Conant summed up the uppity-Man approach with "If I read the book of Job correctly, its lesson is a denial of the assumption that the universe is explicable in human terms; it is a corrective to the presumption of human beings in applying their standards of value to the cosmos."

I find this apology, often put forward in explicating the book of Job, emotionally comforting but intellectually defeatist. It reminds me of the man who says "Ask me about my business," and when his friend asks "How's business?" the man sighs "Don't ask."

The God-given nature of Man is to ask, to learn, to explore, and, if it helps to get answers, to shake his fist at anything that contributes to his damnable ignorance. It cannot be the mission of poet-Job to inhibit this nature—meekly to accept limits to learning, to refrain from asking, to learn to live in the dark. Incomprehensibility is to be resented and attacked, never to be accepted. If we assume that Man was endowed with curiosity for a divine purpose, it follows that enigmas were created to be illuminated by insight and conundrums to be chipped away at by cumulative understanding. Not everything may be solvable now, but nothing is unthinkable, and mind-freeing answers lie ahead to mysteries that now seem unknowable. What did the ancients know of space travel and genetic engineering? And we are the next generation's ancients.

God's opening question out of the whirlwind offers a more satisfying way of coming at this surrender to incomprehensibility. "Who is this whose ignorant words cloud my design in darkness?"[3] (The verb in the KJV has a deeper ring: "Who is this that darkeneth counsel by words without knowledge?"[4]) This implies that God does have "counsel"; the word is not used in the modern, lawyerly sense of "advice", but more as Jeremiah quoted God as saying "Is counsel perished from the prudent?"[5] The synonyms of this early sense are "purpose, plan, design"; the military meaning is "mission". Job has challenged and beclouded God's grand design; by his terrible "oath of clearance", the challenging man has forced his God to act or, by remaining aloof, to forfeit the moral contest and concede that Job's accusations of sloppy moral management are true. God appears with the usual fanfare and immediately asserts he does so have a plan.

The apparent farrago of rhetorical questions that follows is not only a sarcastic blast at Man's presumption—"Where were you when I laid the earth's foundations?"[6]; the questions also illuminate the magnitude of creation. He has the stars organized in the heavens—"Can you bind the cluster of the Pleiades or loose Orion's belt?"[7] These constellations were gods in the pagan heavens, and now they answer to him.

He has laws to determine what the stars do, surely a sign of planning: "Did you proclaim the rules that govern the heavens . . .?"[8] But he is not so busy with the architecture of the universe that he cannot manifest himself by taking care of the details of existence, too: "Who provides the raven with its quarry when its fledglings croak for lack of food?"[9] Just because Job cannot see the plan does not mean there is no grand master plan running the universe.

Job is chastised for obscuring God's counsel, his universal mission. In his speeches from the whirlwind, God takes Job into his confidence: Instead of answering such wounded-pride questions as why Job should be so humiliated before his former slave girls, God broadens his perspective, showing him how much more there is to the cosmos than Man has ever dreamed of. That, and not the thunder of intimidation, renews the man's lost trust and restores his shaken faith.

Although Job has been pestering God with his "whys", the Lord's voice in the whirlwind suggests a question that Job has not thought to ask: "Who has cut channels for the downpour and cleared a passage for the thunderstorm, for rain to fall on land where no man lives . . . ?"[10] In other words, why am I wasting valuable rain on the uninhabited desert? Water was precious to the ancient nomads; throughout the Bible, rain was God's reward and drought his punishment. But here God asserts that he is throwing it away on empty desert, as if to demonstrate that rainfall has nothing to do with human behavior, that Job's morality was no business of God's.

Man is self-centered, but God is not Man-centered; part of his plan, which Man cannot grasp, is to give the life-giving water to things in places where no man goes—and if Man doesn't like that or thinks it is wasteful, too bad. These passages in God's speeches should be of special interest to environmentalists, especially those who will hold up a hydroelectric dam to preserve the snail darter: The plants and atmosphere may not exist merely to serve Man. The animal-rights contingent, even to the fur-haters and vegetarians, will find succor here as well. (I call my two Bernese mountain dogs pets, not "companion animals"; I am their owner and master, not their associate, which they forget all too often as they drag me into a snowbank. But a true Joban receives the message that Homo sapiens is not the only living thing at the center of God's concerns.)

Still, Man has rational and moral senses not vouchsafed to other living things, at least so far as we know. To the question asked by frustrated humans—What sort of God permits injustice?—theologians down through the ages have answered: God's ways are beyond human understanding. We cannot measure God's justice by our own moral standards, because God knows more than Man can ever know, and the acceptance of this human limitation is the beginning of wisdom. Their evidence is hard to refute: When Job was permitted to glimpse the wonders beyond his ken—to "see" God in action running his universe, sometimes struggling with the sea of chaos, sometimes toying with the forces of evil—he dropped his suit ungrudgingly.

Some see this as a surrender of Man's pride. Because he

wanted to control his own destiny, Job at first demanded a sensible, predictable moral order in which people would get what they earned in life. Do good and do well; do bad and be done badly to. Such a neat system puts God at the beck and call of moral Man, delivering prosperity or ruin on order: Man proposes by his conduct, God disposes according to the moral rules. But that justice-on-demand sought by Job is supreme arrogance.

The theme of the speeches out of the whirlwind is: Whose universe is it, anyhow? Man does not rule God, but the other way around; Job has to give up not only his divinely guaranteed justice but also the unacceptably arrogant "will to dominance" that lies behind it. "I am the master of my fate," writes the poet William Ernest Henley of invincible man in a strait gate, "I am the captain of my soul." That is what Man wants but cannot snatch from the fell clutch of circumstance; to Job's demand for moral order, for an end to innocent suffering, for do-good tit for get-good tat, God says: Nothing doing, you don't own me.

In the face of such "children of pride" God discovers other Leviathans to fry. Robert Frost's God thanks Job in the end for releasing him from moral bondage to the human race: by showing that no link exists to chain sin to suffering, "You are the Emancipator of your God . . ."

God is free to be unjust; more accurately, he is free not to concern himself with Man's just deserts. The denouement can be seen as even more upbeat: Job's repentance marks not a surrender so much as a joyful reconciliation between unknowing Man and his all-knowing creator. Out of his love for Man, God pulls his punch at the end lest he destroy Job's free will, which gives meaning to Man's worship.

Even so, no matter how the lesson of the ungraspable big picture is written—and it has been written every which way in all languages—a defensive tone creeps in. The apology (the original sense of that word is "a defense") is too apologetic (its current sense is "expressing regret"). The broader-canvas explanation rationalizes: Sorry, we don't have the answer to this, but maybe we can turn inexplicability into a kind of answer; only God knows, because only he can stand far enough back to see the grand design, and all we can do, with our nose pressed to the details, is trust that the Lord knows what he is doing.

Shining by itself, the unknowability argument does not illuminate the Joban landscape. We will examine the other side of this big-picture coin later, but meantime, consider another message that has been of direct use to many believers:

### 4. Don't blame the victim; suffering is no evidence of sin.

"You will find no one like him on earth," God told the Satan, provoking the accusing angel by hailing Job as "blameless and upright".[11] Yet, to prove the point of the purity of Man's motives, God dispatched the Satan to cause him to suffer. The ancient syllogism of retribution had been clear: If you did wrong, you suffered God's vengeance; therefore, if you were suffering, you must have done wrong. But here was proof in the biblical canon that man was not necessarily to be blamed for his own misfortune.

When one of the Reagan administration attorneys general observed that the poor usually had themselves to blame for their poverty, liberal root-casuists were enraged. There was surely some truth to the truth in Ed Meese's callous observation—many people undoubtedly are poor because they are lazy—but many rich people are lazy, too, and are not poor as a result. Defenders of the homeless or welfare-bound could have grounded their objections in Job: True, many of the poor may be lazy, but many more inherit disadvantage, get little training, and are not exposed to the work ethic in their upbringing. Because they did not seek underclass status, they cannot be legitimately charged with "bringing it on themselves"; poverty, therefore, is no proof of laziness. The cause cannot be assumed from the result. A corollary of this divorce of sin from suffering was equally discomfiting to Calvinists: It held that prosperity was no proof of virtue.

Victim-blaming is still with us, as a way of wishing away the obligation to avenge or compensate for crime. We see it in the "she was asking for it" defense of rapists and the "why do they live in those low-lying areas?" from people who do not want to be bothered with the cost of flood relief. Gypsies, Jews, Kurds, Armenians, Cambodians, and other ethnic or racial groups with memories of mass murder trigger a response of "they brought it on themselves" from rejecters of responsibility for humanity's burden.

Job's wrongheaded visitors presented the then-prevailing doctrine that suffering is evidence of punishment, and therefore punishment must be evidence of sin. Job knew that to be false, as did the reader. God's flat accusation in the epilogue that "you have not spoken as you ought about me"[12] for the first time discredited that suffering-means-sin doctrine. Not completely; the argument is still made that Job sinned in objecting so strenuously to injustice, and Talmudists have created a position that even if Job sinned in that way, a person is not to be held responsible for actions taken or words spoken under duress.

But all the pain that the Satan inflicted on Job and his family was not for anything Job did; on the contrary, the sufferer bore the punishment precisely because he was the most blameless man in the world. Blaming the victim was wrong.

All right, then—what about the homosexual victims of AIDS? The Bible, read literally, judges homosexuality to be sinful—the worst kind of sin, an "abomination". Perhaps the stricture was rooted in the need for the human race to procreate, following God's direction to "be fruitful and multiply". It can be argued that the Bible is mistaken or out of date, or must not be read literally, but the plain and repeated condemnation of homosexuality as a sin is there in black and white. As a result, some moralists and "straights"—homophobic politicians among them—have seen AIDS to be God's relentless scourge of those who break his moral code.

Poet-Job would not agree, at least not in my reading of him. First, the HIV virus is visited not only on homosexuals and on drug addicts using contaminated needles but on hemophiliacs needing blood transfusions, patients of infected dentists, even babies. The suffering is demonstrably indiscriminate, meaning that the punishment, if intended, would be sloppily targeted—hardly the work of a purposeful, omnipotent God.

Second, the essential moral point in Job is that God never has been in the retribution business—at least not on earth—no matter what other portions of the Bible may lead believers to believe. The blameless and upright are tested, or suffer for no apparent reason, along with the sinners and downright wicked. Suffering—in our time, dramatized by the celebrated and often outraged victims of AIDS—is no evidence of sin. Poet-Job's God made it quite clear that traditionalists who argued the contrary in his name "have not spoken as you ought of me".

Sometimes a victim is guilty; sometimes not. The fact of victimhood is not admissible as evidence of moral culpability in the case. The Book of Job stands as a firewall between the victim and the blame; theology was never the same after the notion of retribution got what it deserved.

### 5. Misery has company.

Bereaved believers looking for comfort in the Bible can find it most forcefully in Job. Not only is suffering not to be construed as evidence of sin, as we have just seen, but apparent punishment is not evidence of isolation from God. Nobody needs to walk alone; to paraphrase a line about home, God is the one who, when you have to pray to him, has to listen.

Poet-Job replaced automatic condemnation by virtue of suffering with an unprovable but persuasively comforting assertion: that the sufferer had not been abandoned by God. Job's poignant recollection of "the time when God was watching over me, when his lamp shone above my head, and by its light I walked through the darkness!"[13] touches a chord with every sufferer who remembers better times. "I call for thy help, but thou dost not answer"[14] is read by the believer who knows that God is testing Job and will answer him, just as he will answer the believer in some way in similar travail. If Job is mistaken about being isolated, the bereaved reader thinks, maybe I'm mistaken in my own tragic circumstances.

In the victim's mind, the worst fear is not that he or she is being punished for some unknown but just cause. Job was certain that he had not sinned enough to deserve such a reaction from above, and many victims, including guilty ones, are equally certain their punishment is undeserved or excessive. The greatest anguish they experience is the fear that the suffering is proof that they have been cast off by God.

During adversity, fear of abandonment—of being all alone, Godforsaken, without even the solace of religion—is a shattering thought. Pain and loss are bad enough; on top of that, a sense of rejection by the object of worship is the crusher. In the New Testament, the question asked by the suffering Jesus—"My God, my God, why hast thou forsaken me?"[15]—is the most emotionally searing line in the Gospels.

A central teaching of Job is that the sufferer who may be estranged from his fellow men is not estranged from his God. Although it seems to the person in pain that God is unconcerned, the author of Job shows that he is directly concerned—worried, even, about losing his favorite, though he lets Job suffer without intercession almost to the end. That's one reason why the bereaved turn to Job for comfort; even though they are offered no explanation for the source of their grief, they relate to a suffering human who also thinks he has been left alone but who they know really is not. It may not ease the pain but it does assuage the bitterness.

To Job, in the end, seeing was believing. More important than the severe tone of God's voice was the appearance of that voice, and the theophany did the job of reconciliation. To those denied the safe harbor of worldly retribution, or the postmortal fix, poet-Job offered a soul-satisfying substitute: an opportunity for personal knowledge of the deity. Through Job, who represented questioning mankind, God proved himself accessible to the practical person: The poet had him reveal himself to this irritating blasphemer, to make the point for all time of God's being there.

"Let the Almighty state his case against me!"[16] was Job's cry as he rested his case; and that is exactly what the offended Almighty did. The answering and not the answer is what finally silenced Job, and possibly satisfied him. God's who-are-you-to-ask tone puts us off, and his seemingly off-the-point content causes us a worried wonderment, but it was what the badgered God did, more than what he said or how he said it, that responded to Job's need. What God did was to show up.

The theophany, or appearance of God, is the culmination of the book; the epilogue is an anticlimax. To Job, the representative human sufferer, who in anger and despair at being abandoned by God sought contact again and again—usually arrogantly—God did in the end appear. The lesson here: God came booming along in person when the confused and innocent sufferer needed him most. Detachment is the worst affliction; to a person in the darkness and hurting, this religious confidence gained from Job's example is no small thing.

### 6. Analogy of the animals: The order of nature symbolizes the moral order.

Having been granted the honor of "seeing" God, wasn't Job intimidated and his issue of fairness finessed by a God interested mainly in asserting his power and reveling in his mystery? Wasn't Job's heart too soon made glad by the appearance of a God who had only sarcastic questions and a strange recounting of the splendors of the animal world?

One not-too-respectable exegesis interprets the speeches from the whirlwind as God saying to Man, "Can't you see I've got my hands full?" Frankly, this occurs to a great many readers and has the advantage of being logical to those who think of God as Man writ large. The I'm-busy-now reading is intriguing in its suggestion of the weakening of divine omnipotence, but can hardly be called uplifting.

Some interpreters find a more satisfying lesson in the whirlwind answer. Rather than boasting of his power, God is pointing with pride to the immensity of his responsibilities. Showing instead of telling (which is the best way to teach), God is parading the whole of creation before the eyes of his questioner.

The Lord's first speech was about the building of the universe, conveying some idea of the difficulty of bringing order out of chaos. His second speech delineated the wonders of nature in all the species of animals. These two subjects—the order of the stars in the heavens, the order of the beasts on the earth—are to be taken as a vast analogy. He is calling on Man to maintain his own moral order on earth by exhibiting evidence of his strength in creating and maintaining both universal and natural order. If God can oversee this difficult universe, if he can show intimate concern for such a diversity of his living creations, humanity should be able to run its own small world.

### 7. *Suffering may be a blessing in disguise.*

In the eastern panhandle of West Virginia, where wise Washingtonians escape for the weekend, the radio listener has the choice of country music or silence. After a while, even the sweet solitude of the mountains can get to you, and you find yourself beginning to listen to the country-song lyrics. The surprise to a city dweller of Sunday gospel music is that this "stained-glass bluegrass" contains some eye-opening philosophy in hummable form. You can learn a lot.

Here was this singer with a banjo twanging along about going to a twentieth reunion of his high school class. There he meets the girl who had been his high school sweetheart. As a lovely young thing, she had broken his trusting heart. Oh, how he suffered in those far-gone days; they had planned a home, and talked of their children-to-be, and he had been wrenched by the loss when she left him to marry another. How it had hurt; he thought he would never get over the pain.

He meets her again, and what does he find? She's a dawg: sloppy, mean-spirited, her once-maddening figure long gone to corn fritters and hush puppies, no singing voice, and a total loss to the poor guy saddled with her as a life partner. (Maybe I'm exaggerating, but this is how I remember the song, which I have been listening for in hopes of catching the name, but apparently it has sunk below the Bottom Forty.) Was this what he had been suffering the tortures of the damned about, when he was young? He thanks God for saving him from the burned-out old flame, and introduces her to his wife at the reunion—the wonderful woman he would never have met if he had not been cruelly jilted by the mess-to-be. The message of the country song twangs home: Sometimes we don't realize that what seems like God's injustice or unconcern is really his way of protecting us from mistakes and readying us for what we deserve.

Cornball? Sure. A powerful argument for withholding condemnation of God during inexplicable pain? You bet. When any authority, usually parental, tells a subject "I'm doing this for your own good," the child writhes and accuses the parent of doing it for society's good, or the parent's good, or the older sibling's benefit—never the subject's. When Authority uses that excuse, it is a shorthand way of saying "I do not now have the time, or am not at liberty to vouchsafe to you the reasons for the discipline I am laying on you, but trust in me, someday when you have children of your own you will see why that much licorice or that much time at the electronic slot machine is detrimental to your development."

Eliphaz the Temanite puts it this way: "Happy the man whom God rebukes! . . . the hands that smite will heal."[17] His traditionalist theme about the use of suffering as a means to conversion is developed later by the young Elihu: "Those who suffer he rescues through suffering and teaches them by the discipline of affliction."[18] Not knowing the reason for suffering does not mean there is no reason; it means only that it is unknown to the sufferer.

One function of the prologue in Job is to set up the possibility to believers that God is hiding from them the real reason for pain. As the country lyric suggests, that may seem like injustice while it's happening, but is not, because the story will turn out happily in the end, strum-strum. God knew that girl you pined for would turn out to be a dawg, or that fella romantically tossing beer cans out of the pickup-truck window would get picked up and incarcerated by state troopers. You were being saved even though you did not know it at the time.


## 8. Christianity's secret weapon

About a half-millennium after Job's revolution came the Christian counterrevolution. The followers of Jesus of Nazareth placed great significance in Job 19:25–27, translated in the King James Version as "I know that my Redeemer liveth, and that he shall appear at the latter day upon the earth."

Though not the first to conceive of an afterlife, Christianity found the witness, vindicator, kinsman, interceder, attorney, or redeemer that Job vainly sought. Job wanted help in bringing God to court, lest God's presence overwhelm him and his anger shut him up (as it later did). To Christian believers, Jesus was and remains that intermediary. Addressing the disturbing theme of Job, Christianity took a thought from Elihu and introduced the idea that suffering can be redemptive—one can suffer for the sins of others and thereby lift the guilt from others. As Jesus was innocent and suffered on the cross (like Job, wondering if God had forsaken him), some suffering can have an idealistic purpose. As we have seen, poet-Job taught that Job, though he did not realize it, suffered to show that suffering is no proof of sin, and to prove that God is not concerned with getting even. Christianity teaches that Jesus suffered and died for a similarly redemptive purpose: to assume the guilt and pay the punishment for original sin and the subsequent sins of mankind.

One of the reasons for the worldwide success of Christian theology is that it turned the tables on the demanding, unrelenting, don't-look-to-God-for-your-justice lesson of Job. Most people liked the earlier tradition of trusting God to work things out for Man that held sway before poet-Job came along to adjust religious theory to life's unfair reality. Religious people found satisfaction in the old idea of retribution for two potent reasons: First, unfairness unfixed breeds resentment, and the spectacle of a person whooping it up through the years and getting away with it rankles the breasts of those too good, too quickly tired, or too timorous to live the life of living it up; second, although poet-Job inveighs against praying "for" anything material, most people think a life of ethical conduct and regular worship rates some form of preferential treatment in the afterlife.

Christianity delivered this in a way that could never be disproven by experience: by promising retribution or reward in a life after death. Nobody has ever come back from the dead either to say "there's nothing on the other side" or, as the joke goes, "I've seen God and she's black." By basing much of its reward on faith and hope in the world to come, Christian teaching (and the Islamic teaching that grew out of it) solved the problem of failed retribution by postponing retribution until the hereafter.

It's true that Hebrew Scripture includes the idea of an afterlife in Sheol, a place for departed souls; one of the thirteen principles Maimonides derived from the Bible is that God will resurrect the dead. Moreover, the story of the suffering servant in Isaiah offers a redeemer who "was pierced for our transgressions, tortured for our iniquities".[19] Thus, Christians could find intimations of both resurrection and redemption in the Old Testament and gave new emphasis to heaven and hell in an afterlife in Christian teaching. This offered most believers a more satisfying solution than poet-Job could match, with his ambiguities and mysteries about justice and fairness. William Jennings Bryan, the populist "Great Commoner", understood the appeal of the hereafter to the average person. He would tell his rapt audiences, " 'If a man die, shall he live again?'[20] is the most important question ever asked." With the afterlife a factor, nobody can say for certain there will never be a Judgment Day. As a result, a person's fate again becomes behavior-driven.

Too pat a solution? To many, yes. Christian scholars acknowledged the appeal of the comfort brought to the sufferer by the thought of bliss in the hereafter, as well as the less-exalted comfort in his mind at the thought of the wicked burning in tomorrow's Hell. But H. H. Rowley argued that Job taught a more profound and idealistic lesson: that the reverent sufferer need not envy the prosperous evildoer because "the wicked may have his prosperity, but the pious may have God; and in God he has far more than the other. The inequalities of life belong to man's outer lot; but this is immaterial to his spiritual life."

Christianity may find solace in inequity by turning to God's values in the here and now, but there is no denying that it has long had a secret weapon in the possibility of retribution in the hereafter. Although retribution in the afterlife is less in fashion these days among heavy thinkers, evangelists know it remains a basic attraction to all those people who are lonely, poor, or mistreated in what believers think of as this life.

But not all readers of Job are believers. As indicated in the rundown of artistic reaction to the dismaying compromise poet-Job seems to make at the end, skeptics are drawn to Job, too—both to cheer his unprecedented defiance and to jeer at his sellout to lordly pomp and pressure (which the reverent call his reconciliation with his maker). Let's see how the poet speaks to the skeptic about the key to Job's turnaround.

# 2

## THE MESSAGE TO SKEPTICS

FOR SKEPTICS—people who do not actively believe in God, but would like to hedge their bets in case God exists—the key question in any study of the Book of Job is this: What was the clincher in the second speech of the Lord that convinced Job to reconcile himself with God?

Before the voice boomed out of the storm, we had heard the irate Job speak out in defiance; after that first Yahweh speech, Job put his hand to his mouth and adopted an attitude of what may be sullen acquiescence; but after God's second speech, Job says "now I see thee with my own eyes"[1] and repents.

God's sudden appearance, with all the pyrotechnics of a theophany (biblical writers knew how to bring God onstage), shuts Job up but does not persuade him at first. But at the end of the poetic portion, we see—with our own eyes—that something in Yahweh's final speech turned Job around.

The clincher was not fear; the worst God could do to Job was to kill him, which would put him out of his misery. Nor was Job overwhelmed by love; this was the God of Wrath on display, not the God of Mercy. Nor was he persuaded by an explanation: Not a word was offered by God about the satanic wager or any other reason for earthly injustice. Nor was Job bribed: The sweeping restoration of camels and power and prestige and family members he had lost did not come until after his atonement, and had not been promised by God in the speeches from the whirlwind.

While eliminating reasons for Job's turnaround, add these two about the author and his text: Given the remarkable courage shown by poet-Job throughout, we have no cause to assume his nerve failed him at the end. Nor can we confidently blame the seeming irrelevance of God's fulminations on an evisceration of poet-Job's work by some censorious sage.

Okay, then, what was the clincher? I think Job was humbled only when he had his eyes opened to what God had to teach him about the flow of power and obligation between master and subject, between creator and creation. Through Job, God gives Man a deserved glimpse at his place in the universe and a sense of participation in its workings. God skips the subject of morality and fair treatment because that is humanity's responsibility to work out for itself on the earthly level.

Now we're in the realm of theo-politics, the study of the trading of support and responsibilities between God and Man, between the acknowledged but accountable master and his voluntary but demanding vassal. That produces more stress than solace, more competition than comfort.

Can we find any comfort in the Lord's sarcastic, intimidating, apparently irrelevant speeches out of the whirlwind? Sweet are the uses of perversity. In a provocative piece in a learned journal two decades ago, David Robertson, a professor of literature and poetry, roiled the religious waters with his assessment of Job's hidden meaning to those searching for solace: "While God may be more powerful than we are, he is beneath us on scales that measure love, justice, and wisdom. So we know of him what we know of all tyrants, that while they may torture us and finally kill us, they cannot destroy our personal integrity. From that we take our comfort."

Heated defiance and cold comfort in that. Maybe we shouldn't be looking for comfort at all; sifting through the most faith-troubling chapters in the book, it could be that we are better off looking for meaning. Many modern artists, like the sculptor Ivan Mestrovic—whose statue of the naked, agonized Job haunts the Syracuse University quadrangle—were attracted by the hero's rebellion and rejection. Others found the meaning of life to be that life had no meaning at all: Live for the moment fully, as if standing on the trapdoor of our life; despair should be our mood because alienation was our natural state. If we wait for Godot, we will wait forever, for Godot—God—is not coming. Even worse, he constricts our efforts to move ahead on our own, causing Job's nihilism: "He has walled in my path so that I cannot break away, and he has hedged in the road before me."[2] Thus trapped, facing lives of solitary confinement in a chaotic prison, we are only kidding our sentimental selves about some hidden order; life is purposeless, existential—in a vogue word, absurd.

Not yet. Once more unto the breach: We have to exploit any opening we can find to break through to the "message" of God's daunting speeches from the storm.

Most important in the first speech from the whirlwind—the longest sustained quotation of words attributed directly to God in the Bible—is the way God says he handles the sea. Herman Melville was right: The sea is the key, the symbol of the dark forces of chaos that God had to subdue in Genesis. In a question impossible for mortal answer, God storms: "Who watched over the birth of the sea"—shutting it back behind two doors—"when it burst in flood from the womb?"[3]

Discoveries of scrolls on the Syrian coast have shown that this same symbolism—of God taming the raging seas that existed before he took up the job of ordering the universe—was expressed in the Babylonian creation narrative and the Canaanite Baal myth, as well as in the later writings of the Hebrew prophet Isaiah. Throughout the neighborhood of the Middle East—all of Western civilization at the time—that idea of an ordering god conquering a primal chaos was the received wisdom, and poet-Job refers to it frequently.

Here is God at the creation, but not doing the creating. Underlying these myths is this thought: God is not necessarily the First Cause, saying only "let there be" this and that, but instead is taking an existing mess and trying to straighten it out, creating light and

Our Father which art in Heaven    hallowed be thy Name

Thus did Job continually

There was a Man in the
Land of Uz whose Name
was Job. & that Man
was perfect & upright

The Letter Killeth
The Spirit giveth Life

It is Spiritually Discerned

& one that feared God
& eschewed Evil. &there
was born unto him Seven
Sons & Three Daughters

W Blake inv & sculp

London. Published as the Act directs. March 8: 1828. by Will.<sup>m</sup> Blake N.<sup>o</sup> Fountain Court Strand.

I shall see God

We shall awake up

I beheld the

Hast thou considered my Servant Job

Ancient of Days

The Angel of the Divine Presence

מלך יהוה

Thou art our Father

in thy Likeness

When the Almighty was yet with me, When my Children were about me

There was a day when the Sons of God came to present themselves before the Lord & Satan came also among them to present himself before the Lord

W Blake

inv & sc

London Published as the Act directs March 8. 1825 by Will Blake N 3 Fountain Court Strand

The Fire of God is     fallen from Heaven

And the Lord said unto Satan Behold All that he hath is in thy Power

Thy Sons & thy Daughters were eating & drinking Wine in their
eldest Brothers house & behold there came a great wind from the Wilderness
& smote upon the four faces of the house & it fell upon the young Men & they are Dead

Whitaker inven. & sculp.

London, Published as the Act directs March 8 1825 by Will. Blake N 3 Fountain Court

And there came a Messenger unto Job & said The Oxen were plowing & the Sabeans came down & they have slain the Young Men with

Going to & fro in the Earth

& walking up & down in it

And I only am escaped alone to tell thee.

While he was yet speaking
there came also another & said

The fire of God is fallen from heaven & hath burned up the flocks & the
Young Men & consumed them. & I only am escaped alone to tell thee

W Blake invent & sculp

London. Published as the Act directs March 8. 1825. by Will. Blake N.3 Fountain Court Strand

Did I not weep for him who was in trouble Was not my Soul afflicted for the Poor

Behold he is in thy hand: but save his Life

W Blake inventor & sculp

Then went Satan forth from the presence of the Lord

And it grieved him at his heart

Who maketh his Angels Spirits & his Ministers a Flaming Fire

London. Published as the Act directs March 8. 1825. by Will^m Blake N.^3 Fountain Court Strand

Naked came I out of my mothers womb & Naked shall I return
The Lord gave & the Lord hath taken away. Blessed be the Name of the Lord

And smote Job with sore Boils
from the sole of his foot to the crown of his head

WBlake inv & sc

London, as Act directs Published March 8. 1825 by William Blake N °3 Fountain Court Strand

What! shall we recieve Good
at the hand of God & shall we not also
recieve Evil

And when they lifted up their eyes afar off & knew him not
they lifted up their voice & wept, & they rent every Man his
mantle & sprinkled dust upon their heads towards heaven

Ye have heard of the Patience of Job and have seen the end of the Lord

W Blake inven & sculpt

London. Published as the Act directs March 8. 1825 by William Blake N 3 Fountain Court. Strand

Lo let that night be solitary
& let no joyful voice come therein

Let the Day perish wherein I was Born

And they sat down with him upon the ground seven days & seven
nights & none spake a word unto him for they saw that his grief
was very great

London Publishd as the Act directs March 8: 1825 by Will Blake N° 3 Fountain Court Strand

life in the process. If he has to slam the doors shut on the chaotic sea (and he told Jeremiah, too, "I placed the sand as the bound for the sea"[4]), the ordering force of this pre-biblical myth was involved from the start in a struggle with hostile forces. He did not start from scratch, with a clean slate, nothing around but him. Disorder preceded order. It's hard to get our minds around this thought, but before Nothing there was Something called "chaos". Darkness on the face of the deep—a chaotic, hence evil, mess on the boiling surface of the sea—came first, or at least came at the beginning along with God's mission to put it right.

We don't have to join the debate about whether this theory of creation is true or not, or if natural selection did the ordering of higher life by itself. Many prefer the theory that God came first and created everything, including disorder, darkness, and evil, to help him cast a universal balance sheet. The who-created-evil debate is related to Job's quest for justice, but would take us off into another book. It is enough, now, to recognize that the God-was-presented-with-a-hostile-environment notion was the way a great many of the ancients saw creation, and that poet-Job adopted that divine struggle theory to explain the prevalence of injustice in a universe being put in balance by God.

In his first speech, God says he commanded the sea: "Thus far shall you come and no farther, and here your surging waves shall halt."[5] Was his point to demonstrate that it isn't easy, being God? And in the passage about making "rain to fall on land where no man lives",[6] was he complaining about wasted effort? To some skeptics, God seems to be whining about how hard he has to work, to which their cool response is "It's tough all over; get on with it." But consider what the veteran line manager says to the consultant fresh out of business school: "If you are going to criticize my management, learn something about its complexity and you won't be so arrogant." Rather than complaining about being overworked and underappreciated, God in his first speech is making this point: "You accuse me of having no purpose, plan, design, or counsel, but that is not true: My purpose is to keep sweeping back the waves of chaos, ordering the stars while feeding the squawking little birds and allowing the likes of you to squawk as well. How's that for the meaning of life?"

The first speech out of the whirlwind does not entirely blow Job over. Not wholly convincing, is the way I hear Job's response; he announces his willingness to put his finger to his lips and shut up, but does not apologize. God then lets him have it with Behemoth and Leviathan.

Back when we discussed Herman Melville's use of the whale as a symbol of God's malevolence, Leviathan was described as not merely a whale but the original sea serpent, writhing about in the universal sea, in opposition to God's calming influence. On Judgment Day, according to Isaiah's prediction, "the Lord will punish with his cruel sword . . . Leviathan . . . and slay the monster of the deep."[7] In his final speech to the quieted but still-unpersuaded man in the Book of Job, God recalls "the chief of the beasts",[8] Behemoth, in Pope's translation "which I made as well as you", which could mean "just as good as you" or "as ignorant as you". This was not just the yawning hippopotamus, crocodile, or whale, but the symbol of chaotic brutality—a creation somehow necessary to the universe but surely not on the side of law and order.

God, the cosmic warrior against darkness and the chaos of the sea, is suggesting here that he has a use for evil; moreover, in bringing to mind Leviathan, the mythic coiling dragon who "makes the deep water boil like a cauldron",[9] God answers Job's opening burst of outrage, when the angry man damned the day he was born and added this imprecation: "Cursed be it by those whose magic binds even the monster of the deep, who are ready to tame Leviathan himself with spells."[10] Job, in that early passage of poetic swearing, had been either calling on God to join him in damning all creation, or calling on mythic magicians to reverse God's order by stirring up the sea and its serpents of chaos. Now God answers at the end of the poetry by claiming to have Leviathan and Behemoth under control. Man would be wise to leave such forces to God to handle, and not to presume to take on the monster symbolizing chaos: "If ever you lift your hand against him, think of the struggle that awaits you, and let be."[11]

On the surface, God has stopped crabbing at the top of his lungs and begun boasting of his omnipotence, an equally unworthy exhibition. However, if we give him the benefit of the doubt and plumb for the profundity—and remember, poet-Job uses these iro-nies and double meanings frequently, expecting his readers to dig for design—we find God showing Man that while he permits the existence of evil, and sometimes enjoys jousting with it, he keeps it leashed and does not permit chaos to rattle about unrestrained. In his first speech, God stressed how busy he was keeping the heavens in order, dealing mainly with the impressive architecture of the universe; in the second speech, he uses supernatural monsters to show how he was on top of evil in his eternal struggle.

What about killing the monster once and for all? God's answer to a suggestion that he annihilate evil might have been: I'm not yet ready for Judgment Day and retirement. Precipitating that final battle would destroy the balance between good and evil, freedom and order, creation and destruction, life and death, war and peace, flood and drought, wisdom and ignorance. Conflict and tension is life, Job is shown; total victory over chaos would be followed by a terrible silence. If God were to assert total control, the merry-go-round would stop, the music would end, the dynamic of creation and destruction would give way to the peace of the grave. The last page of history is Judgment Day: Good triumphs over evil, hell freezes over, and an unnecessary God and his dead universe im-plode and vanish into a theological black hole. (I'm reading a lot into that last speech, but the reader is supposed to.)

Poet-Job intimates that his hero grasped some conception of that grand design. The turning point was not that Job finally recog-nized God's power—"I know that thou canst do all things and that no purpose is beyond thee"[12]—because such invincibility had been stipulated throughout his defiance. The clincher, what political pollsters have come to call a switcher issue, was Job's recognition that his root problem was not injustice but ignorance: "I have spoken of great things which I have not understood, things too wonderful for me to know."[13] The last words are often translated as "beyond my ken".

And then Job adds "O listen, and let me speak; I will ask questions, and you shall answer." The NEB translation puts those lines in a footnote, as if not suitable for appearance at that point, but its conclusion exactly quotes a line spoken by God twice in his speeches. Two of the most respected recent translators, Pope and

Good, each make that line a part of Job's final words, but put it in quotes, as if Job is quoting God just before repenting. But that's their guess; we have no evidence that quotation marks appeared in the original text. My guess is that "I will ask questions, and you shall answer" is a continuation of Man's questioning, and is an integral part of Job's reconciliation with his God.

Maimonides, as we saw, was among the first to catch that meaning in explaining that the Book of Job was a book about humanity's lack of knowledge. Today, that strikes us as fairly obvious: The reader knows about the wager in the prologue, but Job is never given to know that God's motive in punishing him is to reveal Job's motive in worshiping God. But when the reader is in Job's shoes, how should he or she react to that lack of knowledge? For fifty generations since Maimonides, interpreters of Job have argued that Man should accept that there are some things mortals can never know.

A different answer, to my mind more to the subtle poet-Job's point, is that ignorance in a person with an inquiring mind creates a vacuum with all the pulling power of the aforesaid black hole. God slapped down Job for his arrogance, but did not destroy his near-divine curiosity; on the contrary, he certified the rightness of Man's defiance and challenge. He took Man to the mountaintop and showed him a glimpse of all he did not yet know, but might begin to learn.

"Ken" is knowledge, not intelligence. The things too wonderful for Job to know, or the wonders "beyond his ken", are not necessarily wonders beyond humanity's capacity to discover. If his aggressive wondering has carried Job this far, why not further— why not all the way to understanding? God's speeches gave him an inkling of those wonders, and when God answered his challenge by inviting him to put himself in God's shoes to do better, Job saw that he could not meet that counterchallenge. But that does not stop him from trying to find out more. If a balance of forces is at the heart of God's management of the universe, then—along with discord and harmony, lawlessness and law—constant mystery and continuing solution are part of that balancing act, with every answer posing a fresh question. At the end of that rainbow of knowledge is a pot of wisdom, and Man is driven to find it.

That is one Joban's attempt to figure out what turned Job

around so abruptly at the end. Job's quest is not only for knowledge (why are you doing this to innocent me?) but also for a say in his own fate (why can't I earn God's grace and a happy life by praying hard and doing good?) and perhaps to gain a piece of the universal action (why can't I develop software to hook Leviathan?). By daring to have his hero accuse God of injustice and unconcern, to summon God to court to answer those solemn accusations, and to have God in the end approve of this sustained defiance even after overcoming it with a challenge of his own, poet-Job has given a biblical boost to human integrity and political freedom that we are only now beginning to realize. Just as doctrinal pioneers, for their own theological purposes, read a prefiguration of Jesus Christ into "I know that my Redeemer liveth", political people can read a dynamic vision into "wonders beyond my ken".

What in the speeches from the whirlwind reconciled Job with God? The searching skeptic need not take the point of the Yahweh speeches as merely "there are things man cannot know" and need not accept Job's acceptance as evidence of the futility of asking. Rather, skeptics can read Job's God as saying this: "There are things you do not know, but I fix no penalty for asking, or even making a nuisance of yourself by demanding—and while some mysteries may never be solved, you can never tell what I'll let you find out if you keep pushing." The bombastic "Who are you to ask?" tone of the voice from the whirlwind, and the series of dismaying put-downs that riddle the speeches, need not demonstrate the insignificance of Man; rather, they can be read to show that God took moral Man's defiance seriously enough to invite him into the universal mind.

God opened the bidding by testing Man's motives; Man raised the ante by challenging God's morality; God showed a quick flash of a celestial hand beyond morality and raised the stakes to control of the cosmos itself; Job cuts his losses, folds, and God takes the pot. But Job won a great deal in losing the hand. The theophany—the commanded performance by the Lord—raised Job's stature to a worthy interlocutor with his chosen God, in ironic contrast to God's who-the-hell-are-you put-down. Time for a test pilot's metaphor: Job pushed the envelope of Authority, and—talk about wonders—the envelope moved.

Poet-Job did not write a book as richly ambiguous and multifaceted as this to get something off his chest or to undermine his religion. On the contrary, he shattered hypocrisy and rigidity and replaced all that with an idea of his own about proper conduct in pain. Modesty and reverence are fine human traits, and befit a philosophy that accepts the inaccessibility of wisdom and the unknowability of God. The prophet Micah cannot be faulted for admonishing us to "walk humbly with thy God". But Job teaches that the arrogance of moral outrage is divinely, not diabolically, inspired; when the sun insults Ahab, he has not just the right but the obligation to strike back. When Job's integrity was insulted by unfair affliction, he did more than dissent; he rightly indicted God's management, impugned God's motive, and criticized God's aloofness. This challenge by an argumentative believer led to contact with his deity, and the content of that contact, intuitively understood, led to his reaffirmation of faith.

Poet-Job was propagating an idea of particular interest to the open-minded: Those needing to engage with God—passionately, sometimes irreverently, always demandingly—are most able to come to "see" God, however awesome or intimidating that insight turns out to be. As a basis for worship, awe is better than fear, and the need to engage is best of all. Job refused to quit protesting until he was permitted to see—that is, to get a quick peek, a metaphysical teaser, at a corner of all he is yet to learn. God may take offense at disrespect, and if he chooses to reveal himself you'll soon know that, but he is more profoundly offended at phony piety—unthinking or wrongheaded orthodoxy. Skeptics catch the divine drift: You may or may not find the answer by demanding to know, but you will surely never find the answer by fearing to ask.

If dissent is Godly; if even blasphemy is blessed when rooted in Godless morality; and if half-informed challenge is not only tolerated but rewarded by God with a glimpse of the unknown— then where have we been all these millennia? "Ranging over the earth, from end to end." That's a fascinating line of the Satan's; he uses it twice, as if the accusing angel knows God will forgive him for playing the innocent and lying about his mission of skepticism. Using that narrowed eye—like Job's defiance, permitted and even provoked by God—both believers and skeptics can follow the first authorized challenge to Authority to try to discern political lessons in Job and the book's relevance to modern politics.

The Book of Job endorses a vassal's right to make demands on his lord. That not only inspired ecclesiastical, artistic, and political rebels to resist totalitarianism, but fanned controversies about the flow of fidelity up and down. When we pledge allegiance, we demand allegiance. Let us put Leviathan on a leash and walk him through the world of loyalty.

# PART III

# BRIDGES TO JOBAN POLITICS

# 1

~❧ ❧~

# THE VALUE
# OF JOBAN LOYALTY

WHEN THE NATURE of the dancing changes, or if an exciting new partner slips into your arms, are you still supposed to go home with "the guy who brung you" to the dance?

Of course, replies the loyalist; a deal is a deal, and the personal commitment made by one human being to another is the most binding deal, overriding all but the most radical changes in circumstance. Such personal loyalty is closely akin to political loyalty: American patriot and publicist Thomas Paine made objects of his contempt "the summer soldier and the sunshine patriot", who shrank from service in the new nation's wintry trial. (Paine also coined the phrase "from the sublime to the ridiculous", which some may apply to the interplay of spiritual and political.)

But what of the times when difference of opinion drives a wedge between friends—when profound disagreement about the teaching of religion or correctness of ideology strains personal bonds? When longstanding loyalty between friends or colleagues comes into conflict with loyalty to some higher political or spiritual authority, cognitive dissonance begins its jangling and the sensitive soul undergoes self-torture. But the afflicted and spat-upon Job, I think, would come up with this axiom: Personal loyalty is a value that transcends theological or ideological disagreement.

Here is what leads me to believe that. After Job damns the day he was born and calls for the replacement of God's light with darkness, the senior of his friends, Eliphaz, gently remonstrates with him for this startling affront to the deity. The infuriated man slams back with a lament that all his friends have betrayed him, and that he was tricked by those he trusted. Job's central point goes to personal loyalty in a do-or-die fight: He demands that his colleagues not merely commiserate with him but support his position in this dispute. Because they are his friends, they should remain loyal to him and take his side—even though he can no longer claim to be a religious person. "Devotion is due from his friends to one who despairs and loses faith in the Almighty."[1] Even when a man becomes a heretic and a pariah, he has a call on his true friends.

Edwin Good's more recent translation puts Job's valuation of personal loyalty even higher: "Who melts away his loyalty from his friend departs the fear of Shaddai [the Almighty]." I read that to mean: Whoever does not support his friend loyally is himself no longer a God-fearing person. Professor Good explores that crucial verse as a picture of life in the harsh desert: "Job elaborates the metaphor of the melting of loyalty (v. 14a) into the image of wadis that flow with water in winter rains, store water in the ice of winter cold, but suddenly go dry in the hot season, bringing death to caravans forced from the road into the desert in search of water. . . . What sort of help can you get from such friends?" The King James translators evaded the controversy by turning "loyalty" into "pity"; the New Revised Standard Version is "Those who withhold kindness from a friend forsake the fear of the Almighty." Read "fear of the Almighty" as an ancient way of saying "religion"; thus, people disloyal to friends cannot be truly religious even when they're arguing in favor of religion.

The best understanding of this loyalist's verse can be found in Norman Habel's 1985 commentary: "Job responds that if Eliphaz were a friend he would be Job's support, even if he [Job] no longer found strength in his past faith, his 'fear of Shaddai' . . . the common denominator between true friends is not a common faith, but a genuine human compassion and loyalty which survives when all else fails."

When political summer soldiers were abandoning the Prime Minister on what they claimed was a matter of principle, Benjamin Disraeli snapped: "Damn principle! Stick to your party." Job would have substituted "friend" for "party". Let's take on the issue as it is posed by Habel—that even if an afflicted person abandons God, he should command the loyalty of his religious friends—and give it a political twist. How long does the congenital loyalist stick with a political ally when he turns out to be a wrongdoer, or at least no longer what the old gang considers a correct thinker? Of the many ties that bind political professionals—shared goals and memories, a sense of belonging to some happy band, a common loathing of amateurs—how binding is the tie of personal loyalty?

The pejorative term for *friend* is *crony;* the pundit Arthur Krock of *The New York Times* put the catchphrase "government by crony" into Interior Secretary Harold Ickes's mouth early in the Truman era, giving personal loyalty within the White House a bad name. A political leader can hang in there too long for an old buddy, as Harry Truman did with his friend Harry Vaughn, who took too many gifts, or as some Nixon loyalists did after proof was produced that the President was dissembling to protect boneheaded but loyal supporters. But leaders can also pirouette away all too quickly, keeping their own slippers unmuddied at the expense of the partners who brought them to the dance. On the scale of support in a storm or mud fight, how much weight should a politician give to personal loyalty?

Job answers that forthrightly: Stick with me, old friends, even if my unjust affliction has caused me to fear God no longer, and you and I are on different sides of the religious issue. You owe it to me because I have been your friend through thick and thin; because you can find no evidence aside from my inexplicable punishment that I am fairly accused; and because my justified doubt deserves at least the benefit of your doubt. This argument cuts no ice in the desert of Uz: Job's eastern powermates promptly bail out, putting loyalty to religious tradition ahead of loyalty to a friend, and making all the arguments of their tradition that he is doing badly because he has done wrong, or that his suffering was a rigorous discipline that had moved him to sinful arrogance. Abandoned, Job then vainly tries to enforce loyalty with a wild threat to his visitors to "beware of the sword" for being disloyal to him by supporting God's injustice.

His colleagues in power do not even trouble to respond to this seemingly ludicrous warning. Here is a worldly leader who once commanded everything, and now has nothing, asking his associates to support his obviously losing cause against the Almighty. Does he suppose they are as crazy or sinful as he is? Job's claim of loyalty vanishes because the associates believe Job must have been broken for good reason by a just God; more pragmatically, they put spiritual-political loyalty ahead of personal loyalty and assert their primary allegiance to the place where the real power obviously now resides.

But now comes the irony that makes a case for personal loyalty: God, who had double-crossed Job by making him a test case for purity of motive, in the end double-crosses three of his own supporters who are Job's disloyalists. "You have not spoken as you ought about me," Yahweh twice tells the three consolers (excluding young Elihu) in the epilogue, "as my servant Job has done."[2] The friends had insisted that God enforced morality, distributing justice with an even hand; Job had argued that God was at best uninterested in human justice, and that human suffering was random, unconnected to moral worth or ethical living. In the end, God pronounced the pious friends wrong and the impious Job right.

This surprise endorsement of his angry accuser cannot be stretched to mean that God subscribes to everything Job said during his dialogue with the visitors, but it raises the possibility that poet-Job was having God endorse Job's startling notion that old friends in power should stick together in adversity—even if this personal loyalty associates them with an avowed nonfearer of God, an irreligionist.

To drive the point home, God gives Job the most puissant patronage in politics: what mobsters would call an intercession contract, or power of life and death over Job's faithless former loyalists. When the friends ask Job to intercede to keep God from "being harsh" with them (Job had once warned his disloyalists to beware of God's sword), Job delivers for them, and God withholds his wrath. Not only does the Lord spare the lives of his consolers, which Job magnanimously asked for, but he doubles Job's previous wealth—which Job notably did not ask for—as a kind of divine tip for all his trouble. Such delicious retribution flies in the face of the main point the book has just made, that Man must not look to God for justice. (As discussed earlier, maybe poet-Job had to toss a sop to tradition and legend to get published.)

If I were Job—as the poet induces all readers to imagine themselves to be—I would have hesitated a long moment before interceding, to savor the sight of my disloyal ex-supporters thinking about twisting slowly, slowly in the wind, in John Ehrlichman's phrase, before pleading for mercy in their behalf. But I would never trust those guys anymore; as the Kennedy family motto goes, "Forgive but don't forget."

Personal loyalty is adhesiveness in action; you either have that sticking quality or you do not. If you have it, the next question is—loyal to what or to whom? Family exerts a pull, as do friendships, employers, fellow workers, cultural and social organizations, your old school and old flame; these personal or group loyalties are crosshatched against the pull of political candidates, the attraction of burning issues like abortion and gun control, and the deep draw of great causes like human rights. The forces rarely line up in a way to let you go with the magnetic flow. For example, you may be a staunch right-winger who happens to strongly favor gun control, and you love your liberal sister whose husband is a pistol-toting leftie; that's a tough enough conflict of loyalties, but what if your brother-in-law reminds you of the help he gave you to start your business and asks for your vote in defeating the candidacy of your other sister's best friend, who is a co-religionist fellow Hungarian right-winger but against gun control? You are in a classic conflict-of-loyalties bind, unable to do anything without selling some allegiance short or short-shrifting a comrade. It happens all the time and it isn't your fault.

People with strong views and controllable emotions tend to put ideological and political loyalty ahead of personal loyalty—ideas and mind-sets ahead of friendships. When you and your friend part company about a sensitive issue—whether abortion rights, or arms-bearing, or jobs versus smoke, or any other profound argument-starter—your friendship is strained. After the first few agreements to disagree civilly, the notion occurs that your friend is far-out, obtuse, or wrongheaded. Your personal loyalty frays when a third party attacks your foolish friend, and you experience that secret, guilty pleasure that Germans call *Schadenfreude*. Pretty soon, these conflicting personal and political loyalties set up a disturbing dissonance in your mind, which you resolve either by acquiescing in your friend's views or by cutting him off—most often, by seeing less of him. Ideological loyalty frequently demands that sort of conformity, and the jettisoning of old personal loyalties can be an aid to political advancement.

But the choice is not as easy as that, because political loyalty often has a personal component. Proximity, gratitude, admiration, longtime comradeship with its shared secrets and potential embarrassments, and the expectation of reciprocal support are strands in the bonds of personal-political loyalty. Although the binding quality of this cord of allegiance may not be as strong as the magnetic pull of stern principle or the seductive tug of fresh opportunity, the virtuous and the prudent do not neglect these old ties or expediently set them aside.

As every person who serves in the Congress knows, the entire institution operates through a network of little loyalties. Anyone promising to sweep out the cobwebs of compromise is looked on with horror: The cobwebs hold the place together. Senators, like lawyers, assail each other on the floor and regale each other around the dinner table; the sound of back scratching in the bazaar of favors and friendships is the permanent buzz of political activity. The same is true in the symbiosis of movers and media, of lapdogs and watchdogs, as useful and sometimes lifelong personal loyalties are formed within the lines and across the lines. This produces an understanding of seemingly hypocritical or inexplicable dealings.

When Nelson Mandela came out of twenty-seven years in a South African jail to appear at his first world forum, he disappointed every speechwriter of every color in the world with a pedestrian political speech, laboriously thanking everybody on the dais. Here was a Joban figure who had spent half a lifetime suffering for his anti-apartheid cause, and who had maintained his integrity by refusing to promise nonviolence in return for his freedom. He was given humanity's attention at last and a place in the spotlight on the world's stage—and he blew the opportunity to deliver an inspiring, profound, at least thematic statement.

Years later, however, with communism collapsing around the world, and with his own prestige secure as the preeminent leader of his people, Nelson Mandela traveled to Cuba to appear at a rally with Fidel Castro. The South African surely knew that the dictator Castro had become a pathetic figure, hoarsely bellowing "Socialism or death!" like mad King Lear on the heath. Public opinion–sensitive colleagues in the African National Congress had surely advised Mr. Mandela that an appearance with this discredited relic of Communist tyranny would offend liberal Mandela-lionizers around the world. Association with a known abuser of human rights might even weaken the ANC's cause.

Yet Mandela went and lifted arms with Castro before the Cuban crowd and world cameras. Why? Because Castro had stood up for him, and his then-ragtag band of followers, at the beginning. Castro had railed and harangued in Mandela's behalf through the decades when the great danger was the world's inattention. To many liberals, that Mandela decision to refuse to abandon one of the last Communist despots was a serious mistake, recalling Dean Acheson's principled but mistaken "I shall not turn my back on Alger Hiss." But I had to admire Nelson Mandela for that display of dogged loyalty, especially since he could do the degenerating dictator little good. (A visit in 1991 to Libya's Qaddafi was not so admirable; that was motivated more by money than by loyalty.)

Affection can be part of both political and personal loyalty; gratitude for past favor or the expectation of future reward goes into it, but most puissant of all is a camaraderie shared in the hungry, early days that is never experienced by the world's perennial careful latecomers. John F. Kennedy, notorious for both party and personal loyalty, said in backing away from one candidate redolent of controversy: "Sometimes party loyalty asks too much." That is hard to dispute (as is his "life is unfair"), but he was talking about the times it was permissible for him to wander off the party reservation, to refuse to endorse candidates of his party whose positions or personality differed widely from his own. When it came to taking the flak for standing by longtime supporters who came under fire, the Kennedy clan tended to put loyalty first.

That is part of what got Richard Nixon into trouble in the Watergate scandal: loyally seeking to block prosecution of his wrongdoing supporters, who he thought acted stupidly but out of loyalty to him. The phrase "team player" came into disrepute during Watergate, and was not rehabilitated until the Bush years.

Many Washington insiders made their political judgment of Jimmy Carter after he was elected and before he took office; in that interregnum, Carter let it be known he would appoint Ted Sorensen, JFK's alter ego and speechwriter, as director of Central Intelligence. Sorensen was the New York lawyer who had swung the influential Kennedy crowd behind the little-known Carter, and who later helped with some good advice and phraseology in the campaign when establishment Democrats were scornfully saying "Jimmy who?" But when right-wingers hollered that his choice to head the CIA would be too soft on the Soviets, Carter expediently but disloyally backed off and humiliated his early supporter. Political semiologists took that as a sign that the new President's term would be marked by weakness; blood was in the water and the sharks began to circle. (Make that "we" sharks.)

Consider the way Ronald Reagan, in octogenarian retirement in 1991, threw three of his most loyal and senior aides off the board of his presidential library. Ed Meese, Martin Anderson, and William Clark had served Reagan through thick and thin (Groucho Marx liked to add cruelly after that cliché, "like leeches"). They had paid their political dues; they had marshaled the conservative movement behind Reagan throughout the seventies, and helped keep right-wingers from becoming too disgruntled during the Reagan presidency. After the battle ends, the small honors of a library board or a special place on the dais of anniversary dinners mean nothing to the public but mean a great deal to the Old Hands who have bronzed their "For [whomever] Before [whatever defining event]" buttons. But Mr. Reagan, perhaps manipulated by a wife eager to avenge old slights or to cultivate new friends, inexplicably dumped the trio of veterans of his campaigns. Why? No deep-seated sense of downward loyalty.

It works both ways. In a column in 1991, I took a pop at the roundheeled way former President Jimmy Carter had taken more than eight million dollars for his presidential library and other personal charities from the "bank of crooks and criminals", BCCI, in return for easing the corrupt bankers' way into high-level contacts. That was a rough charge, and I eagerly braced myself for the return salvo. But what surprised me was the absence of angry letters to the editor, op-ed pieces on what good had been done with the money, or calls to me from Old Carter Hands defending their boss. The Washington woods are filled with former Carter appointees, but very few people proudly identify themselves, malaise and all, as Old Carter Hands. Or Old Reagan Hands. Or Old Johnson Hands, with the exception of Jack Valenti. These Presidents turned out to be loyalty-takers, not loyalty-givers, and when their reputations came under attack, few primary sources came forward with op-ed pieces or books to protect their great man's place in history.

The two Presidents who did inspire lasting loyalty among the troops were Kennedy and Nixon. The "Kennedy people" played for keeps. They understood hardball before that opposite of bean-bag had a name and ran to win before Vince Lombardi called winning the only thing. They zipped their lips tightly when it came to infidelities, shamelessly passed out a Federal bench plum to a Boston political hack, and protected a family legal retainer when scandal struck.

I remember, in the backstretch of the neck-and-neck 1960 presidential race, sitting on the edge of a hotel bed with Nixon campaign director Bob Finch, phoning all over the country trying to get some doctor or Kennedy source somewhere to admit to his candidate's Addison's disease, which required extended cortisone treatment. Our efforts came to naught; the Kennedy doctors camouflaged his serious condition with phrases like "mild adrenal deficiency"; their loyalty ran to their patient, not to the truth. The Kennedy people knew how to stonewall then, and they knew how to keep a solid phalanx nine years later, at Chappaquiddick. Though rarely remarked, it is remarkable that all the women at that ill-fated party have been steadfastly silent for a generation, even during the interest in Senator Ted Kennedy's role in a nephew's rape acquittal in Palm Beach.

There are both a fierceness and a permanence to that political loyalty; though the members of the band are aging and the torch has been passed to a clammy hand, just take a pop at JFK in the press and you'll get a reply—in op-ed print from Ted Sorensen, or in a gibe at a Washington party from the former columnist Charlie Bartlett, or later a scholarly rebuke in a book by the historian

Arthur Schlesinger, Jr. In most respects, I think it's admirable, because I have experienced the same roguish loyalty manifested among hard-core Nixonites.

The Nixon people are more defensive, of course. The Kennedy people begin by saying "Jack had his human failings, but—" The Nixon people, to establish credibility, have to go further and offer "Nixon did some terrible things, and crimes were committed in his name, but—" and only then can we go off into welfare reform, the opening to China, or his long second comeback.

Nixon's loyalty to "us" (himself included) was paralleled by a depth of hatred for "them" (the media especially included), a mistake that he later ruefully admitted was the route to self-destruction. A few embittered Nixon aides still feel that they should have been pardoned, but the majority, two decades later, feel a part of the general Nixon reputational comeback. At a gathering of the clan at the opening of the Nixon Library at Yorba Linda, California, in 1990, the mutual loyalty was palpable amid the wave of self-justification. I took up Barbara Walters's invitation to appear on *Nightline* that night to defend the Nixon record against a grumpy, unreconstructed Nixon-hater, and I felt good about it; if I had not been available, the program's producer would have found a score of others ready with an equally gleeful defiance of Watergate calumny.

Personal political loyalty is not always easy: When tapes were released, a generation after Nixon's fall, containing a series of his anti-Semitic cracks, my heart sank, and I had to remind myself of the Old Man's unwavering backing of Israel and his appointment of Henry Kissinger, Arthur Burns, Herbert Stein, Leonard Garment, and other Jews to his White House staff. His private slurs lessen my opinion of Nixon, as did his unconcern for privacy in his secret taping system, but there is poetic justice in the latter exposing the former, and loyalty can take a few bruises. Same with the Kennedy people after his walls of privacy were breached. But go find that many Old Hands to speak up for Johnson, Carter, Reagan. The jury is still out on Bush; I suspect he's a loyalist but most of his appointments are not.

In this discussion, I have assumed loyalty to be a value, a good thing in a human being, an obligation in an authority or institution.

But you cannot be a nut about this: Loyalty overdone can cease to be a value and become a corruption of values. Allegiance can be egregiously misplaced, as Stalinists and Hitlerites learned, and a mafioso lives and dies by a fearful loyalty to his criminal family; it's a truism that loyalty is a value that can be devalued by fidelity to bad ends. Obviously loyalty when blind is not all, and even a mobster has to be ready to refuse to "go to the mattresses" in an unfamilial cause.

Note the chickenhearted qualification in the preceding paragraph about bailing out of causes that do not advance the values of the family, or country, or ethnic or religious group. Disloyalty to an individual is never excused on grounds of expedience, but is almost always explained as greater loyalty to a principle.

How easy it is to become an overnight ethicist when a colleague is cornered; who wants to snarl with the fox when you can bay with the hounds? At moments of doubt, before evidence of wrongdoing is shown, the genuine loyalist offers the benefit of the doubt, or at least suspends judgment, despite the awful feeling that the ship is sinking. This earns him scorn among the legion of pursuers, and recalls the watchword of pragmatism expressed by FDR's secretary of the navy: "When the water reaches the upper level, follow the rats." But we should not be so quick to castigate the team players, the quick-to-forgive followers, when they refuse to join the chorus of self-righteous derogation led by the goo-goos of starchy tradition or perpetual reform. In everyday politics, loyalty—not mindless or sentimental followership, but the willingness to stick to a proven ally at the cost of some personal embarrassment—is a quality that should and does go into the mix of most political decisions. Abuse for loyalty goes with the territory of leadership.

That's when the hardest evaluation begins: Loyalty is a value, fine, but loyalty to what? To your friends? To your country? What does an avowed loyalist do when political and personal loyalty come into direct conflict?

The choice between friends and country came before Michael Straight, scion of the family that originally financed *The New Republic,* on a Washington street in the early fifties, when he ran into a diplomat he knew from his own secret past to be a member of a

Soviet spy ring. Should he turn this old friend in, perhaps saving American lives during the Korean War—or say nothing, standing by fond past associations? Straight said nothing until years later, when he wanted a government job, but meanwhile the spy escaped to Moscow. The man who put loyalty to a friend ahead of loyalty to his country still defends his decision, and has his lawyer write sharp notes to those who differ, but that strikes me as a perversion of the priorities of loyalty.

This same excruciating choice of friend versus country faced ex-Communists called upon to "name names" before congressional inquiries into internal subversion. What would the poet-Job have done if called before a court of sages and asked to reveal the names of those who had written this blasphemy with him? I like to think he would have taken an anachronistic Fifth Amendment and, if given immunity to remove that protection, risked a contempt citation. Our testimony-refuseniks of the fifties were not being reluctant to alert lawmen to the dangerous work of foreign espionage agents, but were refusing Congress help in ruining fellow dupes; there's a significant difference.

In a recent case of espionage (a world rich in loyalty conflicts), Jonathan Pollard, a Jewish American and fervent supporter of Israel, was caught passing secret documents to help that United States ally defend itself from the likes of Iraq. He pleaded guilty; the prosecution double-crossed him on the plea-bargain and he was given a life sentence. Though this was a case of unlawfully switched loyalty, with more than thirty thousand dollars passed, the betrayal was too often seen to be a case of "dual loyalty", a charge lightly made by anti-Semites at hawkishly pro-Israel Jewish Americans like me. I was glad to see the traitor to the United States go to jail (though I thought his sentence was excessive in light of his plea-bargain), and was sorry to see his Israeli controllers let off with a wrist-slap; they were far more guilty of undermining the interests of their country than Mr. Pollard was of his.

The dual-loyalty charge struck home when my old Nixon speechwriting colleague, Pat Buchanan, charged on a television show in 1990 that the supporters of war against a nuclear-arming Saddam Hussein, after his invasion of Kuwait, were the "amen corner" of the Israeli Defense Ministry. (As a political lexicographer, I knew what the amen corner was: a claque ready to applaud a candidate on signal, derived from the religious enthusiasts sitting in a designated section of church who would shout "Amen!" on cue.) The feisty Buchanan, a recent convert to isolationism especially when it concerned support of Israel, later went on to name the war hawks urging an attack on Saddam's nuclear threat—listing only the names of Jews. (He did not include my name, probably because we had been through the political wars as comrades in arms, but I took offense at being left out—I had been inveighing against Saddam long before he grabbed Kuwait.)

The Buchanan charge collapsed of its own weight; it was obvious that President Bush launched Desert Storm to defend the oilfields of Saudi Arabia and the Emirates and to liberate Kuwait, not for Israel's sake; indeed, Mr. Bush's main concern about Israel was to keep that nation from responding to incoming Scud missiles, lest the Arab coalition withdraw its approval of our assault. But the Buchanan low blow was unmistakable: Jewish Americans were urging the United States to risk American lives, he implied, to serve Israeli and not American interests.

My friend and *New York Times* colleague A. M. Rosenthal promptly denounced Mr. Buchanan as an anti-Semite, deducing that from a pattern in his positions, and chided me in a column for not joining in. I chose to wait until a conservative columnist who was Catholic, William F. Buckley, made the case, which he did more effectively than any non-Catholic could have. Then I opined, more in sorrow than in anger, that Buchanan's dual-loyalty insinuation was anti-Semitic. As it surely is: Loyalties can have crosscurrents, as I have argued above, but must flow to the primary object of allegiance. To impute disloyalty is to make a vicious accusation.

But is there a higher loyalty than to that of a country or a cause or a person? Yes: to the whole truth, to history, and to the highest cause of all, your own integrity—what your conscience tells you that you stand for in life, and without which you no longer feel whole.

That's pretentious to say and not easy to illustrate. Here's an example of a curious admixture of personal and political loyalty, to show the shades of gray in the decision to be discreet and the multicolored hues of being true-blue. My speculative analysis involves a risk-taking President, a beautiful and talented woman, and a counterspymaster; it is about romance and murder and conflicting allegiances, a compound combination that should signal speed-readers to slow down.

Mary Pinchot Meyer, of a distinguished American political family—her father was a Bull Moose party aide to Theodore Roosevelt, her uncle was a two-term Pennsylvania governor—was an abstract artist living and working in Georgetown after her divorce from the deputy chief of the CIA's plans directorate, "the department of dirty tricks". In early 1961, soon after the inauguration of John F. Kennedy, the forty-one-year-old artist and the President began a love affair that lasted for two years. This was no sexual dalliance, such as the one FBI Director Hoover insisted the President end with the mistress of a mafioso. It was a serious relationship with a discreet and caring member of the Kennedy social set whose sister was then the wife of Ben Bradlee, the editor of *The Washington Post* and a Kennedy intimate. Only a handful of the clandestine couple's close friends knew about the affair; one was James Angleton, the CIA's legendary head of counterespionage, a man dedicated to ferreting out disloyalty in others and with a passionate (some muttered paranoid) code of loyalty in himself.

At about noon of October 12, 1964, almost a year after the Kennedy assassination, Mary Meyer went walking along the towpath of the Georgetown Canal and was murdered by an assailant who put a bullet through her head. A drifter wandering nearby was arrested and charged, but later acquitted; the murder has never been solved. The prosecutors at the time did not know that the victim had kept a diary detailing her affair with the President, which might or might not have offered a clue to her murder. Mary Meyer's closest friends, including the President, did know of the diary, which she had said she wanted her son to see when he grew up, and which presumably the President had wanted nobody to see, ever. For days after the murder, Jim Angleton, equipped with the black-bag tools of his trade, led a fruitless search of the victim's home. Finally, the diary was discovered in her studio, probably by her sister, in a steel box also containing letters, and was turned over to Angleton.

He destroyed it. I say that with some confidence because I asked Jim Angleton about it over a long dinner at the Army-Navy Club in Washington in the late seventies, after he had been fired for overzealousness. He acknowledged the deed, asking, "Wouldn't you have done the same?" I said I didn't know; wasn't she his friend, as much as the President was? He grimaced at my retrospective sentimentality, probably assuming it was a device to draw him out: "You would have done your duty," he said. Subsequently, he told a friend of mine who also pressed him about the diary that "it would have destroyed the Presidency", but the great counterspy tended to get overdramatic.

Working from that set of facts (which we can hope future memoirs will amplify), we have an array of conflicts of loyalty. The overriding imperative, of course, would be to turn over to the police any evidence bearing on the investigation of the murder. But for the sake of argument, assume that you—a Federal official charged with protecting national security—find nothing in the diary that might be germane to the killing. Assume that the contents of public interest are tasteful but detailed descriptions of a love affair, with corroborating documents in the President's handwriting also in the strongbox. In the counterspy's mind, these are the loyalties likely to pull toward destruction of the diary:

1. The reputation of the dead President's character, as well as his place in history, would be dragged through the mud, and his widow would be unnecessarily embarrassed and hurt. Remember, this is 1964. The nation is still staggered by the assassination, not totally convinced of the single-killer conclusion, but holding the martyred President close to its heart. You are unaware of any other Kennedy romance because the FBI's Hoover hates to deal with the CIA. Why allow the golden memory of JFK's brief term to be sullied by scandalmongers who would surely fail to see the sad tenderness of the President's private love?

2. The institution of the Presidency would be demeaned. In 1964, the longtime secret affair of Franklin Roosevelt and the correspondence revealing the wartime romance of Dwight Eisenhower had not yet been made public. This first proof of

adultery by men who were recently President might send a shock wave through the nation, weakening the Presidency during Vietnam wartime, with the Soviet threat ever-increasing.

3. Kennedy had been a friend whose support of your boss at the CIA had protected you, and was a friend of friends who had turned the material over to you knowing that you would protect his personal reputation.

The loyalties pulling against destruction of the diary included:

1. Mary Meyer was a friend, too, the former wife of a fellow spook, whose expressed wish it was to preserve the diary to show to her son when he was old enough to appreciate her role in United States history.

2. Never does history appreciate a decision to "consign to the flames" (the shredder was not yet in common use) primary-source documents that would shed light on the motivation and moods of the lives of the great. If the fact of the destruction became known, discredit would fall on Angleton's beloved Agency. Relatedly:

3. There is such a thing as loyalty to the truth. If you must shave that loyalty to stay true to some higher purpose (misleading a mob about the whereabouts of a man it wants to lynch), there is a moral and often legal difference between outright lying and refraining from telling the truth. Destroying the diary is a lying act.

Where you come out on this depends on which loyalties are most important to you. To an Angleton, known within the Company as "Mother", deception was as mother's milk; the end, not the means, was his concern, and while he might have felt a twinge of conscience at ignoring the wishes of his dead friend, he believed his overriding loyalty went to the protection of the nation and the institution of the Presidency, which he felt must not be weakened lest the Communists exploit it.

His decision, though internally consistent and at least defensible at the time, was wrong. What would have been right? He should have let Mary Meyer's sister and friends think he had destroyed it, but preserved the diary somewhere, with instructions to a bank or other trustee to deliver a strongbox to her son, Quentin Meyer, with a copy of its contents to the Library of Congress or the Kennedy Library a generation or two later, perhaps after Jacqueline Kennedy's death. (Who knows? Maybe he did.) In 1964, that would have been the outcome of my reaction to that conflict of loyalties; others may hold prompt disclosure paramount and would have turned it over to the police, or run it in a newspaper, or carried out the deceased's wishes as faithful executor, or destroyed it or not, based on any other calibration of loyalties.

That time, however, is not this time. In retrospect, what harm would have come from learning from a firsthand account of this love, just as we later learned of the love affairs of other past Presidents? Knowledge of the affair with Lucy Mercer has not tarnished the reputation of Franklin Roosevelt; the public auction of Kay Summersby's suggestive correspondence with Dwight Eisenhower has not diminished our evaluation of him as general or chief executive. White House adultery in retrospect is tame stuff; only when presidential playing-around may be in prospect do we suddenly apply the blue nose to the scent. Spin doctors do their thing on present reputations and images, but history's relentless revision catches up to all the manipulations and suppressions.

Hindsight's crystal vision suggests that the loyalty that should have taken precedence in this case was personal loyalty to the murder victim. The Kennedy willingness to run personal risk would have come out, as it did, in a different episode. Paradoxically, had the news of a Kennedy love affair been centered on a sensitive and remarkable woman rather than a mobster's moll, the image of Camelot would not have been so sullied. The President's human failing did not shatter the reputation of the whole administration, nor did it undermine the Presidency. The Oval Office itself is hard to bend out of shape.

Job's castigation of disloyal friends got us into this topic; let's see how he would lead us out of it.

The pre-fallen Satan of the prologue was the accusing angel, not the Devil of later fame; his assignment from God was to prevent the tainting of the celestial court by any impurity of motive. The

Satan's power is strictly derivative but enough to do the job, roughly analogous to the powers given to the head of counterespionage for the CIA, who is required to suspect everyone to prevent the corrupting penetration of the Agency by a "mole" of a foreign power. Jim Angleton would have taken that comparison to the Satan, mischievously protective of his superior, as a left-handed compliment suitable to his sinister world.

The disloyalty of the would-be consolers to Job was based on their misconception of a higher loyalty to the supreme authority— theirs was a blind allegiance to God, or at least allegiance blinded by a mistaken notion of a God concerned with meting out justice on earth. Job's selfish and resentful point was that true friends should be steadfast friends when troubles strike, but more significant to students of loyalty was that an innocent man has a right to expect his friends to believe him when he insists, in pain, on proclaiming his innocence. In the end, God agreed with him on that, refuting forever the notion that suffering is evidence of sin. Before abandoning a crumbling colleague to curry favor with the power that has toppled him, a couple of lines in Job seem to tell us, consider the possibility that the ultimate authority will side with him against you.

Shakespeare buttressed the need for central, rather than higher, loyalty in *Hamlet,* with Polonius advising his son: "To thine own self be true, / And it must follow, as the night the day, / Thou canst not then be false to any man." The first loyalty—ahead of God, country, family—is to your own integrity, to your sense of what you fiercely believe to be right. Pledge your allegiance to that and all the subsidiary pulls of loyalty sort themselves out.

And what did this stiff-necked loyalty to personal honor get Job? It got him all the things that God could give: his camels back twice over, his replacement family, the satisfaction of sparing his false friends, and a transforming personal appearance from the deity himself. But it also preserved what it was not God's to give, more important to Job than anything else: the stubborn loyalty to his own integrity we call self-respect.

# 2

## MEDITATIONS BY LINCOLN AND JOB

NOBODY IN AMERICAN history was more concerned about loyalty than Abraham Lincoln. When it came to allegiance to authority, he was the opposite of a dissident.

Elected by a plurality, he was a determined majoritarian who was willing to put the nation through its bloodiest war to establish the idea of majority rule in the world's new democratic experiment. When abolitionists like *New York Tribune* editor Horace Greeley were willing to say to the seceded states "erring sisters, depart in peace", it was the newly elected sixteenth President who insisted that no minority defeated in a democratic election would be allowed to "set up shop for themselves". He was convinced that if the majority did not assert its rule, a nation would divide and subdivide until anarchy prevailed and dictators arose. As a result of this conviction—not shared by most members of his own Cabinet—the Union made war the price of secession.

Lincoln, the enforcer of allegiance, was an implacable crusher of Southern dissent. Yet, like Job, he bore the sobriquet "the Man of Sorrows". Grief was his frequent companion: "In this sad world of ours," he wrote in condolence, "sorrow comes to all." As the embodiment of a sundered nation, agonizing through what he drew on biblical imagery to call its "fiery trial", Lincoln can be seen as our most Joban President. Like Job, his conduct throughout four years of sustained calamity was to refuse any compromise of the principle of majority rule that would end the suffering. Like Job, Lincoln wondered about God's purpose in putting innocent and guilty alike into the crucible of fraternal slaughter. And like poet-Job, Lincoln was moved to compose a meditative fragment that fits uneasily into his collected work and makes us wonder what he was really getting at.

We have some historical evidence that our sixteenth President read and reread the Book of Job. When it came to his own relationship with the power he quietly called "my maker", Lincoln was more circumspect and respectful than the biblical figure he studied—Lincoln was, after all, a politician—but the President twice revealed that he suspected that Man's purpose and God's might not be the same. He suggested guardedly, both in private and in public, that God's will was unfathomable, apparently inconsistent, and—reading between his lines—perhaps unjust. The same faith-troubling suspicion, we have seen, was a reason for the schism between God and Job.

September 1862 was the worst of times for Abraham Lincoln. The war was going badly for the North. John Pope, the impetuous general he had counted on to replace the cautious George McClellan, had announced grandly that "my headquarters is in my saddle", prompting wags to suggest that his headquarters was where his hindquarters should be. Pope turned out to be a bombastic incompetent who led the Union to disaster at Second Manassas. To avert the loss of the war, the humiliated President had to turn again to McClellan, a popular general whose political aim was to negotiate peace with the Confederacy rather than to win the war. The open-ended conflict, brought on by Lincoln's determination not to let the Union be divided without a fight, had caused more death and destruction than he or anyone had imagined. On top of that national burden, the periodic melancholia that afflicted Lincoln was worsened by personal losses: the death of his eleven-year-old son Willie, who had been the light of his life; and the incipient madness of his wife.

He was also on the brink of his most desperate gamble: proclaiming the slaves in the states in rebellion to be free. Lincoln was well aware that abolition would be the largest property seizure in the history of the world; that it was probably unconstitutional and possibly an invitation to uprisings and massacres; and that it was surely a decision that would kill all talk of peaceful compromise. Lincoln's preliminary proclamation of emancipation of slaves within the rebellious states would make a bloody fight certain until one side or the other bled to death. The combination of pressures showed on him; his attorney general noted in his diary at that dark time that the President "seemed wrung by the bitterest anguish— said he felt almost ready to hang himself".

Lincoln was profoundly familiar with the Bible, and drew on its cadences and images for his speeches: "a house divided against itself cannot stand", the oratorical centerpiece of his keynote address in the 1858 debates with Stephen Douglas, was his quoted paraphrase of the New Testament Mark 3:25 ("If a house be divided against itself, that house cannot stand"). The man known in Union song as "Father Abraham" was never a churchgoer, a fact noted by his legion of critics, and he tacked on a reference to divine providence to the proclamation of emancipation he had been drafting, but only after his devout Treasury secretary suggested it.

Elizabeth Keckley, a free Negro seamstress who made dresses for Mrs. Lincoln, recorded in her memoirs an occasion when the President came into the bedroom looking deeply dejected, and said, "No good news. It is dark, dark everywhere." According to Mrs. Keckley, "He reached forth one of his long arms, and took a small Bible from a stand near the head of the sofa, opened the pages of the holy book, and soon was absorbed in reading them. A quarter of an hour passed, and on glancing at the sofa the face of the President seemed more cheerful. The dejected look was gone, and the countenance was lighted up with a new resolution and hope."

The modiste's memoir continues: "The change was so marked that I could not but wonder at it, and wonder led to the desire to know what book of the Bible afforded so much comfort to the reader. Making the search for a missing article an excuse, I walked gently around the sofa, and looking into the open book, I discovered that Mr. Lincoln was reading that divine comforter, Job."

Did that really happen? Mrs. Keckley's book, long treated as a prime inside-the-White-House source by historians, was ghosted by a journalist, just as most such memoirs are today. The ghost-writer probably asked his stoic and strong-minded subject if the President ever read the Bible; when told about her discovery of Lincoln's reading the Book of Job, he might then have embellished the story by adding the dramatic bit about how that particular part of the Bible had brought light to what was widely called "Lincoln's mournful countenance". But the reading of most of Job—the folk-tale ending aside—moves few of those who read it to sudden relief or rejuvenation. The sufferer may identify with, but is rarely cheered up by, the travail of Job. Nobody with Lincoln's long legal background would find instant solace in that book. On the contrary, I believe he would be drawn instead to the moral disputation between opponents at law, and his experience as a defense attorney would probably cause him to side with the afflicted plaintiff.

Even taking with a grain of salt that part of the Keckley account that describes Lincoln's beatific reaction to Job's travails, we can give credence to her discovery that Lincoln's Bible was open to the Book of Job. The reason can be found in two of the most mysterious but revealing pieces of Lincoln's writing.

After the assassination, Lincoln's secretaries came across a fragment written in Lincoln's hand that they estimated had been written in the fall of 1862. They asserted that it "was not written to be seen of men"—neither part of an unmailed letter nor a draft of a thought for a speech. Nor did Lincoln keep a diary; this fragment was an intimate rumination in writing that does not exist elsewhere in his extensive collected works. John Nicolay and John Hay labeled this private religious thought discovered in the President's papers "a Meditation", the sort found in prayer books. Here is the complete text of the brief essay, unique in Lincoln's collected works for its theological puzzlement, with the italics reflecting the President's underlining:

The will of God prevails. In great contests each party claims to act in accordance with the will of God. Both *may* be, and one *must* be wrong. God can not be *for,* and *against* the same thing at the same time. In the present civil war it is quite possible that God's purpose is something different from the purpose of either party—and yet the human instrumentalities, working just as they do, are of the best adaptation to effect His purpose. I am already ready to say this is probably true—that God wills this contest, and wills that it shall not end yet. By his mere quiet power, on the minds of the new contestants, He could have either *saved* or *destroyed* the Union without a human contest. Yet the contest began. And having begun He could give the final victory to either side any day. Yet the contest proceeds.

The "meditation" ends there; a great, accusatory Joban "Why, God?" is implicit.

The secretaries, in preparing their uncritical biography and eager to counter post-assassination aspersions on Lincoln's religiosity, seized on the fragment as evidence of the President's private piety. This expression of Lincoln's innermost thoughts, like a diary entry not intended for publication, seemed to them to be proof of Lincoln's belief in God. Didn't it begin with the devout words, "The will of God prevails"?

That sentence, the context suggests, contained an ironic intent. The meaning of that topic sentence, as I read it, is an exasperated "They all say 'The will of God prevails', but—" because it is followed by Lincoln's wondering why God does not make his will clear and support the side of the right, so that the carnage can end. That was Lincoln touching on the notion of retribution, but the underscored "may" in "Both sides *may*" put this in the conditional mood. It is deemphasized by the delayed infinitive, as if he could not accept that explanation of inexplicable suffering.

The sense of abandonment and isolation is central to Joban suffering. The mystery of God's absence in the nation's hour of need troubled Lincoln. So did the evidence of God's inexplicable purpose, or lack of any purpose at all, in punishing not only those guilty of "monstrous" slavery but also those in the North seeking to end it. In the line in his meditation—"I am already ready to say this is probably true"—the pronoun "this" refers to the thought in the next sentence: that God wills the continuation of the cruel bloodletting. Was this an attempt by Lincoln to shift his feelings of guilt for deciding to fight a civil war that had turned out more destructive than he ever contemplated? Was he trying to align his presidential will to wage war with God's will to let it continue? I think it reflects his anguish at God's apparent injustice: in an image he would use later, blood was being extracted by the sword from those who never wielded a lash.

Lincoln was already on record, in his defining pre-presidential speech at Cooper Union in 1860, as espousing the idea of ultimate moral retribution: "Let us have faith that right makes might . . ." Two and a half years later, slavery's wrong was asserting its might, and midterm elections were showing a widespread fraying of that faith in both conservative Republicans and war Democrats. At that low point, Job's ancient accusing question came through Lincoln's pen: How could a just God inflict the bloodiest punishment on slavery's supporters and foes alike? Why does God continue the unnecessary bloodletting of the innocent along with the guilty? The beleaguered President already had practical military and political reasons for shifting the focus of the North's cause from the less appreciated "preservation of the Union" and the abstract principle of majority rule to the morally rallying and politically reinvigorating crusade to "abolish slavery". But this meditation suggests he also felt the need in September 1862 to express his pained bewilderment at the arbitrariness of God's will.

He raises the humbling notion that "God's purpose is something different from the purpose of either party", because God could—but does not—make either party the instrument of his purpose. "And having begun He could give the final victory to either side any day," the lawyerly reasoning went. "Yet the contest proceeds." The purport of that last line can only be: How can this be consistent with Man's idea of justice and morality, of right making might? Why is God's punishment falling indiscriminately on the guilty and the innocent?

His apologist-secretaries hoped that "the will of God prevails" in the lead of the Lincoln meditation would be taken to mean that the nation's people must subject themselves to whatever that will was. But I believe Lincoln was sending a different and not nearly so submissive a message. He was crying out, "If the 'will of God prevails', why does this carnage continue? Why doesn't he let 'his' side prevail?" Far from being unquestioningly reverent, Lincoln was playing part of poet-Job's song—not the damn-the-day verse cursing God's creation, but the Joban message about the frustrating inaccessibility of God's design, the existence of which grows more doubtful as the innocent suffering increases.

The Lincoln meditation has been treated by most historians as an incomplete thought, a rumination composed when the President was afflicted with the depressive mood he called "the hypo". I think it is central to his wartime religious development. My evidence is in his reprise of this Joban thought, this time with a possible answer, in his most mature and mystical speech.

Lincoln's second inaugural address was delivered in March 1865, five weeks before the surrender of Robert E. Lee and his own assassination. Most Americans can readily recite at least the opening of its peroration, beginning, "With malice toward none, with charity for all, with firmness in the right as God gives us to see the right, let us strive on . . ." The magnanimity in this magnificent sentence is what the speech is best remembered for; forgotten is the theme of the short sermon, explicitly stated in the line: "The Almighty has his own purposes." The implicit theme: God's purpose may not be ours.

North and South, Lincoln said after taking the presidential oath for the second time, "read the same Bible and pray to the same God, and each invokes His aid against the other. . . . The prayers of both could not be answered." That followed his earlier meditation. To find a way out of this dilemma, he cited St. Matthew's Gospel: "Woe unto the world because of offences; for it must needs be that offences come; but woe to that man by whom the offence cometh."[1] Matthew was quoting Jesus' words about the type of persecutor who committed offenses—crimes or sins—against God's children, particularly those who believed in him. For such a miscreant, "it would be better for him to have a millstone hung around his neck, and be drowned in the depth of the sea".[2] This was a Jesus being protective of his vulnerable followers.

Lincoln then applied that admonition to the nation's offense of slavery against the Negro: "If we shall suppose that American slavery is one of those offenses which, in the providence of God, must needs come, but which, having continued through His appointed time, He now wills to remove, and that He gives to both North and South this terrible war as the woe due to those by whom the offense came, shall we discern therein any departure from those divine attributes which the believers in a living God always ascribe to Him?"

That's a long and complex question, more suited to a college seminar on metaphysics than to a political speech from the steps of the Capitol.

Its first premise is that, as St. Matthew said, "it must needs be that offenses come"—that is, ill fortune as well as good comes from God, and lasts for as long as the time God appoints for it, presumably as a "fiery trial", as Lincoln once called the war, or divine discipline for each person. (This is one of the rationales for suffering put forth by Eliphaz and Elihu.)

The next premise is that the carriers of this evil of slavery are all Americans, both North and South, who are being punished for being the vehicle of the offense sent by God for our trial. Lincoln's questioning clause, beginning "shall we discern", is ambiguous: It may agree with the legend's view of the patient Job, "Isn't this the retribution religious believers expect of a moral God?" or it may agree with an uncomprehending, impatient Job of the Bible, "Isn't this undiscerning affliction of both the proslavery South and the antislavery North quite different from the justice that religious people have been led to expect?"

In the end, having raised a metaphysical question for the first and last time in presidential inaugural addresses, the not-quite-certain Lincoln submits to taking his punishment of war without objection, as Job did when blasted by the voice from the whirlwind. The wartime President accepts the unforgiving, random retribution from the God of Wrath: ". . . if God wills that it continue . . . until every drop of blood drawn with the lash shall be paid by another drawn with the sword, as was said three thousand years ago, so still it must be said, 'The judgments of the Lord are true and righteous altogether.' "

In citing that psalm of David (19:9), the President did not object to the arbitrariness of God's punishment of the whole nation, especially those fighting to preserve and to abolish human slavery. His proposed solution to the problem of the otherwise inexplicable randomness is to apply moral retribution not to individuals but to the whole nation (an answer that moralists have long given to the problem of the torture of innocent Job). But the disquieting part of Lincoln's message, delivered with extraordinary humility on the verge of the bluecoats' victory, is that the purpose of the Union, or of mankind, may not be God's purpose: "The Almighty has his own purposes," he reminds his fellow citizens, purposes unrevealed to us, beyond our ken. That is why we will strive "with firmness in the right as God gives us to see the right"—a human being's limited vision, not God's much wider vision—but only the part of the right that God permits us to see.

That is my reading of Lincoln's reading of the message of Job, as he took the opportunity of his inaugural speech to deliver an unexpected sermon undergirding the appeal for magnanimity. "Charity for all" in his memorable peroration was not a promise of rehabilitating handouts to everyone, but was meant in the New Testament sense of "charity"—God's love for mankind—directed by Lincoln to his fellow victors.

The publicly expressed theology in his 1865 inaugural was rooted in his 1862 meditation. From the early ". . . it is quite possible that God's purpose is something different from the purpose of either party", his phrasing moved only to "The Almighty has his own purposes," a safer thought for public presentation. But his theology was marching on: At first, Lincoln saw the nation suffering as Job suffered, subject to arbitrary and indiscriminate punishment; at the end, he found a possible moral purpose in God's national punishment for the sin of slavery, but concluded that the victors should be generous to the losers because no human could discern the divine purpose of the terrible war.

By making ignorance of God's purpose the central point of his second inaugural address, Lincoln signaled its importance to his own soul-searching. When the Albany political adviser and editor Thurlow Weed complimented him on it, the President replied on March 15, 1865, that he expected that short speech "to wear as well as—perhaps better than—any thing I have produced; but I believe it is not immediately popular. Men are not flattered by being shown that there has been a difference of purpose between the Almighty and them. To deny it, however, in this case, is to deny that there is a God governing the world."

Like Job's consolers, Lincoln understandably saw evidence of the national sin in the national suffering. After all, Lincoln was a man of his time, and the prevailing interpretation of the Bible still leaned toward retributive justice, with God enforcing the moral law. But Lincoln had read the contrarian Book of Job for himself, and probably concluded that something was morally unjust about the length and indiscriminate terror of the war. He then reached for and accepted the Joban explanation that we are not permitted to see God's design in all the suffering. That led him to enjoin his fellow citizens to the Old Testament psalmist's submission.

Unable to explain God's apparent cruelty and arbitrariness on earth, both Lincoln and Job ultimately came to reconcile themselves with God by resigning themselves to the unknowability of his grand design. In Lincoln's meditation, we find no early acceptance of God's frustrating inaccessibility; his rumination is a believer's "but why?" In the Book of Job, however, the reader gets an inkling of his ultimate acceptance (or cave-in, if you prefer) in a meditation of his own—a reflective, philosophical, mood-breaking interlude in his angry disputation with the false consolers.

Every interpreter of Job notices that this curious, calm passage doesn't seem to fit anywhere in particular in the book. "Extraneous" is the word most often used to characterize this much-abused chapter. Not only is this hymn, poem, or meditation pacific rather than stormy, its style suggests to some that it was not written by the same hand as poet-Job's. And philosophically, it comes out of left field: Job—the original insurgent, a rebel with the greatest cause—uncharacteristically seems to call here for the meek acceptance of human ignorance of the ways of God.

But not everybody derogates this hymn to "God's unfathomable wisdom", as the NEB titles it. Robert Gordis believes it to be the early work of a young poet-Job, inserted into the book because it contains some beautiful images. He sees this independent piece, though not an integral part of the book, inserted as an intermezzo—a kind of musical interlude between the disputation with the friends and Job's final soliloquy summing up his case.

Let's subject selections from Job's meditation to the same kind of analysis we gave Lincoln's. The opening image of Job's hymn to wisdom is of a miner digging a shaft deep underground:

> *There are mines for silver*
> *and places where men refine gold; . . .*
> *the end of the seam lies in darkness,*
> *and it is followed to its farthest limit . . .*

Seeking that treasure, mining that ore, human beings are capable of amazing technological and scientific achievement:

> *Man sets his hand to the granite rock*
> *and lays bare the roots of the mountains;*
> *he cuts galleries in the rocks,*
> *and gems of every kind meet his eye . . .*

Having shown humanity capable of using technical skill to gain great knowledge, poet-Job poses the question that demeans the value of mere information about even the most precious material things:

> *But where can wisdom be found?*
> *And where is the source of understanding?*

The answer is neither in the mind of skilled mankind nor in the disorder of the deep:

> *No man knows the way to it; . . .*
> *and the sea says, "It is not with me."*

Can wisdom be bought?

> *gold and crystal are not to be matched with it,*
> *no work in fine gold can be bartered for it, . . .*
> *and a parcel of wisdom fetches more than red coral;*

To the repeated question, the poet now gives a positive answer:

*No creature on earth can see it,*
*and it is hidden from the birds of the air.*

*Destruction and death say,*
*"We know of it only by report."*
*But God understands the way to it,*
*he alone knows its source; . . .*
*even then he saw wisdom and took stock of it,*
*he considered it and fathomed its very depths.*

That's what most modern scholars believe to be the end of the hymn. "It" is wisdom, an understanding of the workings of the universe accessible only to God, beyond at least the present grasp of the most knowledgeable or technologically skilled human. That's the grand-design point made in the speeches from the whirlwind, although an opening is given there for Man to learn more, and this meditation provides what a television producer would call a teaser or billboard for the book's conclusion.

But to early reverent minds, Job's meditation lacked a snapper—a specific answer to the repeated "where can wisdom be found?" A need was perceived to give the frustrated reader more satisfaction than "God knows." That was when an editorial splice, in prose, may have been made—"And he said to man"—followed by a suspect conclusion, a pitch about how you, too, can find wisdom right at home.

*The fear of the Lord is wisdom,*
*and to turn from evil is understanding.*[3]

That's hardly characteristic of the persnickety Job we have come to know and puzzle over, and often to identify with. Many exegetes, delving into the early manuscripts, find that this pat answer directly contradicts the spirit of the book. As Marvin Pope notes, "After the poetic elaboration of the point that wisdom is inaccessible to man, the definition of an entirely different kind of wisdom seems rather abrupt." Not merely abrupt, but outright atypical; the scribes and sages who were poet-Job's editors twenty-five hundred years ago apparently added a conclusion that flies in the face of the book's theme.

"Fear of the Lord" is the ancient locution for religion. And to the ancient Israelite, "to turn from evil" meant to live the ethical, commandment-following life—that is, one upholding the moral values espoused by, and following the traditions and rituals protected by, the religious establishment's understanding of Scripture. The "answer" of the meditation—one that many suspect was inserted or tacked on, which demonstrates the beginnings of what might now be called the Job cover-up—says that the only wisdom Man can achieve is through unquestioning religious observance; the only understanding he can gain of the meaning of life is through the practice of morality. Thus, most modern scholars say, toss out the final couplet as phony and misleading.

But hold on. There is another way to come at this jarringly soothing ending that shows poet-Job, while sounding like the voice of tradition, to be as rebellious as ever. In the prologue, the "blameless and upright" Job was stipulated to be one "who feared God and set his face against wrongdoing". That is precisely the prescription given in the meditation as the route to wisdom: "fear of the Lord" and "to turn from evil". The same words appear, leaving no argument about mistranslation. That could mean that Job, at the beginning of the book, was in a state of wisdom, or at least well on the way to understanding. Talk about the arrogance of outrage: As Edwin Good puts it, Job's hymn to wisdom "adds to Job's powerful assertion of unassailable moral righteousness the claim to a divinely certified wisdom". According to this ironic reading, the concluding lines about how everybody can now get wisdom may have been stuck in by another hand, but whoever did it was a rebel who knew what he was doing.

But let's stick to the consensus reading of the whole Joban meditation. Its message foreshadows the lesson driven home in the speeches of God. Poet-Job is saying "here is the point I am about to make," or, if he wrote the meditative poem early in his life, "here is an idea for a book about wisdom's inaccessibility to Man." Inserted in the middle of the Book of Job in the way a dramatist lays a dagger on the table early in a play, the only-God-knows message tips off the philosophy of the end, when God booms out that he is the all-knower and Man is a most minor knowee. Humans may get smart, even attain great knowledge about the world around us, but when it comes to heavy-duty wisdom—final answers to the metaphysical whys about injustice—only God knows, and he's not saying, at least not yet.

What does that answer do for us?

Sometimes meditatively, occasionally poignantly, mostly insolently, Job wondered why justice was perverted. Lincoln (the type of resolute legal moralist Job sought as interceder in taking God to court), in his meditation and the inaugural sermon based on it, more respectfully asked why political morality—in his case, majority rule enforcing racial justice—was not allowed to triumph with a minimum of bloodshed. In Job the dissident and in Lincoln the avatar of authority, we find this in common: a refusal to accept the logic of an amoral God, or a capricious Fate, or a human future that cannot be changed by Man's rejection of enslavement and his demand for access to understanding. The force of Joban wonderment keeps us grasping for wisps of wisdom unnecessarily denied.

# PART IV

## WHAT LEADERS CAN LEARN FROM JOB

WHY DID GOD select Job, out of all the people on earth, for testing by the Satan?

I submit it was because Job, at the moment of testing, had reached the earthly pinnacle of power. In "the East"—presumably the center of some ancient establishment, viewed from the West—Job was a towering presence, not necessarily in physical size, but in social and political influence and in moral stature. His decisions, more than that of any other human, affected the lives of others. He was not merely the best and richest, but the most *powerful* man on earth. That meaning is worth pinning down because his preeminence as a man of power is what made him just right for God's experiment.

The standard answer to "Why Job, of all people?" is that the man from Uz was the best of the good. The first word used to describe his life, in the book's opening lines, is "blameless". Other translators chose "perfect", in its disappearing sense of "complete, whole". God really had the time and inclination to finish creating this man, and is manifestly proud of his handiwork. The second adjective in the ancient text describing Job, "upright", is rooted in "straight", with its connotation of morally straight, virtuous, as opposed to crooked, in both the standard and modern colloquial senses of that word.

Those meanings in the text are not in dispute: Job, in a judgment attributed directly to God in the prologue, was one straight shooter.

At the end of this section about what leaders can learn from the Book of Job, we will challenge the notion of such a no-fault man, but for now, set perfection aside; in the test God proposed about Man's motive, of far greater interest to the Satan would have been the extent of Job's power. To compare the strength of the antagonists in the struggle between God and Man, consider the next word used by God to describe his servant Job: "greatest".

"The *greatest* man in all the East"[1] is the way the NEB reads the ancient text, reinforcing the choice of "greatest" made nearly four centuries before by the King James translators. But the poet-translator Stephen Mitchell and the Anchor Bible's Marvin Pope prefer "richest". The difference, to those of us in politics, is substantial: Wealth is not power unless put into action. (Whoever said "soak the great"?) For a ruling on *gadol,* the Hebrew word in question, I turned to professor of Judaic studies Jacob Neusner, the modern Talmudic scholar who could best give Job instruction in iconoclasm; he translates that word as meaning "eminent authority" in rabbinic literature, with no connotation of wealth. Edwin Good, in his 1991 book on Job, agrees: " 'Wealthy' is not the primary meaning, though one would not exclude it. The main idea is 'big', which can include personal 'greatness'. 'Wealthy' seems too narrow, 'great' too broad. Reference to power might approach the idea . . ."

That's it, in my book: Job's status as leader of his world is the reason the news of his affliction drew three other leaders—kings of neighboring nations, or at least chieftains of nearby tribes—to console him. To think of the three visitors as "friends", as they are usually called, is misleading. More likely, the men come to commiserate were his colleagues at the top, his fellow world leaders. A short stretch of the imagination lets us envision their gathering as a summit meeting at a dungheap, around a superpower's bed of pain.

Why did poet-Job make his human hero the most powerful man in the East? Not merely because the designated victim would then have the highest position and most material wealth to lose; the dramatist wanted to present the strongest, most prestigious, and most morally reputable human adversary in the coming moral conflict with the all-powerful.

When you humiliate the humble, it's not a real contest and nobody wants to watch; but when you grind down the proud and powerful, you can count on a mighty explosion. Because Job had been given the most, he had the most to lose. The furious reaction of Job to his mistreatment by God would be in character with a man of power, who, when attacked, would fearlessly counterattack.

At the same time, God is shown by poet-Job to be an authority figure less than completely certain of his authority. Why else would he send the Satan to roam the world and spy on its inhabitants? Why else would he provoke his doubting agent, the prosecutory angel, to test the sincerity of Job's worship? The simple-sounding Joban prologue suggests that God is neither omniscient nor omnipotent. We can sense political weakness; God seems like Authority that has been in office too long, and needs reassurance.

By presenting a conflict between a possibly self-doubting Almighty and a mortal as self-righteous as he is powerful, the dramatist introduces the possibility of an upset: On first reading, the outcome of Job's testing is not a sure thing. Surprises seem to be (and are) in store.

Will the most powerful human being suffer in silence and prove God's wisdom in trusting his motive, as the folktale did—or will Job curse God to his face and thereby defeat God's design for the universe?

Will the human mind confront God and be crushed—or will it cease to believe and thereby, as far as mankind is concerned, destroy its creator?

The drama's suspense is palpable and effective; that's why audiences in every land and every medium have been riveted by it down to the latest generation. God might be seen as commanding the universal Ins, while Job, a former top In, stands now as champion of the Outs. The first profoundly dissenting human being is, then, like Leviathan, "King over all the children of pride"—the pride of the mavericks, the representative of an ousted elite restless under authoritarian control. Job stands for those outsiders who are persuaded that they are victims of inequity and have no friend in court. In this political construct, the reader becomes more than a passive taker of moral instruction; the reader is encouraged to be an active decision maker about the issues presented.

With that assessment of the relative strength of the contestants as prelude, we can examine a few Joban political lessons to modern leaders who are in, or aspire to, authority.

To use Theodore Roosevelt's prizefight metaphor, our "man in the arena" with God is Job. Our political arena is a society in which people freely delegate their sovereignty to a government, but with this proviso: that Authority protects their property without taking away their individual rights.

Of course there is a great difference in the relationship between lord and vassal in the spiritual world, and the tension between Authority and Subject in the political world. But biblical writers encouraged believers to apply the lessons of one to life in the other. Therefore, accept—for the sake of history's longest-lasting argument—the analogy of the path between God's celestial court and Job's dungheap as the earliest corridor of power. That leap of metaphoric belief will help us examine some political truisms to see if they are falsisms.

### 1. Use it or lose it.

From the State Department's Foggy Bottom to the place Pentagonians call the Puzzle Palace, diplomats and defense officials playing the game of nations find themselves presented with one of the most ancient national security rationales: "Use it or lose it." When George Shultz, as Reagan's secretary of state, used the phrase from his old marine days, a few etymologists raised their eyebrows at its sexual origin, but most people felt that the saying delivered a truth with a punch. Put more precisely in its application to national power, that admonition means: "Test it or don't trust it."

Though the Book of Job is mainly about a subject's conduct

under pressure, it is partly about Authority testing its authority. In the modern political world, we are often struck by an issue of testing of power. Authority must be confident of its power, and others must be certain of that power's existence as well as a will to use it; otherwise, power will atrophy as the certainty of its efficacy erodes.

Apply this principle to nuclear weaponry. In the deepest freezes of the cold war, proponents of strategic arms control argued that doubt was an asset. If a nuclear power, thinking of starting a war, is not totally confident that its weapons will work, its rational leader would not be likely to launch missiles that will invite retaliation; such self-doubt is thus a force for stability and peace. That's the reason for test-ban treaties. But in the dubiety derby, more important than the doubt in our own minds whether our weapons will work is the certainty in the mind of our potential adversary that our retaliatory weapons will work all too well.

I recall a discussion about nuclear warheads that was held in the White House Situation Room in the early seventies. Henry Kissinger, in usual mien of mournful Joban exasperation, confronted a group of hawks who were concerned that our bravado exceeded the capacity of our nuclear deterrent: "Look, it doesn't matter if we have talcum powder in our warheads," he argued, "—if the Russians think those warheads contain bombs, that's what counts."

In deterring nuclear war, misplaced confidence in the other side's power was as stabilizing as self-doubt about one's own power. What for four decades supported the theory of MAD— mutual assured destruction—was not so much the West's certainty of its ability to retaliate massively but the East's doubt that its own first strike would be the only strike.

About doubt: Consider the tut-tutting strain that runs through much of the modern commentary on Job. Wasn't God cruel to let the Satan rain down torments on blameless and upright Job just to prove a point about the motives of his worship? Extending that complaint to our lives today: Isn't God callous and unfeeling to wipe out all those people, good and bad, in earthquakes and other uninsurable "acts of God"? Let the psychiatrist Carl Jung, second only to Freud in the alienist pantheon, put the question as he did:

If the Supreme Being, whose supremacy should logically produce the most serene self-confidence, showed a curious need to test the most blameless man—wasn't this the Almighty's confession of self-doubt?

In the theological dealings between Lord and vassal, doubt (so often derogated as debilitating) can be equally constructive: A healthy skepticism can impel a renewal and deepening of trust. Doubt tends to be a stage rather than a permanent state; out of the seed of doubt sprouts the testing that produces either faith or disbelief. God incited the Satan to express aloud his doubt about the motive behind Job's piety; that gave God cause to test Job, to discover the depth of Man's fury at injustice, and to recognize the need for a whirlwind visit. Job's increasing doubt about God's interest and justice led not only to Job's self-righteous blasphemy but also to a peek at the big picture and a reconciling renewal of trust.

This mutual suspicion took place despite agreements between God and Man that had long before been set down in writing to remove all semblance of doubt. The creator's relationship to his human creation had been set up in patriarchal times as between protecting lord and willing vassal. The powers and obligations of God in his suzerainty were bound by a solemn covenant. That covenant also spelled out the responsibility of the people to worship God as their exclusive spiritual lord, abjuring all others. But as time passed, doubting and testing began annotating that agreement. Israel tested its Lord frequently, even as that people depended on his aid for its preservation. God returned that doubt, which led him to test the quality of the worship of the best and most powerful man in the world. This need for testing showed that God was realistic about the need to renew his authority—in other words, to use it or lose it.

Realism pervades the work of poet-Job. In his real world, he says, "The land is given over to the power of the wicked, and the eyes of its judges are blindfold."[2] No justice is dispensed from on high, which we take to mean that moral man must work out a rough justice for himself. In our modern real world, Job's plaint is repeated in a more colloquial "there ain't no justice". Half the population doubts our government's ability to guarantee equal-opportunity justice while the other half doubts its capacity to enforce criminal justice. That suggests to me that modern political leaders have to learn to put doubt to work. To prevent a stage of doubt from freezing into a permanent state, Authority must engage in the testing that leads to mutual confidence. The leader must gain trust in his own efficacy and his followers must gain belief in the leader's power and his will to use it.

The political test should not be confused with the taking of the public temperature by means of polls. Sampling is not testing, in its sense of "putting to trial". God did not send the Satan to Job with a questionnaire. The test that will answer doubt is the leader's willingness to expend political capital in some costly cause. The test is to engage those who are politically active in a controversy about the best way, even though the lazy legions of the politically inert prefer "the easy way".

In the week before President Bush launched an air attack on Iraq to expel Saddam Hussein's forces from Kuwait, the feeling in Washington was palpable that a compromise was in the works. In the U.N., the Soviet Union was pressing for a deal to allow the Iraqi dictator to save face while he withdrew from most of the country he had sacked. Gorbachev's negotiator Primakov was shuttling between Moscow and Baghdad. Most television commentators reported the likelihood that the feared bloodshed of allied troops would be averted in some last-minute triumph of diplomacy.

Before the spirit of appeasement could take the name of action by the throat, Mr. Bush struck by air. Most of the U.S. public, which had previously told pollsters it wanted to avert a war, quickly approved the spectacular display of accurate, destructive power. Then, after a month-long bombardment by air, political and diplomatic pressure again mounted for nonmilitary sanctions against Iraq in place of a potentially costly overland attack. Again Mr. Bush tested his support by ordering the storming of Iraq's dug-in positions in conquered Kuwait. Again American public-opinion support materialized. This surge of backing came partly because of the low-cost success of the air attacks, and partly because early emotion is to support the troops no matter what the policy, but mainly because the President's unwavering resolution gave people confidence.

News analysts dwelt on the testing of the President in a crisis. But the deeper testing was the reverse: the testing by the President of the American public's willingness to support armed intervention a short generation after its agonizing defeat in Vietnam. Mr. Bush's authority was enhanced by the public reaction to this test of itself— we did the right thing and it actually worked—especially when victory was quick and, to us, relatively cheap.

But would the American public have continued to support "Bush's war" if the blitzkrieg had turned into a quagmire? The President—more Vietnam-sensitive than the public—evidently did not think so, and so he declared victory prematurely. He had put the public to the test: and while he heard some antiwar dissent, mostly what was inspired and revealed was broad-based support. Only when Mr. Bush flinched from further testing, and two million panicked anti-Saddam rebels had to flee for their lives, did public enthusiasm wane and the public's estimate of the Bush Presidency begin its long march downward.

What a Joban moment that was: On February 28, 1991, with Iraq's elite Republican Guard routed and running to escape retribution, President Bush, at the urging of Joint Chiefs Chairman Colin Powell, and with the soldierly acquiescence of General Norman Schwarzkopf, determined that geopolitics called for a ceasefire while the Iraqi forces were still intact. This historic blunder was based on a strategic concern that Iraqi Shiites and Kurds might be encouraged to separate their territories from the land misruled by the elite Sunni sect from Baghdad. Sure enough: The repressed minorities staged an uprising; and remnants of Saddam's most loyal regulars—strengthened by helicopter gunships permitted to operate by an admittedly "suckered" General Schwarzkopf— slaughtered them. The injustice done to the rebels was palpable, but Mr. Bush, his advisers, and our Saudi ally had a bigger picture in mind. Their big-picture strategy was to bring order to the region by replacing Saddam Hussein with a less belligerent military dictator, thereby averting "dismemberment" of Iraq—that was the horrific vogue word in use—through the chaos of self-determination.

At the time, Western pundits who had long association with the hapless Kurds objected at the top of our lungs. As Saddam's gunships massacred the freedom fighters, we called Mr. Bush's abandonment of the rebels he had been urging to rise to be an act of immorality and injustice, but as White House Chief of Staff John Sununu smugly told *Newsweek:* "A hundred Safire columns won't make us change our policy." He was probably right because protest in print, unsupported by mass media coverage, can usually be deflected by those in power.

But the White House staff did not reckon on the countervailing power of color film televised from a scene of carnage and suffering on a Joban scale. The sacrifice of innocents might have passed unnoticed, as had the poison-gassing of five thousand Kurds a few years before at Halabja—except for the intrusion of an unexpected human element: the terrified migration of two million exposed, terrified souls. Their exodus, widely described as "biblical", was brought into American living rooms on television. At that moment, the strategic big picture was covered over by real pictures—images of dying babies, sobbing mothers, accusing fathers. White House worry about partition of Iraq was swept away by the dread of political repugnance at home. The Bush policy was belatedly changed and the refugees were given both food and a zone of their homeland with at least temporary allied military protection.

Twice the President had tested the nation's mettle and gained reassurance from support given by the majority of the public. But the third time, his testing of support was based on a calculation justified only by concerns beyond the public's ken. The uproar caused Authority to back off. Ironymongers will note that all this testing took place about events that happened in the land of Uz: The ancient Mesopotamia that makes up part of modern Iraq was the site of the Job story.

In my review of modern Jobs, I will come back to one of the Kurdish leaders, but my point about tests and fiery trials is this: Democratic leadership draws unmatchable strength when it puts itself and its public to the test. A totalitarian system, enshrining stability and promising security, resists such testing because it is fearful of any exposure of public doubt. In yesterday's Soviet empire, the hard shell of communism's authority concealed a mushy fear of testing. In today's China, the "mandate of heaven" is the term for popular faith in leadership's alignment with good fortune; but when natural or economic disaster strikes, or when ruling cliques fall out, the mandate is sure to pass from a fearful gerontocracy to leaders readier to take the test of public support.

Every person in command needs to be kept in touch with the source of his or her authority by the force of doubt. That force can bring about a new confidence of strength or a necessary awareness of weakness. In Job's case, doubt from above stimulated doubt from below; God's doubt of Job's motive resulted in Job's doubt of God's justice. This triggered the testing of each other and, after the hollering back and forth, a hard-to-explain closing of the chasm between Authority and Subject.

Long ago labeled "divine discontent", self-policing doubt is the antithesis of smugness in leaders. Such doubt divides not to conquer but to restore. In the political leader's need for a renewed mandate, as in God's need to engage in a power struggle with Job, creative doubt at the top is the irritant that builds the pearl, a stimulus to mutual measurement, an incentive to reject the cool comfort of aloofness for the hot prodding of proximity.

Now, about that proximity:


### 2. "Close" counts only in horseshoes and hand grenades.

In the 1960s, as the selection of party nominees for President shifted from national conventions to state primaries, a slogan was born: "He cared enough to come." Whenever a campaigner concentrated his time elsewhere, or tried to appear above the battle, an opponent on the scene would blanket the neglected state with the politics of personal presence.

The comedian Woody Allen raised this point to a philosophical adage with his advice to young playwrights fearful of getting produced: "Eighty percent of success is showing up." (When President George Bush misquoted this as 90 percent, I queried Mr. Allen, who replied: "The figure seems high to me today, but I know it was more than sixty and the extra syllable in seventy ruins the rhythm of the quote, so I think we should let it stand at eighty.")

We have seen how Job teaches leaders to reach out and renew their strength by testing their sovereign publics. Now we will examine how leaders can succeed by showing up—by caring enough to come. Authorities must let subjects reach out and touch them.

We are talking not about pressing the flesh but pressing the spirit. Thomas Hobbes, the most illustrious English political scientist until John Locke came along, took a name out of Job for the title of his most famous book. *Leviathan* was published in 1651, just after Oliver Cromwell overthrew the monarchy. You remember Leviathan—not the literal crocodile, or Melville's Moby Dick, but the mythic fire-breathing dragon. In ancient Ugaritic texts that preceded or paralleled the Hebrew writings, the good god Baal conquered Lotan, the symbol of evil, described as "the serpent Twisty, the Tyrant with seven heads". In Hebrew Scripture, the sea serpent surfaces again, as the voice of God asks from the whirlwind: "Can you fill his skin with harpoons or his head with fish-hooks?" He asks this question as a way to belittle Man's power, warning: "If ever you lift your hand against him, think of the struggle that awaits you, and let be."[3]

The security-centered Hobbes used the name Leviathan to label a commonwealth, or state, "which is but an artificial man". He constructed an elaborate metaphor about a monstrous body politic. First Hobbes described humanity in a state of nature, without government, and with the life of man "solitary, poor, nasty, brutish and short". (Great name for a law firm.) This Leviathan's strength is the wealth of its members; its nerves are reward and punishment; its reason is law; its soul is sovereignty; its business is the public safety; its sickness, sedition; its death, civil war. Those were the days a political thinker could really extend a metaphor.

Political Man, according to Hobbes, conceived this Leviathan state for the purpose of self-preservation: By putting their sovereignty into one awesome pot, individual citizens could supposedly guarantee the good behavior of all. The Hobbesian choice was between despotism and anarchy, and Hobbes came down hard in favor of despotism. For the sake of the individual's safety and the preservation of his property, absolute monarchy was required; in a strict, Hobbesian world, no elections would be held that might undermine the people's awe of their collective sovereign. Only if the Leviathan state failed to provide safety to life and property did its subjects have the right to overturn it.

Did subjects have the right to resist the laws of Leviathan? They could disobey only when conscience told them secular law came into conflict with the laws of God. Through "right reason", people choose to accept God's rule, and here again Hobbes made a case for absolute power: The natural right by which God demands obedience comes not from anything as soft as Man's gratitude for being created, but from God's "irresistible power". Obedience is attracted by that magnet: "To those therefore whose power is irresistible, the dominion of all men adhereth naturally . . . not as Creator and gracious, but as omnipotent."

Hobbes must have been impressed by the overpowering, who-are-you-to-argue-with-me voice from the whirlwind. Three and a half centuries ago, this spokesman for absolutism turned to the politics of Job in order to deal with why evil men prospered while the good suffered. The problem was topical then as now: "it hath shaken the faith, not only of the vulgar, but of philosophers and, which is more, of the saints, concerning the Divine Providence." Hobbes wrote to stop the shaking: "And Job, how earnestly does he expostulate with God for the many afflictions he suffered, notwithstanding his righteousness? This question in the case of Job is decided by God Himself, not from arguments derived from Job's sin, but His own power." Innocent suffering? A manifestation of God's works, to be choked down by saints and sinners without complaint. Hobbes teaches that power alone, not grace or morality, commands obedience, and he cites Job's authoritarian God as his authority.

Thomas Hobbes turned out to be profoundly mistaken about both the source of authority and the lesson of Job. Let us turn, as poet-Job did, to life's reality to draw an analogy. Experience has shown that absolute power in Leviathan, the monster state, is a bad idea. It is unproductive and corrupting. Instead of protecting people from afflicting each other, a system of unrestrained central power invariably produces a dictator, unaccountable to the source of sovereignty, who afflicts the people.

In the twentieth century, Hobbes's absolute-security theory was given a seventy-year trial, and was disproven by the internal decay and ultimate collapse of communism. (Hobbes might argue that communism's demise fits into his loophole, which allowed a people to overthrow a regime that did not protect property. But anybody trying to extend his concept of property protection all the way to financial security or national prosperity would be shouted down on any panel show.)

If, in the political world, omnipotence is demonstrably wrong in the relationship between Authority and Subject, why should might make right in God's dealings with Man in the spiritual world? Power balances in the secular and spiritual worlds are hardly the same, but let me try to make the case that Hobbes read Job incorrectly, and as a result built his philosophy of political absolutism on spiritual sand.

The Book of Job does not teach resignation to inexplicable muscle-flexing. Blind obedience to omnipotence is hardly its message. Rather, renewal of faith comes from the opposite direction: If God is not to be merely believed in but trusted, he cannot escape the necessity of responding in some way to moral challenge.

Throughout his dungheap ordeal, Job continues to try to bring God to account. The visitor Elihu may have been inserted later, by poet-Job or some other hand, to explain why God would never appear: "the Almighty we cannot find; his power is beyond our ken".[4] The young intruder could assure Job only that this *deus absconditus*—the forever-hidden God—was using suffering as a prophylactic in scourging the innocent man, dissuading him from some future sin. That's like smacking your kid for what he hasn't done yet on the assumption that he's bound to get into mischief someday.

This idea of an unreachable God was an ironic setup by poet-Job, because in the very next chapter, exactly the opposite happens: God reveals himself to Job in a bolt from the blue. It's the old read-me-upside-down trick: We can take this surprise theophany, in direct contradiction of Elihu's tirade, to be a signal that the opposite of what Elihu said was true. That leads us to conclude that we can find the Almighty, and that his power is not beyond our ken. By immediately showing Elihu to be wholly mistaken about God's unwillingness to appear, poet-Job suggests Elihu's other messages are mistaken as well: We then take the point that God does respect clever, or inquiring, minds; and by extension, that he will at least pay attention to an indignant moral appeal.

Stepping on Elihu's lines, God opens up to Job, in the first stormy speech, with a broadside of rhetorical questions to make Man seem little and God big. As we have seen, the more he goes on this way, the more God reveals about the workings of the universe. He does not answer Job's questions about morality and justice, but answers questions the challenging man never knew to ask about metaphysics. The tone of God's first speech from the whirlwind is undeniably sarcastic-bombastic, but the meaning is far from absolutist. I hear: "You dare to judge me? Here are a few criteria you never thought about—how I would judge me." Job, more impressed than persuaded by the first speech, replies he will now shut up, but his dissatisfaction shows at first in his withholding of repentance.

God, held accountable for his cruel punishment of the blameless man, goes into the balance-of-nature argument in his second speech. That convinces Job, who is at last a player and not a playing card, that he has glimpsed the elemental forces that keep the world in balance. The awestruck player then folds his hand, but God, having been forced to extend himself by appearing, overcompensates in the epilogue by generously letting his opponent rake in the pot.

At any gathering of world leaders, the question put by pundits to each other at the end is: "Who won?" In his whirlwind confrontation, Job wins by getting (for himself and for the rest of us questioners) a fleeting indication of the wonders now beyond his present ken. His sustained challenge brought God out of hiding, thereby demonstrating to the world's citizenry that no authority is beyond reach of the governed. God wins, too, by keeping Man's worship, the human support that poet-Job seems to me to think God needs. (Lincoln's secretary of state, William Seward, giving in to his President's desire to issue a written proclamation of emancipation, asked wryly, "What's liberty without a pole?" In the same way, what's God without worshipers?) The conflict between remote God and blasphemous Man turns out, thanks to the blessed human badgering that leads to an inkling of divine accountability, not to be a fight to the finish.

In biblical power-plays as in modern political life, when Authority is forced to give an accounting of its stewardship, the accounting is rarely given with good grace. Any reporter who has ever used the Freedom of Information Act to pry embarrassing facts out of a government agency is subjected to this institutional sulkiness. Job's God expresses his irritability in no uncertain terms, grumping at having been called away from important work by this minor creation. In modern political life, the adept political authority tries to mask this resentment at the uppityness of its challengers, whether in Question Time in Parliament or at news conferences in the White House, but the strain is always there.

I just used the term "news conference", now preferred in all the stylebooks. Some readers will recall when the meeting of press and public official was called a "press conference". The change was made in 1969 not, as most reporters persuaded themselves, to embrace electronic media as well as print journalists; it was changed to "news conference" because Richard Nixon privately insisted that the President's conference with the press did not belong to the press but to the President, to make news. He was wrong about that—the confrontation is a way for the governed to make Authority more readily accountable—but the name-change stuck and it's too late to argue now.

Accountability may be grudging, but Authority is obligated to remain engaged, to be reachable, in order to stay alive. To be "enlivened by debate" is more truth than trope; the heated clash of ideas, parties, philosophies, and interests keeps a political system from icing over and stopping cold. This includes opposing what most of us consider to be vice; indeed, the effective politician attributes evil, darkness, unraveling organization, and impending disaster to his opposition so that he can shine in contrast. No bad, no good, says the theologian; the practical politician turns that justification of evil into: He's bad, I'm good. The comedian Henny Youngman, asked how his spouse is, replies "Compared to what?" When nearly good needs to look better, it tries to make pretty bad look terrible.

When Jimmy Carter's press secretary, Jody Powell, was asked about the closeness of a defeat of some challenge to the President, he replied with a pointed if lugubrious adage: " 'Close' counts only in horseshoes and hand grenades." This usually means that in most races, to lose by a little is to lose all. But in a wider sense of maintaining accountability, close counts for plenty.

"All politics is local," goes another truism; the leader who loses touch with his roots in the people soon loses his perch on high. Modern courtiers think that proximity to power is power, and vie for the recognition by their rulers that is now called "face time". As a result, aides who are put in place to facilitate communication from the center can become a palace guard blocking access from suspected rivals on the periphery. A leader's carefully cultivated sense of closeness counts a great deal in delivering the assurance of accountability. That assurance—tangible, visible—is indispensable to the maintenance of Authority. Out of reach, out of touch, out of office—three outs and the side is retired.

" 'Close' counts only in horseshoes and hand grenades," in its sense as a derogation of intimacy, is a falsism. Closeness to the source of power is indispensable to the maintenance of power. To hold a subject's allegiance, Authority must remind itself, as poet-Job's God apparently did, that face-to-face persuasion of the subject—by reasoning, intimidation, or awe—cannot forever be avoided. "I knew of thee then only by report," says Job, whose too-filtered vision contributed to his estrangement, "but now I see thee with my own eyes."[5] Job stayed loyal because God cared enough to come.

### 3. Losers keepers.

"Show me a good loser," went a phrase I unfairly attributed to Henry Kissinger in the 1970s, when I was sore at him, "and I'll show you a loser." Contrast that hardball cynicism with Lincoln's poignant observation after losing an election, cited by Adlai Stevenson in his second concession speech to Eisenhower, "I'm like the little boy who stubbed his toe on a rock and said, 'I'm too old to cry and it hurts too much to laugh.' "

Is suffering a defeat good for a political person? The run for office is a short run, and the loser is not likely to find comfort in talk about the long run. But can rejection at the polls be fairly presented as what condolence-bearers sardonically call "a character-building experience"?

First, let's recognize that to suffer a political defeat is not to endure real suffering. In its personal impact, defeat at the polls is a setback to a career, not a personal tragedy, and it happens to at least one candidate in every contest.

Second, there is no denying that the majority's rejection is a painful blow to the ego. Even if the candidate begins as a long shot, by the time Election Day rolls around, the underdog is almost always persuaded that the polls are wrong and an upset may be in the works. The bruise of loss affects a person's self-image and has turned extroverts inward.

I believe that losing a campaign early in political life is constructive. Blessings in disguise were disparaged by no less an authority on the vagaries of victories than Winston Churchill, but the taste of defeat near the start makes subsequent victory all the sweeter. And a therapeutic trouncing introduces a little real humility into candidates who must at least profess humility. Bill Clinton won his first race for governor of Arkansas while still in his twenties: He swaggered around the state trying to impose elitist solutions to everyday problems, until he was beaten next time out. He and his wife, Hillary, regrouped; they attuned themselves more closely to the habits and desires of local voters (though an ardent feminist, she adopted his last name), and went on to reoccupy the governor's house for a decade. The experience of getting up off the floor helped Clinton survive the ignominy of ridicule of his too-long 1988 convention address (the only applause came after his words "And to conclude"), and made it possible to avert an early knockout from a one-two punch in the 1992 presidential primaries.

Ted Kennedy has been breezing through a lifetime of elections in Massachusetts, where a Kennedy could do no wrong. The ease of victory helped to undo him; the discipline of an early defeat might have made him a President, just as the prospect of defeat next time is making him a better senator. His older brother JFK went all the way without a loss, but I believe he would have been an even better President with a little of the royal cockiness knocked out of him in his thirties. Ronald Reagan's loss to Gerald Ford in the Republican convention of 1976 was, at age sixty-five, thought to be a career finisher, but he was unready for retirement.

The comeback quality—the law of political return—is current in our leadership. George Bush was running against Lloyd Bentsen for the Senate in Texas in 1970. Pat Buchanan and I were on temporary duty from the Nixon White House writing alliterative speeches for Vice President Spiro Agnew, barnstorming the nation in that midterm election, and the straw boss on our campaign plane, Bryce Harlow, offered the young Bush the red-hot Agnew's aid. Out of political conviction, misjudgment of the Texas electorate, or a desire to make it on his own, the moderate Bush turned down the conservative Agnew identification, and lost. Chastened, Mr. Bush became more conservative, later accepted the party chairmanship from an embattled Nixon (I am tempted to write here "and was never heard of afterward"), and went on to turn primary defeat in 1980 into a successful association with Reagan, leading to his own Presidency.

Defeat, if it doesn't destroy them, tempers leaders. After reaching deep within for internal resources, they can rightly claim to have grown as a result of what the voters have taught them. In the art of comeback, one lesson is not to insist that voters admit they were wrong last time, even if their choice of candidates turned out to be inept or corrupt in office. On the contrary, the putative comebacker should compliment the electorate on having been right in spotting his own shortcomings in policy or personality or presentation, which have been corrected—with no compromise of principle, of course. Last time's losers should assert with pride that they have learned enough to become next time's winners.

Nixon learned that during his first comeback in the mid-sixties, when interviewers slyly asked if he was a "new Nixon". By calling up that manipulative phrase, the reporter was suggesting that the two-time loser had revamped his partisan image to strike a statesmanlike pose. For a time, Nixon angrily denied having put on a pleasing persona, claiming to be the same old misunderstood Nixon. I was in the public-relations business in those days, and hit on a way to deal with the media's suspicion less defensively. When the subject of his changed views—say, a new approach to "Red China"—was broached, Nixon would say "You really want to know if there's a 'new Nixon'. Well, of course there is! Times change; there's a new America, a new world, a need for new policies . . ." The refreshing admission worked. After a while, the candidate would insert his "new Nixon" answer into every interview, whether the questioner was interested or not. In the course of so doing, Nixon identified himself with Churchill and De Gaulle, who had also suffered rejection and made comebacks. The forever-renewing Nixon came back, too; at this writing, a generation after the Watergate fall, he's still coming back.

But before the rebound, there is that seemingly endless stage of loserhood. More often than not, the candidate is blamed for his own defeat by his own supporters. The derision leveled at Michael Dukakis for dissipating a seventeen-point lead in 1988 is nothing new; Senator Everett Dirksen rose before the Republican convention of 1948, pointed his finger at Thomas E. Dewey and his crowd of eastern establishmentarians, and boomed: "You led us down the road to defeat!"

If the Book of Job has a ready audience in politics, it is among the legion of losers. Nobody has expressed the empty feeling after the loss of power more bitterly than the battered and abandoned Job: "If I could only go back to the old days . . . like a king encamped with his troops. Whoever heard of me spoke in my favour . . . But now I am laughed to scorn by men of a younger generation, men whose fathers I would have disdained to put with the dogs who kept my flock."[6]

Eliphaz the Temanite, kindest of the remonstrating visitors, had offered a way out. "Happy the man whom God rebukes! therefore do not reject the discipline of the Almighty. For, though he wounds, he will bind up; the hands that smite will heal."[7] We know that such a promise of divine retribution was false, that poet-Job's point was that the hand that smote was under no obligation to heal. Yet "do not reject the discipline of the Almighty" makes us think twice, especially when it is followed by Elihu's "Those who suffer he rescues through suffering and teaches them by the discipline of affliction."[8] The brash intruder reminds Job of his smugness in his days of power: "Will that wealth of yours, however great, avail you, or all the resources of your high position?"[9] Job had been riding high, passive in his contentment, never doubting or testing the sources of his sovereignty. In his own recollections of his days of power, Job comes across as having been self-satisfied, taking his exalted position as his due.

Although Job had been described by God in the prologue as "blameless", it could be that God was mistaken. Certainly it seems from Job's words that he had been more than a little smug and pompous when he sat atop a world rather than atop a dungheap. Loss knocked that smugness out of him; in that regard, his unjust misfortune did him good. It made him a rebel; his monumental loss forced him to reexamine his life and admit to having been less than perfect, though not as sinful as his punishment made it seem. Loss also drove Job to make demands on his God that Elihu did not find conceivable. The young man had asked rhetorically, "Can any man dictate to God when he is to speak? or command him to make proclamation?"[10] Elihu's meaning was that no man could summon God, but only five verses later, God appeared—as if on cue—to respond to Job's terrible oath of clearance. Man did command God to make proclamation, and God showed up to do just that.

What was behind God's appearance? I think that the force that caused the theophany was the same force that motivated Job's rebellion: an infuriating sense of loss. Just as Job lost his family, property, health, and influence, God lost his human worshiper—and as the sarcastic fury in the whirlwind speeches makes clear, God does not like to lose. Preventing the loss of Man's worship was evidently very important to him.

Man and God had this in common: Neither was willing to accept his loss. Neither would acknowledge defeat. There stood Job, demanding an explanation of injustice; there stood God, demanding Job worship him without explanation.

Out of this impasse came a compromise that enabled both to make a comeback and to claim a victory. The rebellious human won an appearance by God and an end to his despairing isolation, not to mention a glimpse of the grand design; in these ways, Job won respect. The irritated God won his worshiper back, and won his bet with the Satan: In the end, as God had hoped, Job did fear God for naught. Only after Job's demonstration of disinterested piety did God shower him with gifts in the epilogue—because God was grateful, or felt like celebrating his avoidance of defeat (or because poet-Job did not want to lose all his work to pious redactors).

The seeming losers came back and won. No wonder so many despondent or defeated politicians can be found thumbing through the Book of Job.

### 4. Not even God can be the judge
### in his own case.

When Billy Carter, the President's brother, was exposed acting as a kind of agent for the dictator of Libya, I labeled the minor scandal "Billygate" and called for the appointment of a special prosecutor not beholden to the Carter administration. Instead, the Justice Department retained what it called "special counsel".

That reminded me of a riddle Lincoln liked to pose: If you call a tail a leg, how many legs has a dog? Answer: four, because calling a tail a leg doesn't make it a leg. Calling a counsel "special" doesn't make it special; only the appointment of a prosecutor removed from the normal Justice Department chain of command makes it special. The purpose is to avoid even the appearance of conflict of interest.

The founders of the American system took a leaf from Britain's way of limiting the king's self-judging power and created the independent judiciary. A judge not beholden to the prosecution came between the prosecutor and defendant, laying a hand of restraint on both. In theory, a grand jury is also supposed to act as an umpire between citizen and prosecutor, deciding if the government's evidence is worthy of indictment. But that restraint has been broken down by manipulative prosecutors, who describe panels that do not do their bidding as "runaway grand juries".

In a case of wrongdoing within modern government, however, Job's age-old problem with an unjust God arises. Authority must be required to reach out for Job's "umpire", which we call a special prosecutor. No matter who is in the White House, the Department of Justice attacks the Ethics in Government Act, triggering outside counsel as being unduly suspicious of regular prosecutors. The department's civil servants take it as an aspersion cast on their professionalism, but sometimes professionalism asks too much.

Special prosecutors with genuine independence came onto the Washington scene in the Nixon era after an attempt to suppress a subpoena led to the "Saturday Night massacre", a series of resignations in protest that ended with Solicitor General Robert Bork, who remained at his post to do the deed. The newly empowered law officers were immediately hailed as heroic, almost Promethean figures who would do battle against the power-crazed Zeus. The term for them has since been changed to "independent counsel", to prevent the early assumption by the public that prosecution would surely follow investigation.

The heroic image—especially after the unsuccessful prosecutions of Oliver North and John Poindexter in the Iran-Contra affair—has been slightly tarnished. Independent counsel, appointed by the courts and answerable to nobody, do tend to build empires, and some of them catch the arrogance they have been hired to cure. I recall my own run-in with Leon Jaworski, soon after I left the Nixon White House to go to work for *The New York Times.* The Texas legal establishmentarian had been chosen to conduct the Watergate investigation. Jaworski's methods of intimidating grand jury witnesses seemed to me to be as high-handed and unfair as the charges then being made against the Nixonians, and I inveighed against the new reign of terror, stressing the irony of abusing civil liberty in the name of its defense.

The *Times,* to the eternal credit of Arthur Ochs Sulzberger, let me blaze away at Jaworski's publicity-conscious pomposity, on the theory that even a pack of antimedia conspirators deserved one defender on the opinion-molding *Times* op-ed page. The special prosecutor, however—unaccustomed to any coverage short of adulation—did not see it that way.

Al Haig, then White House chief of staff and official contact with the Special Prosecution Force, sidled up to me at a cocktail party to murmur, "Leon says to lay off him or he'll pull you in before the grand jury." As it happened, I had a thing or two to hide, the memory of which I have since successfully repressed; I felt that clutchfist of fear in my chest that everyone feels at the prospect of torture and ruination before the Inquisition. My concern was soon overcome by suspicion—why was Al Haig, supposedly Nixon's defender, carrying the Jaworski threat to shut me up?

I did the most effective thing I could do: The next day, I wrote in detail in the *Times* about the attempt at intimidation. Wiser heads around the special prosecutor got him to back off. Years later, I zapped Jaworski for a conflict of interest in profiting from his memoirs, eliciting red-faced expostulations from the old hypocrite.

This story is recounted herein to establish my credentials of antipathy toward the go-get-'em goo-goos. But we need them to protect the public's trust in its government; the frequent insolence of these officers is outweighed by the function they perform. The principle of the thing rolls over the personalities: If a prosecutor can be fired by his target, he serves that master as well as the public, and nobody can properly serve two masters. Result: suspicion never resolved, faith in justice weakened.

The best attorneys general understand that. In a polemic urging that Griffin Bell, Jimmy Carter's attorney general, recuse himself from some case involving the president's brother, I used the verb—*recuse*—that is so easily and often turned into a typo. At a Cabinet meeting, Judge Bell said, "It says here in the *Times* that I should 'rescue' myself—and that's exactly what I'm going to do."

Conflict of interest is rooted in antiquity. At the heart of Job's struggle with the Almighty is a conflict of interest: Who is to judge the supreme judge?

Job is so angry at the raw deal he has been getting that he wants to sue. The legal metaphor runs throughout the Book of Job, as befits an ancient culture that laid such stress on the written law. Job is aware that such a legal challenge is absurd: "He is not a man as I am, that I can answer him or that we can confront one another in court."[11] Still, Job indulges himself in wishing he had an attorney who could intercede for him under some rules of adjudication: "If only there were one to arbitrate between us and impose his authority on us both."[12]

This daydream of an arbitrator or umpire had a specific pre-biblical source: In ancient Sumerian theology, each person had a personal god, much as a modern exercise freak has a personal trainer. This junior deity served as an advocate, licensed to practice before the council of the great gods, who were too busy to deal with the preparation of individual cases. (The story comes to mind of a rich Texan who appeals to God for help in making the biggest deal of his life; next to him, a poor man is praying for food for his family. The oilman hands the indigent a twenty-dollar bill and says, "Here, don't bother God with that now, he's working on my deal." This apparently began as an ancient Sumerian joke.)

Poet-Job was among the first to identify the conflict inherent in Authority's self-judgment. By pressing for a trial, with its bizarre notion of God splitting into both accused and judge, or ultimately into both accuser and judge, Job showed that the relationship between God and Man had nothing to do with retribution, the fair settling of accounts; on the contrary, the way the conflict had to be resolved ensured that there could be no impartiality, therefore no justice even in the review of injustice.

Job sees himself as the aggrieved party in a law case, and files his petition to get his day in court: "Let me but call a witness in my defence! Let the Almighty state his case against me!"[13] Not only does he demand a response, but he wants his opponent-at-law to answer him in writing—"If my accuser had written out his indictment, I would not keep silence . . ."[14] (The famous translation in KJV, "would that mine adversary had written a book", misses the point of a legal indictment that informs the accused of the charges in detail.) This need for particulars is often felt by targets of modern investigations being ruined by leaks from publicity-hungry prosecutors; the accused, like Job, wish the government would get specific about its allegations, and say which laws were broken.

Job's problem in this legal conceit is that his opponent is also his judge; "no man can win his case against God."[15] How can impotent Man prevail against the monopolist of power? That is why Job teases himself with a helpless wish for an intermediary who could "impose his authority on us both"—that is, an advocate able to stop an arbitrary God from concluding the trial with a lightning-bolt decision. "If I am to be accounted guilty, why do I labour in vain?"[16] he complains; even so, near the end of his suffering, Job issues his ringing exculpatory oath, the traditional declaration of innocence by the accused in the petition for trial. In effect, Job summons God to judgment—but with God serving as God's own judge, a happy arrangement for the accused deity but not for the human complainant.

In a book so much about human conduct in the face of injustice, this goes to the core of the abuse of power. In any well-run courtroom, between the disputants there sits an impartial party, a judge, treating litigants equally. But when the judge becomes a disputant, or when a prosecutor is a defendant, or when a relative or business partner of either is charged, Job tells modern leaders that some special arrangement must be made to avoid a conflict of interest.

### 5. Be kind to the jaywalking wounded.

*Symbiosis* is a word politics has usefully borrowed from biology. The word originally meant "the living together of dissimilar organisms"; it sometimes referred to a parasitic relationship, such as a flea on a dog; another sense denoted a mutually helpful relationship, like an ant acting in harmony with an aphid; now the extended meaning is "cooperation on the basis of mutual need". Armed with this voguish sense, we are prepared to grind an axiom: In the symbiosis between Authority and Subject, if either finally wins, both lose. When the game is won, it's all over; each side loses its purpose, and the result is Hobbesian absolute rule, or anarchy.

If Authority gains too much power, it loses the power of consent; if the Vassal, or subject, or governed, undermines Authority, then disorder and anarchy reign and darkness is on the face of the deep thinkers.

Poet-Job made a point never before attempted in any preserved literature: Omnipotence can be as feckless as impotence. Too much power is as unusable as too little.

To maintain control, to govern a living universe, Authority has to give a little leeway to disorder. Consider Behemoth and the above-mentioned Leviathan, the pre-biblical, legendary male and female forces of chaos, straining at the bonds. Why doesn't God, if he is as orderly as he is almighty, solve that problem once and for all by killing them and the force of disruption they represent?

Any mythmaker worth a pillar of salt can provide the answer to that: God cannot slay Leviathan and her sidekick without destroying the creative tension needed for the vitality of the universe.

In his whirlwind tour, Yahweh showed Job that governance of creation is a vast balancing act. By conjuring the horrors of chaos—the monsters Behemoth and Leviathan—he showed how only he, and not any of his creations such as Man, can keep them in some sort of control. If Job had not so quickly caved in and repented after God's second speech, he might have asked, "If you're so powerful, then why not kill the monsters of chaos once and for all?" God's answer might have been: Running the cosmos is on a different order of magnitude than running the earth, requiring wholly different standards. What works for you in your strict moral order in one small world would not work if that morality were applied to my whole universe—indeed, the destruction required in carrying out retribution for evil on such a grand scale might endanger creation itself.

Myths aside, human experience demonstrates a certain tension between order and chaos in politics. The tension manifests itself in the eternal battle between tyranny and anarchy, between stability and freedom, between stultifying security and dog-eat-dog self-reliance. The presence of one defines the other; crack-up leads to crackdown; unless a spectrum goes all the way from one end to the other, it's no spectrum.

Hold on, now—that spectrum metaphor may hold for good and bad, but can we legitimately equate order with tyranny, and freedom with chaos? Equate, no; compare, yes. Order and freedom are values that turn evil when carried to their extremes; put another way, tyranny and chaos are evils that have a good effect on each other.

The appearance of the Satan in the Book of Job caused philosophers to write of two inclinations in Man, toward the good and the bad. The pull in the good direction is not altogether good. That pull starts out toward order, emulating God's actions in bringing light to the darkness, and giving system and purpose to what had been chaos and confusion. However, "too much of a good thing" can be demonstrated: such control ceases to be good when the pull to order goes too far—to absolute monarchy, to fascist or Communist totalitarianism, to any form of tyranny. When that happens, the light of order ceases to be enlightening and becomes blinding: The monster of chaos is defeated by an equally destructive monster of control. Poet-Job's Leviathan, a frightening symbol of destructive freedom, would be defeated by Hobbes's Leviathan, the absolute monarchy, no less monstrous for being orderly.

In the same way, the pull in the bad direction shown by the presence of the Satan—toward the darkness of chaos—is not altogether bad. (Modern "chaos theorists" are trying to find a hidden system that underlies seemingly random fluctuations in the physical world; perhaps even chaos has its own rules.) In the Book of Job, the Satan is introduced as an agent of God, by no means the incarnation of evil; he represents the universal tendency toward doubt, through darkening shades of gray all the way to chaos. In politics, we express chaos as anarchy, but well short of that deep end—at about the same place on the spiritual spectrum as doubt—is individual freedom.

The great political questions of our age are Joban questions: How much order is stultifying? How much freedom is possible without slipping toward chaos? Where do you strike the balance to let in enough light to see the big picture and permit enough shades of gray to make the design grand?

Tension is one answer. Stress, maligned as the scourge of our age, may be the by-product of the creative tension that limits Authority's natural urge to place limitations on its subjects. This is not religion's tension between doubt and faith—Job's faith in the existence of God never wavered, even as he castigated his maker for breaking faith with him—but the tension between the more elemental, myth-bottomed poles of order and chaos.

Freedom needs the brakes of order to keep it from slipping down the slope to anarchy, which is a way of saying Man needs God; at the same time, order needs the dynamism of freedom to keep it from sliding into the abyss of absolutism, which is a way of saying God needs Man. (That scrupulously well-ordered sentence lacks dynamism. Freedom can drive you batty; order can put you to sleep.) Because God has shown he needs Man, he is forced to negotiate with him; to do so, the almost-Almighty must be prepared to make some concessions in the way of control.

Poet-Job does not permit his God to exercise total control; first he introduces the Satan, the testing angel who reflects what an alienated alienist called God's self-doubt. Next, poet-Job has his God express some pride and joy in the raging Leviathan—"the grace of his proportions"[17]—even while complaining how hard it is to control the universe. The voice from the whirlwind celebrates the violence of nature in a world of conflict.

What's the point of this almost-Almightiness? I've come around to thinking that God is not merely browbeating Job, though his words also have that effect. Nor is God merely complaining about his workload or bragging about his power, though at times he seems to be. What poet-Job has God doing, as I read it, is demonstrating his celestial restraint, showing Man that life requires struggle to be lived. Conflict is not only necessary to drama but central to living; good and evil exist to compete; and it is tension, even more than love, that makes the world go round.

In this book, we are wearing political more than theological or philosophical glasses. Reject as politically indefensible the notion, long put forward by some apologists, that God is too busy with more important matters to bother with the moral concerns of humanity. The precinct worker will have none of that from the boss: If the one at the top is omnipotent, the excuse of being too busy is absurd; if he is deliberatedly unconcerned, he has broken the covenant, and wannabelievers ought to elect a deity or leader who wants the job and will deliver his end of the deal.

Take another look at the zoo parade in the speech from the whirlwind. God's extended harangue about the animal creatures under his keeping could be an argument by analogy. As Robert Gordis has posited, humanity should keep its moral order, just as God keeps his natural order—controlled not by force from the center but by a subtle balance of forces—and the view has both a literary shape and logical appeal. Now extend that zoological analogy celebrating the necessity of balance to cover the political sphere: The One in Charge must keep the power-pot boiling, and must create power centers or species to play off against each other.

Bring that springy tension into political real life. The symbiosis of press and state is a striking example of the power of sustaining suspense. We all hail the "adversarial relationship" as healthy for our system, but each adversary, aware of its own weakness, privately wishes the other would stop being so damnably domineering. The mutual antagonism is not a charade, nor is the ritual respect a minuet: Government's respect for the media is edged with unadmitted contempt (those whining, unpatriotic naysayers, they're always out to get us), as media respect for government is tinged with apprehension (those abusers of power are manipulating the truth and weakening the First Amendment every day).

Do not be misled by the camaraderie of correspondents and

Cabinet members at annual white-tie gatherings of the Gridiron Club. Do not be bemused by the revolving door containing officials and commentators, as press secretaries become pundits and reporters become speechwriters. A game of musical chairs is played to the tune of a political adage: "Where you stand depends on where you sit." The amazing thing is how the gorge can rise in the same way in the same person as the seating shifts.

During all but the final months of the Nixon administration, I sat in Room 123 of the old Executive Office Building, a high-ceilinged room which was then along Speechwriters Row in the Office of the President. One day in the early seventies, as a parade of dissenters with booming loudspeakers massed a couple of blocks away to derogate my work product, I picked up the phone to be hectored by a journalist. When I tried to beg off, she reminded me that "we pay your salary", referring to the taxpayers' money. Oh, the arrogance; worse, her articles and television appearances had helped to whip up that crowd outside, to my mind encouraging our enemies and prolonging the war. (Come to think of it, she was on public television, and I was paying her salary.)

At that point, steaming, I appreciated the cleverness of some of my more nefarious co-workers. Without causing the slightest protest, they had denied the demonstrators the use of Lafayette Park, a location that would have offered protesters the perfect television backdrop of the White House. How was this accomplished in front of the very eyes of the world's watchdogs? Our conspirators pretended that the aesthetics of the historic park would be improved for future generations by the replacement of asphalt walks with hand-laid brickwork. This necessitated the fencing-in of the area for repairs, which lasted about two years, with no dissenter the wiser. Even the environmentalists were taken in; after all, the Nixon people were improving a park, and it was widely assumed that everything takes forever when you're dealing with a bureaucracy.

To add secret insult to the unnoticed injury, my demonstration-hating associates arranged for local schools to decorate the fence with the inspired graffiti of schoolchildren. Even the kids were enlisted in this coverup. The closing of an historic area for dissent for an extended period of time was thus disguised as a contribution to the beauty of the nation's capital. The barrier concealing the incredible slowness of the work was made to appear to be an outlet for youthful artistic expression. It was all a fraud, a great clean trick (not, of course, a dirty trick—those came later). Whenever I felt besieged as a government official, unappreciated as a public servant, I secretly savored that duping of the persnickety media. The denial of a dramatic backdrop to dissenting demonstrations was a master stroke of minor duplicity.

Today, decades later, I leave my *Times* office in Washington to walk on those so-carefully laid bricks only two blocks away, and to sit on the Bernard Baruch Bench of Inspiration in Lafayette Park, next to the statue of Andrew Jackson. Nobody in my business or in that park remembers that trick, or the glee I felt, back then, of the way we foiled the noisy demonstrators and their media allies. But now, like the returning character in the Housman poem who can no longer find the meaning in the whispering of the aspen's leaves, I think of ways to see through the feints and half-truths and clever releasing of portions of a story emanating from the house across the park. I'll invite one of the new insiders out for a sit on the famous bench, in hopes of penetrating the veil he or she is persuaded is in the public interest to maintain, and I'll inwardly burn at stonewalling by little men in big jobs or misdirection by neophytes who think they invented the technique. Although I like to inveigh against moral relativism, it is hard to deny the truth that where you stand on disclosure does depend on where you sit. You think one way as an inside doer of good, privy to big pictures and delicious secrets—but quite another way as an outside seeker of truth or at least truthfulness, unvexed by governmental responsibility.

More and more, street-crossers between government and media—the jaywalking wounded—come to understand the adversarial tension that exists between those power centers because they have felt the surges of resentment in both directions. David Broder, the *Washington Post* columnist, disagrees with me on this. He thinks that the crisscrossing corrupts the crispness of the adversary relationship, and that readers and viewers are confused by the mixed motives of opinionmakers who shuttle back and forth. And sometimes the revolving door reaches a dizzying speed: In 1992, columnist Pat Buchanan became a presidential candidate while former President Mikhail Gorbachev became a *La Stampa* columnist, as former White House Chief of Staff John Sununu was inserted into the Buchanan slot of a TV talk show.

How, in this media-political mishmash, is virginity preserved or objectivity guaranteed? My answer is that the symbiosis cannot be denied, and that the way to illuminate its darker side is to fully disclose the background and bias of the commentator. I cheerfully recall episodes of my manipulative past. When Ross Perot entered the 1992 presidential campaign posing as a political outsider, I recollected in print the days two decades before, when the businessman seeking government contracts offered to help White House aides rally the Silent Majority against the dissidents. Concealment encourages exposure, but disclosure disarms.

This stroll down selective-memory lane now intersects the broad highway of theodicy. That's the word for the doctrine that seeks to justify the existence of evil in God's world. It says: Abolish sin by divine fiat and you take away the free will that gives moral meaning to virtue; without the piquancy of the possibility of evil, goodness loses all its flavor.

If there were a doctrine called political theodicy, it would seek to justify the inequality, corruption, and general mess we sometimes make of things. It would say: Abolish injustice by governmental redistribution of wealth and you take away the individual's incentive to build a better world for himself; without the possibility of failure, there exists no success. Abolish corruption once and for all and you take the wind out of the process of reform and destroy the need for the good-government types we have been calling goo-goos for the past century. Political theodicy would go on to say: If you constrain all enterprise, including government, with a web of rules, regulations, and detailed behavioral guidelines, then you offer no leeway for personal ethical judgment, or chance for the assertion of individual character, or the opportunity to get a new idea off the ground. You're a giant Gulliver tied down by Lilliputians, God restricted by Job's moral straitjacket.

Just as there can be no order without danger of dictatorship, there can be no freedom without danger of anarchy. In the political whirlwind, the first rule is: Stop lusting for the permanent relaxation promised by reform and enjoy the tension introduced by the provocative possibility of corruption.

### 6. *A little hobgoblin is the fooler of consistent minds.*

"Steady as she goes," says the captain, and every passenger feels better about the man at the helm, except those who can see the iceberg directly ahead.

George Shultz, then Reagan's secretary of state, who likes to sail, gave me the etymology of the word *telltale* at a dinner one night: it's the little strip of cloth a sailor ties to the mast to see which way the wind is blowing, or a device to indicate the rudder's changing position. As an old speechwriter and confirmed symbiotic, I told him that would make a nice metaphor; he soon built a speech around "We must steer the ship of state by the compass and not by the telltale."

Steadiness is a trait that we used to think put the *author* in *authority*. Abide with me: Unwavering purpose, dependability of execution, grim resolution to prevail—all these unwaffling, enduring elements characterize the words and actions of protagonist Job and antagonist God.

Ironically, all this consistency leads to one surprise after another; every development in the interplay of power gains meaning from an unexpected twist. God surprises us at the outset by his doubt, as he requires a test of Man's motive in worship. The pious Job of the prologue surprises us by exploding in a curse at God's creation. After the visiting Elihu assures us no personal revelation is in the works, God surprises him and Job with his appearance. God again surprises us with his refusal to deal directly with Job's challenge; Job surprises us by suddenly caving in; the epilogue surprises the reader by delivering perfect retribution, directly against the point of the book; and God stuns us one last time by threatening to clobber his own apologists and by saying he agreed with at least a portion of Job's seeming blasphemy all along. Even considering the poetic portion of the book by itself, and without the contradictory prose before and after, readers get the feeling that the Book of Job keeps jerking us around.

From a literary or dramatic viewpoint, the value of surprise needs no exposition. It gives books legs, and keeps readers and viewers turning pages, or at the very least awake. Same with military strategy: As General Norman Schwarzkopf delightedly pointed out in his briefing after the stunning initial success of Desert Storm, the coveted element of surprise enables a commander to concentrate his attack against an inferior force of a numerically superior enemy.

But what works for page-turning literature and flank-turning warfare is usually said not to work in politics. In the taking of positions on hot issues, the case is usually made for the value of consistency—"no surprises". The pejorative term for an unexpected shift is "flip-flopping", from the metaphor of a gasping fish on a deck trying to escape over the side to water. When the government decides to reverse field, it is euphemized as "a natural evolution of policy", just as General George McClellan during the Civil War described his retreat from Richmond as a brilliant "retrograde maneuver". Mind-changing is frowned on: If a candidate thinking about abortion shifts from absolute pro-choice to pro-compromise, or a longtime advocate of the right to bear arms votes for a requirement for felons to register when buying howitzers of 105 mm and over, that candidate is excoriated for the worst kind of tackiness—tacking to the winds of change, catering to public opinion. An outright change of mind is seen by partisans not as an honest reexamination or a maturation of mind but as proof of slipperiness, of unconcern for principle, and the image of that fish slithering on deck is immediately conjured.

Just as politicians are advised by their television handlers to "bounce your eyeballs"—that is, to look down before looking across at another panelist, lest you come across to the viewer as shifty-eyed—they are told by campaign strategists to change views very slowly or not at all lest they be seen as acting out of expediency rather than conviction. As a result, we see much steering by the telltale: steadfastness motivated by expediency.

Such consistency is better described as paralysis dictated by public opinion. Job teaches that surprise—when delivered with a sledgehammer—is more convincing.

Raising his voice for the first time from the dungheap, the man we expect to be the patient Job damns an unjust God's daylight. He thereby asserts his integrity, scandalizing the trio of believers who thought it theologically unseemly to demand any form of accounting, much less a personal appearance, from Providence. Surprise: God crosses up the friends and speaks out of the whirlwind, not to give Job the explanatory word about how he was the winner of the celestial wheel of fortune, but to deliver a stern lecture on arrogance instead, followed by a coded message about how to keep order. The reaction of the shocked and reshocked faithful is mostly a bewildered but dogged "That's God for you—inscrutable ways."

In political life, the "city on the hill" invoked by John Winthrop, Ronald Reagan, and Mario Cuomo cannot be Dullsville. "Steady as she goes" for too long and she sinks, or, if you're rigidly holding the wheel of a car, off the road she goes. Just as the potential for evil gives moral force to virtue, the looming possibility of surprise gives strength to consistency. Joban surprise can support rather than undermine the faith of the constituency, provided those in authority remember that to attain the power of unpredictability—rather than to appear to be aimlessly lurching around—the leader must have (a) the dramatic and widely watched moment of expectability, and (b) the will or the perversity to do the unexpected when least expected.

Example I witnessed up close: the Nixon "shokku" of August 1971, when that lifelong exponent of free markets suddenly imposed wage and price controls, slapped on a border tax, and suspended the convertibility of the dollar into gold.

Inflation was running at 5 percent, which seemed like a lot at the time; jawboning, as the usual economic wishing was called, was doing nothing to bring it down; and for technical reasons a run had begun on our gold. A Sanhedrin of lifelong laissez-fairies secretly assembled at Camp David. As the speechwriter for economic addresses, I was hustled up in a helicopter next to economics adviser Herbert Stein, who whispered that this could be the most significant weekend in the economy since March 4, 1933. When the guy on my other side, Paul Volcker of Treasury, heard that it meant the closing of the gold window, he sighed and put his head in his hands; I remember wishing I knew what the gold window was.

"In this discussion," Nixon told John Connally, Arthur Burns, and the rest of us, "nobody is bound by past positions." Within a few hours, the last free-market holdout, Burns, gave in, and a group of conservative Republicans assumed more peacetime control of the American economy than had ever occurred in our history. Mr. Nixon, unconcerned about the philosophical shift, was delighted at the chance to take decisive command in what seemed to be a crisis (and he was prepared to go on the air calling it his New Economic Policy until we discovered, in the nick of time, that was the name Lenin had given his plan in the 1920s).

I then knocked out a draft of the speech that knocked out the markets in Tokyo. Henry Kissinger was not at Camp David that weekend, but said later that the sudden change of position contributed to the "madman theory", which helped him persuade the Soviets and North Vietnamese that to upset the President was to court who-knew-what. Most of us involved in that well-received "shock" of two decades ago now pretend it was useful because (a) controls were at least administered by people who did not believe in them, and (b) the controls achieved nothing, proving that the nation should never do that again. But the unexpected boldness surely contributed to the general admiration for Mr. Nixon's daring and delicious unpredictability, which resulted in an electoral avalanche in 1972 before all that snow turned to mud and slid down the drain.

Example of statecraft surprise I witnessed from afar: Mikhail Gorbachev's decision in 1989 to lift the Iron Curtain.

For four years in power, that apostle of *perestroika* had only been talking about reform, not actually changing the system. Although his concurrent policy of *glasnost*—a real reduction in repression—had gained him the popularity he needed with the Soviet intelligentsia and the outside world, he had refused to move on the reduction of arms spending or the central control by the corrupt, lethargic Communist apparatus. In time, hard-liners in the United States realized that the Gorbymania here was sadly misplaced; that this man was a Leninist still, a predictable Communist apparatchik with a marvelous feel for packaging and a great sense of public relations.

And then, stunning us all, this principle-free improviser let Eastern Europe go.

It happened suddenly: The East German government could no longer count on Soviet troops to keep it in power; the Poles were no longer menaced by a Red Army takeover at the first sign of Solidarity independence; the Hungarians and Czechs would not suffer another crushing by tanks in Budapest or a phony "Prague spring". The hated Soviet occupation was over, even if many troops who had no housing to return to remained. The Berlin Wall was then torn down by jubilant Germans shouting *"Freiheit!"*—freedom. That was a surprise that infused everything else Gorbachev did later—and much of what he failed to do, until the coup attempt and countercoup—with an element of unpredictability. After he jerked the rug from under the East German Communist hierarchy, we never really knew about this man; in an updating of the "madman theory", he might or might not deliver on his promises of radical structural reform. As a result, and despite the last warnings of Andrei Sakharov and Yelena Bonner, Gorbachev kept the world off balance and himself in power far longer than his indigenous support would ordinarily have permitted.

Simple inconsistency shows only a lack of principle, but calculated inconsistency demonstrates Authority's understanding of the potency of public puzzlement. "There can be no power without mystery," Charles de Gaulle wrote in *The Edge of the Sword.* "There must always be a 'something' that others cannot altogether fathom, which puzzles them, stirs them, and rivets their attention."

Poet-Job introduced the governed to that mysterious "something"—the power of a leader's unpredictability—in the voice from the whirlwind. God's tone was surprisingly angry; neither Job nor the reader could anticipate that his message would be both dysresponsive and symbolically revealing. We are still trying to work out what it means, which I think was the subtle author's intent.

In the 125 generations since, people being governed have been lauding steadiness and consistency—"no surprises"—as desirable elements of a command presence. But exciting leaders who have a grasp of the power of the unexpected know better.

THE FIRST DISSIDENT    163

### 7. Nobody but nobody is perfect.

A satirical button from the 1976 presidential campaign offered a battered but creative ticket: "Agnew and Eagleton—Nobody's Perfect". I saved mine, and like to pin it on whenever moralizers pose as moralists and gussy up gossip-mongering with invocations of "the character issue".

We hate to admit that moral standards change lest we be branded moral relativists. In 1988, Appeals Court Judge Douglas Ginsburg felt he had to withdraw from consideration for appointment to the Supreme Court because a colleague revealed he had smoked marijuana as a young college teacher; that was seen to be disqualifying. Senator Al Gore, Democrat from Tennessee, promptly made known that he also, like most people of his generation, had "blown dope" in his undergraduate college days. That inoculated the senator from such a revelation during a possible run for the Presidency in the future; having admitted youthful misdeeds, he reduced what was once seen as wrongdoing to insignificance. Moral judgments are made not just on what is done, but on what the circumstances are, and how and when the person deals with the "wrong".

Most people who hold premarital intercourse to be wrong will acknowledge that it is less wrong for people in their twenties than those in their teens; singles who maintain their virginity into their thirties, unless as a result of a vow of celibacy in connection with a religious life, are thought by most Americans today to be conducting their lives in a way that calls for counseling. The standards about adult virginity are changing only slightly behind most people's behavior. But when it comes to extramarital intercourse, political candidates are held to more rigid standards than are practiced by most of those who judge them. The gap between standards for politicians and practice by human beings is wide.

We have seen how the accusation or exposure of infidelity—especially by an angry or money-grubbing partner with tape recordings or photographs—can, especially if mishandled, kill or at least damage a candidacy. A small, stern segment of the public feels that any playing around by any candidate reflects the character flaw of inconstancy, and is germane to its judgment about a potential leader. Practical politicians wholly uninterested in moral or privacy questions worry about the lost votes of that unforgiving segment.

Arkansas Governor Bill Clinton, fighting Paul Tsongas for the Democratic presidential nomination early in 1992, gave a qualified denial of infidelity that sought to bring strict standards into conjunction with current practice: "If the standard is perfection," he said candidly, "I don't qualify." His intentionally fuzzy comment seemed to say that though we are all sinners, he had not sinned much, and not recently, and that marital matters were the private concern of his wife and himself. A politician is wise to assert general imperfection; that's the state the voters are in. But he or she may be unwise to assert imperfection on marital fidelity; enough voters are absolutists on that issue to make a difference.

How does Job stand on the perfection issue? He asserts the purity of his own sexual morality in his oath of clearance: "If my heart has been enticed by a woman . . . may my wife be another man's slave . . ."[18] On that score, he swears he is virtuous. We already know, from God's direct testimony, that Job is "blameless, upright, perfect". But Job goes beyond that to take an absolutist stand on morality in general: Man and God have a covenant, and Job's suffering is proof that God is not enforcing morality by punishing the wicked and rewarding the good. The perfect man is entitled to perfect justice.

That strains credulity. Does any mortal qualify for perfection?

I submit that Job does not. Before the testing began, and notwithstanding God's generous stipulation about his favorite human to the Satan, we see a serenely comfortable man—perhaps too certain of his righteousness, which would count as imperfection. After his ruination, he curses God's daylight and implicitly God himself, which may have been forgivable under torture but is hardly evidence of perfection. And in his final speech, Job backhandedly admits to misdeeds throughout his life: "Have I ever concealed my misdeeds as men do, keeping my guilt to myself . . . ?"[19] His confession of wrongdoing may have wiped the slate clean, but we have it from the man's lips that he had done wrong.

So Job was not perfect or totally blame-free. The morality he insists on from God cannot be black and white, cut and dried. Where there is life, there is incompletion, and anything unfinished is not yet whole, complete, or in that sense perfect. Morality cannot be absolute because it does not tie itself to the mooring of perfection.

The voice from the whirlwind also rejects moral perfection by offering the complainant, Job, a view of the compensating sloppiness of the universe. God invites us to consider his creation, the ostrich: "She abandons her eggs to the ground . . . She forgets that a foot may crush them . . . (for God has denied her wisdom and left her without sense) . . ." But try to catch an ostrich on the run: "she struts over the uplands, scorning both horse and rider."[20] Stupid this animal may be, and she flaps her featherless wings wildly to no avail, but with the wind behind her, the voice of God explains, the ostrich knows to spread her tail feathers like a sail and can then outspeed the hunter on the fastest horse. Some creatures are stupid but fast; others slow but smart; still others vulnerable to the point of helplessness but amazingly well camouflaged. God's point is that little in creation is flawless, or even designed to do more than survive.

In response to Job's book-length appeal for the absolutely fair distribution of justice, and to the consolers' wrongheaded discourses on the inexorable working of moral retribution, God attacks Job's demand for juridical tidiness as a mistake. Man does not have to be either all right or all wrong. God's justice does not have to be wrong for Man's justice to be right. "All or nothing" is not the way the universe works.

God drives this point home to Job with a direct challenge: "Dare you . . . put me in the wrong that you may be right?"[21] That central verse is translated by Pope as "Would you . . . condemn me that you may be justified?" and even more vividly in translations of the recently found scrolls known as the Qumram Targum, "Would you make me guilty so that you may be clean?" Job, in the eyes of God, is no longer a paragon. The character-building experience he has been through has left its bruises and exposed a few faults.

Okay, so Job is not, and maybe never has been, perfect; but surely God is perfect, isn't he?

Not in the sense of "complete, finished, unchanging", as he appears in poet-Job's conception. The deity has some of the virtues of Job: outraged eloquence and the ability to react strongly to provocation. He also has some of the vices of Job, particularly the tendency to lose his temper. (The supreme judge should have a supremely judicial temperament, and poet-Job's sarcastic, slashing voice from the whirlwind falls short on that score.) The dramatic development in the character of the Lord in the Book of Job is inescapable. The God of the prologue is cruelly cold, not only ready to subject his servant to the Satan's torture but unconcerned with the killing of innocent bystanders in Job's family and household. But the God of the whirlwind, in his theophany, demonstrates that suffering man is not isolated, and that he is a caring God ("he cared enough to come"). Though his tone is bombastic, his speeches—the longest, most detailed and evocative in the Bible—are profoundly concerned with opening Man's eyes. The character of God at the end of the Book of Job is—whatever the interpretation—considerably different from the God poet-Job portrays at the beginning. Even more than the change in Job, the change in God propels the story. This is a living, growing God, not a static, "perfect" one.

Job does not have to be wrong for God to be right. Metaphysics is not what in our generation came to be known as a zero-sum game, a theory that required a loss for one player to compensate for a gain by the other. Nor is real life on a teeter-totter, poised at some point of equilibrium between innocence and guilt, good and evil, righteousness and sin, day and night; instead, we have periods of dawn and twilight, mixed feelings, ambiguous motives, rough justice, good people with flaws in their characters, miscreants with saving graces, and dopey ostriches with their clever tail-feather trick.

Where is it written that political life has to be perfectly fair? Why should a career be ended by an Election Day rainfall, or a series of bank overdrafts that were common practice down home but are plain wrong to big-city ethicists, or a dalliance with a publicity-hungry model connected to some peephole reporters?

Those last two career-enders refer to a couple of political figures I have come to know and like. Bert Lance was a target of my reporting and calumniating when he was the Carter administration's budget director. Gary Hart was an ideological adversary starting with the McGovern campaign against Nixon in 1972 and extending through his years as a liberal senator advocating fundamental change in our armed services. (The only idea Hart and I shared was an oil import fee that would have broken OPEC, but few others agreed.)

Ol' Bert, to toot a pompous note, played Firpo to my Dempsey in 1977. I won respectability among my peers, who had been leery of my White House service, for belting Bert out of the Washington arena, at least for a long count. Lance and Attorney General Griffin Bell were the most level-headed and worldly of the Carter people, and former banker Bert had Jimmy Carter's promise to appoint him chairman of the Federal Reserve. But Bert was of the informal, go-go era of Southern rural banking that ran afoul of some ethics rules and bank overdraft regulations. Some of us got on his case, and then the Senate and the controller of the Currency reluctantly did, and finally a grand jury indicted him. The petit jury acquitted him on a handful of counts and hung on the rest; properly, the prosecutor gave up, because the broken Lance had paid with his political career for whatever banking corner-cutting he may have done.

We began a correspondence with a couple of biblical citations. Bert sent me a Christmas card that said "Love those who despise you" (Matthew 5:44) and I sent back John 8:32: "Ye shall know the truth, and the truth shall set you free." We have been chewing the political fat for years since then, often in Milton Pitts's Washington barbershop. The mournful-looking big man who made famous the adage "If it ain't broke, don't fix it" tried for a Democratic political comeback several times, and each time was doing fairly well behind the scenes until some publicity-hungry prosecutor or bank regulator or unforgiving journalist (who did not kick him when he was up) brought him down again. I think this shrewd and pragmatic politician deserves a chance at a comeback (Old Nixon Hands have to believe in redemption), but life is only occasionally fair. Bert Lance is a devout Christian and tries not to let these late hits from scandal-scavengers embitter him; he tells me that the part of the Bible he has paid much attention to in recent years is the Book of Job, particularly Job's relationship to his friends.

"Folks are quick to turn on you when circumstances turn against you," he observes without rancor. "They assumed because Job was in such deep trouble, he must have done something terrible.

It got so bad he had a few doubts about maybe having sinned himself. That's why, in the end, when God put the friends' lives in his hands, Job could understand how they'd been mistaken and he let 'em off the hook.

"I've been there. When you go through the public pillorying, you have doubts, you begin to wonder—what in the world did I do? Maybe you did something wrong and never knew it. So you forgive your friends for their doubts, it's only natural. If I were Job and given the chance to get even, I'd pull my chin a little and take it under advisement—but then forgive."

How does a person under siege survive, all alone? "Job couldn't do anything to get loose from his predicament," explains Bert Lance, "except see it through. He didn't fear God anymore because there wasn't anything else God could do to him, except take his life, which would have been a relief. When you come under fire that way, you get frustrated, but you reach an understanding with yourself on being where you are—if you don't, you can't survive. Job knew who he was, what he stood for. When your friends run out, and you can't get in touch with God, you have to find yourself—then at least you're not isolated from yourself.

"See, Job got angry with God, as he had every right to do, but in the end, that anger has to turn to acquiescence. You can't fault God for circumstances," the man from Calhoun, Georgia, concluded, "because that's not what God's about."

Gary Hart, a Yale Divinity School graduate, former senator from Colorado, is another student of Job I've run across in politics. Hart would have been the Democratic nominee for President in 1988 were it not for a sea change since the days of JFK in journalistic attitudes toward the privacy of candidates. If I were Hart, I would wallow in the parts of Job's peroration that show the public's fickleness: "If I went through the gate out of the town . . . men in authority broke off their talk and put their hands to their lips . . . The man threatened with ruin blessed me . . . But now I am laughed to scorn by men of a younger generation . . . Now I have become the target of their taunts . . ."[22] Gary Hart does not linger over this reversal of fortune, as Job did; on the contrary, he dismisses this passage as Job whining ignobly. The Job whom Hart sees in these verses is a man selfishly pleading for personal restoration, a goal unworthy of the man who has shown the moral courage to challenge God on the transcendent issue of universal justice.

Over a fast lunch in a crowded Washington café, Hart and I had a talk about Job's personal pride. (Reporters at the next table, accustomed to straining to overhear leaks and critiques between source and pundit, probably thought the biblical citations were some sort of code.) Afterward, the former senator and now close student of the new Russia faxed me some "unsystematic meditations" that I'll excerpt here. The Job quotations are from Stephen Mitchell's poetic translation.

Gary Hart on the Christian approach to injustice: "The doctrine of original sin ('All have sinned and come short of the glory of God') was a virtual necessity for the Christian Church as a means of accounting for the suffering of the innocent. ('For by Adam has sin come into the world . . .') You simply declare there is no such thing as innocence. If human nature is inherently sinful and, therefore, guilty, then people deserve what they get. In this case Eliphaz the Temanite is the first Calvinist: 'Man is the father of sorrow, as surely as sparks fly upward.' But even so, there is the problem of how innocent children are able to form an evil intent and, therefore, earn the punishment that too often befalls them."

On pride and the establishment: "Job's 'friends' don't want simply a confession of guilt, they want humility. The issue of pride in the Job story is a powerful but often overlooked one. Pride, as someone once pointed out, is the only human quality that is both an attribute and a fault. Too much pride is arrogance; too little pride is self-humiliation. The case made against Job by his 'friends' is really a case against his pride, pride based upon a claim of innocence.

"Zophar gets to the heart of the indictment," observes the former senator, "when, after cataloguing the dire punishments in store for the sinner, he says, 'This is the fate of the sinner; this is the rebel's reward.' For the conventional, institutional, 'consensus' mind, the greatest sinner is the rebel. The three 'friends' today might well represent the Church, the Party and the Corporation— in short, the Establishment."

Interesting, from the reformist candidate the Democratic party regulars feared in 1984 and were prepared to accept early in 1988.

What does Gary Hart see as the gospel of this trio of establishmentarian friends?

"Neither question nor challenge authority. Orthodoxy ('conventional wisdom') is crucial to establishment mentality. Originally an establishment man, under great pressure Job joins the insurgency. He challenges orthodoxy and thus threatens the very foundation of his friends' existence.

"Job is a rebel. He is motivated by pride, saying of God: 'He may kill me, but I won't stop; I will speak the truth, to his face.' Surely this declaration places Job in the pantheon of the Great Rebels. Predictably, this enrages the three friends: Job threatens the system by which they have organized their lives. By forcing the issue of injustice, Job the rebel challenges the central pillar of orthodoxy. The friends' belief in their own rightness becomes self-righteousness. It is they who are guilty of arrogance, the sin of excessive pride. And it is they whom God ultimately humbles, insisting they plead for Job's intercession and forgiveness for 'not telling the truth' about God."

I will not belabor his point by underscoring the political parallels, except to note that establishment nominees Mondale and Dukakis were ultimately clobbered. The reason for bringing my friends Bert and Gary—senators from the Outcast State—into this discussion is partly to show that I have company in a rueful political application of, or occasionally outraged identification with, the Book of Job.

Indeed, there may be enough silently seething Jobans out there to start a "Nobody's Perfect" party.

I can see it now: an unconventional convention held in a vast celestial megadome . . . .

Standing on a dungheap platform with its pro-dissent and anti-isolation planks is an array of long-suffering candidates. . . .

Circulating among the delegations are volunteers on three thousand camels and she-asses handing out "Damn the Day!" straw hats and bumper stickers reading "Life Should Not Be Unfair" . . . bobbing throughout the crowd are signs that proclaim "Nobody's Perfect". . . .

On the giant screen, a TV spot shows the *Rachel,* the ship in *Moby-Dick* that picked up the drowning Ishmael, symbolizing a political party that celebrates a tolerance for human foibles too quickly condemned by the old politics as character flaws, sailing along and ingathering all the orphan children of pride. . . .

In the symbiotic press gallery, the spin doctors of dissidence stick close to the Behemoths of the media, murmuring their creative inconsistencies. . . .

Snaking down the aisle to the microphone, a delegate on the most thrilling mission of his life stands on a chair waving wildly, is recognized, and cries: "The grrr-reat state of Leviathan . . . home of the chaos that undergirds our freedom . . . casts two votes for Eliphaz the Temanite [small cheer from traditionalists] . . . seven votes for Elihu the Buzite [louder yelling from youthful delegates] . . . and to put him over the top . . . seventy-seven votes for the man from Uz!" [pandemonium].

# PART V

## PURSUING THE JOBAN LIFE

A CLASSIC GEORGE PRICE cartoon in *The New Yorker* magazine shows an exhausted zookeeper in a monkey house trying to get his cap back from the gleeful monkeys, with a lady outside the bars tapping her cane and demanding to know: "Who's in charge here?"

The struggle to understand the creator's obligation to command and his creation's power to obey, we call theology; the unendable contest for control between Authority and Subject, we call politics. The common denominator of these joint ventures in governance is power—the exercise or abuse thereof, the dissent therefrom, or the acquiescence thereto. Even when sovereignty is vested in the vassal, somebody has to be in charge.

Job not only teaches Authority a nonobvious thing or two, as the previous section sought to show; the book offers free people some useful instruction in Vassalhood 101—the stimulation of wise followership, the prevention of abuse of authority. (Keep in mind that *authority* as used here, capitalized when a specific power, derives its power from the consent of the hard-to-govern.) In this section, we will examine some secular lessons that the voter who wants to better appreciate the qualities of the dissident, and the person who wants to live a Joban life, can draw from the negotiations leading to power-sharing in the Book of Job.

Wait a minute—why would anybody want to "live a Joban life" if that means sustained innocent suffering, ignorance, and isolation? My definition of *Joban* is not "irreverent, blasphemous, stubborn, ignorant, and self-righteous", though Job was at times all those things. The Joban life, in a political reading, is the life spent maintaining personal convictions: "I will not abandon my claim to innocence. I will maintain the rightness of my cause, I will never give up."[1] This determination to cling to integrity does not flag under duress: "If he would slay me, I should not hesitate; I should still argue my cause to his face."[2]

In an age that celebrates accommodation, people with that sort of grim resolve are often looked on as unduly argumentative and confrontational. Often their "in-your-face" attitude makes it harder for them to get in our consciences. Their frequent martyrdom makes us feel inadequate, timid, guilty—and angry at them for all that. Some come on the scene as Job did, railing and cursing, self-righteously wallowing in their victimhood and striking us as "holier than thou", in Isaiah's phrase. Others appear with the quietly insistent integrity of Mohandas K. Gandhi, one of this century's most successful dissidents, who nonviolently turned around a subcontinent and had a profound effect on an American disciple.

Sensible, pragmatic people who see themselves on the cutting edge of change see Jobans as over the brink; only a generation or two after the battle are persnickety Jobans regarded as inspirational. But where would we be without the Jobs, those people whose tenacity to their principles, right or wrong, stakes out firm positions that later compromisers can take as constants? The essence of Jobanism is to refuse to accept injustice from any source— family, culture, nation, or God—and to press inquiry into inequity beyond what others accept as the limits of the knowable.

Who are the Jobs of our time? The best way to begin to consider Joban qualities for us to emulate, or at least appreciate, is to see them in action in the lives of a few of the men and women who found injustice unacceptable—and who would not let their demand for answers be put off by "it's not for you to know."

### 1. *Maintain your Joban ways.*

To belong to the political club of Joban dissidents, a person must (a) have suffered grievously, either by circumstance or by a personal decision to support an unpopular cause; (b) have reacted angrily, while in the wilderness or prison, to the immorality of such hardship inflicted by those in aloof authority or cruel command; (c) have refused to be browbeaten or tortured or intimidated by anyone into silence or acceptance of unjust punishment; and, on rare occasion and not requisite for membership, (d) have been reconciled to Authority after having glimpsed the big picture or after having gained some share of its power. Members of the dissidents' club are required not to understand why any of these disasters has happened to them, though it is the custom to repeatedly demand, "Why me?"

Not all dissidents are Joban; those who fling their bodies in the way of freedom or shout down those with whom they disagree give dissent and dissidence a bad name. The purpose of dissent as well as its quality determines its value.

Dissidents to communism in what Alexander Solzhenitsyn called the "Gulag"—an archipelago of prison camps—became our time's foremost prisoners of conscience. As a presidential aide at the 1972 Moscow summit, where détente was being heavily promoted, I heard from some of those dissidents. Max Frankel, then a *New York Times* reporter and now its editor, called me at the heavily bugged hotel where the President's staff was staying; we talked in circumlocutions until I suggested we meet at the "top o' the Marx", a wordplay on the bar atop San Francisco's Mark Hopkins Hotel, which he correctly took to be the penthouse bar of the Hotel Rossiya. Because Nixon aides were sealed in a cocoon, "refuseniks"—Russian Jews persecuted after being refused a request to move to Israel—had to rely on reporters as intermediaries. Frankel handed me a letter from a dissident's wife to forward to Mrs. Nixon: "The tone of this letter will sound dissonant to the atmosphere that surrounds you here. Last Monday, early in the morning, four men broke into our house and dragged away my husband. The reason they gave for this was our 'intent' to violate public order during your visit. Very respected Mrs. Nixon! I address your mother's heart . . ."

I gave the original of this letter to Mrs. Nixon, to show to her husband, and a copy to Henry Kissinger; the intrusion of a fact of Soviet brutality introduced one note of sobriety into the official euphoria. A few years later, as a *Times* columnist disabused of détente, I wrote about this episode, and also in passing about another dissident, Anatoly Shcharansky. His resolute wife, Avital, promptly showed up at my office—no intermediary, no call in advance—ready to wait all day to ask what I could do for her imprisoned husband.

I wish now that I had done more, but I wrote something about their plight, and she went on calling on others for years, was present as conscience at every summit conference, composed, determined, a Madonna-like force for remembrance. He was the dissident in jail, she was the dissident as witness; they were like a dollar bill torn apart to be matched in some recognition code at the moment of freedom. Before the Soviet court that sentenced him to jail for treason, her husband, the computer scientist and human-rights activist, refused to confess to the trumped-up charges. "If I agreed to cooperate with the investigation for the purpose of destroying the Jewish emigration movement," Shcharansky said to the press and spectators when the judges allowed him to speak, "they promised me freedom and a quick reunion with my wife. . . . I never compromised my soul, even under the threat of death."

The chief judge tartly asked if he had anything to say to the court. The dissident turned to the tribunal that had handed down their predetermined verdict after a farce of a trial, and coolly expressed his contempt for that world's justice: "To you I have nothing to say." Such contempt for concession to falsity was a reprise of Job's answer to pious friends who tried to get him to submit to the apparent will of the Almighty by confessing to sins he did not commit: "I swear by God, who has denied me justice . . . I will not abandon my claim to innocence. I will maintain the rightness of my cause, I will never give up."[3]

After years as a prisoner of conscience, Shcharansky was released, unrepentant, in what the pre-breakup Soviets claimed was a spy exchange. Today, the former dissident couple and their children live in Israel, where—with his name now spelled Natan Sharansky—he has a political constituency of Soviet Jews who were allowed to emigrate after the dissidents helped begin the process that ultimately broke the Communist system.

In the mid-sixties, many of us saw the Reverend Martin Luther King, Jr., as a Joban figure, provoking and suffering indignities and insisting on the dignity due all human beings—even while he was being wiretapped and bugged by those he thought were his protectors at the Department of Justice in Washington. As a volunteer press agent for the New York lawyers' committee helping to spring him from Southern jails, I came to admire the man who became the American Gandhi. (He was a good writer, too, I discovered when he edited one of my press releases.) This brief association later caused me to castigate Attorneys General Robert Kennedy and Nicholas Katzenbach for signing and extending the FBI wiretaps that they claimed were installed only to prove Dr. King innocent of Communist taint. (Save us from friends tapping our phones for our own good.) Standing with him on a Fifth Avenue street corner, I was troubled by the obvious FBI surveillance; the civil rights pioneer shrugged it off, treating the shadowing agents in a car across the street as a kind of protection.

At that time, Dr. King's opposite number in the black community left me cold. Like most whites, I thought the black militant who called himself Malcolm X, and who reviled Dr. King's nonviolence, was an extremist discredit to his cause. But three decades later, on the occasion of editing an anthology of speeches, I read much of what the provocative Black Nationalist had to say, and I now think that Malcolm X also belongs in the Joban category. Although his original espousal of racial separatism was self-defeating, his later message of pride and mutual service was uncompromising and fiercely eloquent.

Malcolm X turned out to be a double dissident. First he threatened counterviolence, which angered whites; then he accused the Black Muslim leader, Elijah Mohammed, of hypocrisy, which infuriated many militant blacks. Malcolm X told interviewers he was targeted for assassination, which was true; some followers of Elijah Mohammed shot him dead soon afterward, as he was making a speech. The dissident maintained his ways against all authority—white and black.

Václav Havel has a more current and popularly heroic claim to

Jobanism. The politically active Czech playwright who spent years in a Communist prison—refusing the key of silence offered him by his tormentors—became President of Czechoslovakia when the Soviet tide receded. He is now enjoying the Joban epilogue stage, though his triumph was marred by the need to preside over the breakup of his country. "Living in truth" is the phrase Havel uses to describe his alternative to both communism and capitalism; living within a lie was to live within a totalitarian state that destroyed individual integrity.

Writing in the late seventies during a series of stays in prison, Havel worried about a "post-totalitarian system", which was not the happy day of West over East, but the triumph of a morally moribund consumer society over political dictatorship. This sort of question, in *The Power of the Powerless* in 1978, earned Havel little support from the usual supporters of dissidents and other consolers: "Is it not true that the far-reaching adaptability to living a lie . . . has some connection with the general unwillingness of consumption-oriented people to sacrifice some material certainties for the sake of their own spiritual and moral integrity?"

The world turned; the jailbird-playwright became President of Czechoslovakia. At a Blair House breakfast with a few pundits before going to see President Bush across the street, the worried-looking new politician fielded political questions too guardedly; his face lit up only when I asked him if the play of his life had a third act with a happy ending. He said the final act had not yet been written. Westerners and democrats may think he is going our way, but Václav Havel is a political philosopher going his own way.

This credentialed Joban argues that "there is too much to know." In 1992, he told economists in Switzerland that communism had been "based on the premise that the world is objectively knowable" and that we must now "abandon the arrogant belief that the world is merely a puzzle to be solved." Because even democracy's mechanisms "are so linked to the cult of objectivity . . . that they can annul human individuality", he urged "humility in the face of the mysterious order of Being"—reminiscent of Job listening to God's second speech from the whirlwind. Putting understanding of the spirit over the acquisition of objective knowledge, Havel writes his own wisdom hymn in spelling out what a politician today must have: "Soul, individual spirituality, firsthand personal insight into things . . . above all, trust in his own subjectivity as his principal link with the subjectivity of the world."

Of all the famous dissidents who lit up the anti-Communist political landscape—from Poland's Lech Walesa to Lithuania's dissonant musicologist Vytautas Landsbergis—none will throw a beam farther into history than Andrei Sakharov, the nuclear scientist whose scruples turned him against Soviet tyranny. Working together with his life's partner, Yelena Bonner—as Joban a dissident as her husband—the man who created the Soviet H-bomb spent the rest of his life arranging for the detonation of an explosion of freedom within a corrupt despotism. After Sakharov and Bonner were freed from "internal exile", an apt phrase, he came to the United States to speak to a group of American scientists. They expected a statement of political belief; instead, he gave them a talk on molecular arcana, and some of us laymen in the audience strained to find a far more subtle message about the unity of scientific knowledge. Afterward, the tall, slow-moving, near-blind hero looked closely at me through thick glasses that magnified his pupils and solemnly opined that those who wrote political commentary were doing some of the world's most important work. I still take that as a blessing.

During the last week of his life, he rose in the Supreme Soviet to warn against the Communist party's monopoly of power and to call for popular elections. An imperious Mikhail Gorbachev at the lectern shut him up—"Finish up, Andrei Dmitriyevich . . . sit down!" When the most moral Russian on earth tried to continue, Gorbachev barked to an aide: "Turn on the other microphone." Three years later, on the same podium, the fading Gorbachev was humiliated by Boris Yeltsin, who jabbed his finger at a written statement and forced Gorbachev to read it aloud. When some Westerners tut-tutted at this public put-down, I remembered the contemptuous Gorbachev treatment of Andrei Dmitriyevich Sakharov.

To be a Joban is to be outraged by injustice and to be determined to right Authority's wrongs. To be a Joban prisoner, a figure must be more than an innocent in pain, more than a prisoner unjustly incarcerated or a hostage like AP reporter Terry Anderson, cruelly held by Iranian terrorists for six years. For a person in solitary confinement, physical or spiritual, the Joban element is summarized in the phrase "prisoner of conscience"—in jail for political beliefs, often kept there because of a refusal to recant and to serve the oppressor by denying those beliefs.

In China in 1979, a Joban named Wei Jingsheng disappeared into the secretive system of prisons and labor camps. He was not yet thirty; he had worked as an electrician at the Beijing zoo before becoming the editor of an unauthorized magazine called *The Explorer*. Wei had tested the limits of the Beijing regime's tolerance by leading the "Democracy Wall" movement. A gray wall running a few hundred yards down Chang An Avenue blossomed with wall posters calling for more democracy; in a short time, these posters, avidly read by passersby, focused on the need to make the regime's power accountable to the people. That first glimmer of free debate was soon put out by a Communist government that has featured a savage crackdown in each of the last five decades.

Wei was convicted of "counterrevolutionary activities" and sentenced to fifteen years in jail; he is said to be still alive. Wei is remembered not because visiting Western leaders ask for information about him—they never do, lest they lose access to Chinese leadership—but because China's paramount leader, Deng Xiaoping, was reported to have said scornfully that Wei's incarceration had not damaged China's reputation. That single boast reminded the world that to forget a dissident was to invite greater political repression.

Mr. Wei's ordeal has not yet approached Nelson Mandela's twenty-seven years in a seven-by-seven-foot cubicle, but it is proof to his compatriots of a high cost of protest. The massacre of protesters in Tiananmen Square in 1989 was led by students like Chai Ling, then twenty-one, who knew that if she was caught after the tanks rolled, she would suffer the fate of Wei Jingsheng—torture, brainwashing, long years of isolation. She escaped to Paris; dissent needs both martyrs and publicists. Some dissidents are both: Benazir Bhutto, daughter of the Pakistani Prime Minister executed by a military dictator, spent more than five years under arrest, steadily defiant, until she was elected the first woman Prime Minister of a Muslim nation. I spoke with her after her ouster and the jailing of her husband; the only guilt she feels about her sustained political resistance is the time it takes from nurturing her two children.

Unwavering dissent needs extraordinary singleness of purpose. In Hebrew, the word for "freedom" is *herut:* It is the name assumed by the largest party in the political coalition of the right. A pun is involved: A similar-sounding Hebrew word, *herat,* means "engraven". The political point of the name, say some Likudniks, is that the only thing graven ineradicably in stone is freedom.

A recent world leader who meets the Joban criteria set forth at the start of this chapter is Menachem Begin. "I survived ten wars," he would say, "I survived Soviet concentration camp, five years in the underground as a hunted man. I survived twenty-six years in opposition in Parliament, never losing faith in a cause." He suffered the loss of his family to the Nazis in the Holocaust, led the militant Irgun in establishing the State of Israel—battling another founder, David Ben-Gurion, all the way—then seemed to settle into permanent minority leadership, holding fast to his faith in his cause. In Jerusalem in the mid-seventies, I was interviewing government officials from the Labor party that had dominated Israeli politics since the nation's modern reincarnation. The press office asked, as a favor, if I would see the opposition leader, a man widely thought to have little power and no future. For three hours, with not much else to do, this gentlemanly, old-worldly former guerrilla fighter spoke of his dream of a vigorous, growing, peaceful Israel, protecting Jews everywhere from the pogroms he remembered. (Like a dope, I didn't take a note; who knew?) On the way back to my room at the King David Hotel, I told the elderly elevator operator that I had just seen Begin; he smiled and said, "I was here when the hotel was British military headquarters and Begin and his men blew the place up."

After leading his nation to peace with Egypt's Anwar el-Sadat, Prime Minister Begin left the world stage more suddenly than he entered it; "depression" was psychojournalism's judgment, but his departure was caused by a combination of assuming responsibility for the failure to make democracy safe and Maronite Christianity secure in Lebanon, and the death of his wife. Although I do not think he saw himself as suffering for any sin he had committed, Prime Minister Begin went "into the silences", as the Mormons say, which lasted until his death in 1992. Like Job, he had his mastery and his joy inexplicably wrenched from him; unlike Job, who lost everything only once, Begin lamented in private.

The most Joblike man I ever met was Mulla Mustapha al-Barzani, leader of the Kurdish people. Physically, he could have been Job's brother: a desert chieftain from the same neighborhood in what was ancient Mesopotamia, wiry and short with a proud stance that made him taller. His tough skin was darkened by desert sun and ethnic heritage, and his eyes could cast a fierce warrior's glare. His mind-set was an amalgam of vast resentments, the wariness that comes from being consistently double-crossed by a variety of national interests, and a curious trust in the United States of America.

That trust, when we met in a CIA safe house in Virginia, had just been violated horrendously. The twenty million Kurds are a distinct people, neither Persian nor Arab nor Turkish, with their own culture and language; their Kurdistan has always been part of other countries, and is now split up among Iran, Iraq, Turkey, and Syria. Their fighting arm is the Pesh Merga, which stands for "Forward to death"; its apt slogan is "Kurds have no friends." Mulla Mustapha al-Barzani saw an opportunity in the early seventies to exploit the superpower conflict and a regional battle between Iraq and the Shah's Iran to carve out some autonomy for his people. The Shah wanted a Kurdish uprising in Iraq so he could gain full control of a waterway to the Gulf; he had agreed to provide weapons to Barzani's mountain forces, purchased from the Americans. But Barzani did not trust the Shah; he sought, and received, guarantees from the Americans that they would not leave him high and unsupplied in the crunch. Sure enough, the Shah made a separate deal with Iraq and cut off the hapless Kurds, but the Americans—in a betrayal that Henry Kissinger profoundly regrets to this day—did not hold the Shah to his promise. The Kurdish rebellion was wiped out. Barzani, broken and ill with cancer, was allowed to come to the United States to die.

But the tough old bird wouldn't die on schedule. Emaciated, his hair fallen out after radiation therapy, he was the image of affliction: "My bones stick out through my skin, and I gnaw my under-lip with my teeth."[4] Though his visa was dependent on his public silence, the Kurdish chief cannily managed to wage a quiet campaign to urge the United States government to press the Shah to help preserve the remnants of his guerrilla force, so they could fight again another day. Only a strong resistance, he felt, could induce Iraq to abandon the systematic genocide that the emerging Saddam Hussein had in mind. Here was a geopolitically irritating cause, of no interest to the world media, headed by a grimly determined Joban figure; of course I enlisted.

Mulla Mustapha had been told by his interpreter that I liked pistachio nuts, one of the few exports of his region besides oil. A quiet young man, who I later learned was his son, set a large jar between us. As we talked, I shelled my share and popped the kernels into my mouth; Barzani shelled his, ate none, and made a stack of the nuts on a cocktail napkin.

He seethed with resentment at the sellout, but sensed that the Ford administration authorities could be influenced by a moral appeal to the American people. I assured the Kurdish leader he was right about that; morality and sentiment, more than geopolitics or oil, drive American public opinion. He made a military observation that I was to remember years later: that Kurdish fighters in the rugged terrain could hold out against and ultimately defeat far superior mechanized forces—if they could have some way of holding off air attacks. I think he had in mind the new hand-held anti-aircraft missiles. (He was right about that, too; just as Stinger missiles enabled the Afghan guerrillas to hold off and outlast the much stronger Soviet army, some means of grounding the deadly Iraqi helicopters would have made the difference in the Kurds' abortive 1991 anti-Saddam uprising.)

At the conclusion of our talk, formally conducted as if in a desert tent, the old warrior pushed his stack of shelled pistachio nuts across the table. The little pile of kernels was Mullah Mustapha's personally prepared gift to a consoler who understood his quest.

It turned out I was mistaken about the moral appeal, at least in the absence of live television pictures. A few of us—Smith Hempstone at *The Washington Star*, Jonathan Randall and Jim Hoagland at *The Washington Post*—inveighed hotly in print at the scandal of the sellout of the Kurds, but we lit no fires. No visual impact. Then the Kurdish cause was overtaken by the event of the Shah's downfall; Barzani, with no prospects to give him strength, died. Of course, a dozen or so years later, when the Bush geostrategists sold out the Kurdish people again after the half-defeat of Saddam Hussein, the biblical exodus of two million panicked Kurds had a tremendous television impact, described earlier in this book. The thousand-year injustice inflicted on Kurds suddenly began to be recognized.

I was glad to see that the anti-Saddam forces in Iraqi Kurdistan were headed by Massoud Barzani, Mulla Mustapha's son, the young fellow who had set out the pistachio nuts that day in Virginia fifteen years before. In the end, if there is political poetic justice, a descendant of Mulla Mustapha will be the freely elected President of an autonomous, perhaps independent, Kurdistan.

## 2. If access is what you need, find a go-between.

In the sublime relationship of Man to God, or the secular relationship of citizen to governor, the same question arises: How do we get access?

We know whom we want access to: the one who is the source of knowledge and judgment. But even if we get that access, what happens when we get in the presence of the source? We worry that he will trick us with an evasion, or even blow us over in rage.

On the most mundane level, reporters face that need for access all the time. As deadlines approach, sources who have the answers disappear behind a screen of secretaries who play dumb and aides who have only the information that will not embarrass the source. At that moment, we cease being the children of pride and scramble around for an intermediary who can get us access.

We sometimes use bizarre means. For a quarter century, my barber has been Milton Pitts. He has been the barber—hairstylist, he calls himself now—to four Presidents. Two days a week he snips at the bigwigs in the White House basement, and the rest of the time he handles outside customers in a hotel barbershop.

I had a story that only a particular agency chief could confirm. Even if he denied it, I could tell whether to go with the story by observing his reaction eye-to-eye. But he ducked my calls and I thought it would be undignified, as well as an invasion of his privacy, to stake out his house. My last hope was Milton, who would usually touch up this fellow's hair—a quick trim, comb, and spritz—in the hotel shop before a television appearance. The White House barber is notoriously discreet (loyally lying about Ronald Reagan's hair color for years) but agreed to call me when he thought I needed a trim.

Sure enough, next day the man whom West Wing aides have long called "the faithful Figaro" phoned to say he had an appointment available. I hustled over (my hair, in fact, was fairly shaggy) and found the slippery source immobilized in the barber chair, sheet tucked around his neck. Feigning surprise, and feeling a little like the Mafia torpedo who hit Albert Anastasia in a New York barber's chair, I cheerfully pulled up a manicurist's stool and enjoyed my seemingly accidental "access".

Everybody needs a door opener now and then. Intermediation can be overdone: In the 1980s, Mr. Reagan's aide, Michael Deaver, walked through the revolving door of the White House to personify the "age of access", until the line between selling know-how and peddling influence was drawn by a *Time* magazine cover story.

A politician leaving office may be owed favors by those remaining inside, but it is unethical, and may be illegal, for him to hire himself out to turn those favors into cash. And many old pols know the silent, unrecordable gesture of the influence seeker who wants to know if a certain official will take a payoff: the gentle rubbing of the thumb against the forefinger, meaning "can he be reached?"

But not every means of access is corrupt. Before climbing into the arena, it pays to know the ropes—which staff aide or veteran bureaucrat, for example, is the real decision maker in whatever arcane program is the arena. A skillful interceder will know how to refine his client's argument and align his private interest with at least a portion of the public interest, to pick up support. This is not a technique quickly acquired by the complainant or supplicant.

While writing this chapter, I took a break to attend the adult bat mitzvah of my niece Ellen. As the congregation read responsively, I heard myself saying, "Blessed be he, lord of the universe, who separates the sacred from the profane." That's hardly what

I've been doing in this book. On the contrary, I have been using the sacred to illuminate the profane, trusting that readers will not take the juxtaposition of spiritual and political to be a trivialization of Scripture. That's especially true at this point, as we leap from scrupulous barbers and unscrupulous flacks to a subject that Christians hold central to their religion: the interceder between Man and God that multitudes believe is Jesus of Nazareth. The Book of Job, written three to five centuries before the birth of Jesus, contains discussions of intermediation that many have considered a preview of the Messiah. I don't deal with that, or the use of prophets or saints as interceders, here; my interest is in the origin and value of the idea of go-betweens in political relations.

The middleman, now a sexist term, spans the spectrum of civilization. Ancient Greek solons had their official interceders; British parliamentarians had their lobby agents; modern pressure groups have their trade associations and lobbyists; victimized consumers have their Naderite advocacy groups.

What Job wanted in his campaign for fair treatment and vindication was more than a lawyer or a lobbyist. He wanted access to what Washington superlawyers like to call "an attorney for the situation"—a lawyer who would represent the potential solution rather than one of the disputants. He wanted an umpire, in the sense of that word held by a baseball fan: an arbiter working for neither pitcher nor batter but for the game itself.

The visiting Bildad assured Job that "God will not spurn the blameless man, nor will he grasp the hand of the wrongdoer."[5] But Job knew that God did reject the upright—namely, himself, the certifiably blameless man. In his reply to Bildad, Job toys with the idea of arguing face-to-face with God, but then puts that presumption aside: "If I summoned him to court and he responded, I do not believe that he would listen to my plea."[6] How, then, to make his appeal? A curious notion comes to him: "Would there were an umpire between us, To lay his hand on us both . . . then I would speak and not fear him."[7]

We have discussed how this idea of an umpire was rooted in ancient myths about a council of gods that was too busy to pay attention to the individual cases of mortals. The ancients offered the idea of a personal god. To be heard, a human turned to this personal god to act as his advocate in the grand council.

This umpire was not a "vindicator" or redeemer mentioned elsewhere, the kinsman sworn to seek blood vengeance. Nor was Job calling for a judge to decide a case between contending factions, because who could judge the judge of the world—or why would the supreme judge submit to judgment by a lesser one? Rather, the umpire sought by Job would act the way an outside arbitrator does in a labor-management negotiation: He draws his mediating authority from a preliminary agreement of the contending parties to conduct their dispute in the ordered setting of a formal arbitration. In Job's case, the purpose of an umpire would be not only to gain access to the celestial court but to keep the power of God's voice from blowing Job over during the dealings.

Long after Job first floated out the idea that "my witness is in heaven; there is one on high ready to answer for me,"[8] the cheeky Elihu returned to the notion of a personal god to represent Job: "If an angel, one of thousands, stands by him, a mediator between him and God, to expound what he has done right and to secure mortal man his due . . . then . . . he will return to the days of his prime."[9]

Neither of these intriguing ideas—umpire or advocate—comes to fruition. Twice poet-Job raises the idea of an intermediary between fearful Man and terrifying God and twice he drops it. He has Job raise it in the conditional "would that", placing the wish as a condition contrary to fact, like a man saying "if I were king" when he knows he is not. Maybe poet-Job, who often likes to let the reader know what the characters do not know, is exercising another grand irony: The only umpire or interceder in the celestial court with the gumption to stand up to God is the Satan, and he is not speaking on behalf of Job but against him.

When God does appear, no umpire is present; sure enough, as Job predicted, God's presence cows the man to silence, and finally to awed submission. Would the original dissident have done better with an advocate? Although Job, representing himself, did not have the proverbial fool for a client, he would have been better off with an unawe-able mouthpiece. Imagine what a trained lawyer could do for human wisdom if he could examine God in a discovery proceeding.

In the same way, the governed should have access to independent help in confronting the governing power. The third branch of government, the judiciary, is one Joban umpire that enables the citizen to contend with the executive or legislature in court. Another umpire in the court of public opinion is the media, which offer bullhorns to the unfairly treated or to skillful manipulators. But they are not Elihu's idea of an intercessor, a personal angel or go-between to facilitate a hearing and to help present the best case.

The most effective middleperson has been the most derided: the professional or registered lobbyist, who can be a steadfast advocate for honorable hire or a sleazy influence peddler ripping off both client and public. Beyond these techniques quickly acquired with an intermediary comes the Joban need: to be accompanied in a quest for a fair hearing by someone who is not intimidated by the biggest of big shots. Just as many former prosecutors perform well as defense attorneys, former government officials often do well as power brokers; the phrase is "coming to do good, staying to do well".

The perfect interceder would be a retired accusing angel, pushing his way through a revolving door in the clouds; the Satan would make a fine personal god at home in the celestial court, combining skepticism of human motive with an irreverence toward Authority and a have-wings-will-roam attitude. That is because misery, which may love company, needs company with clout.

Enter one of three types of modern interceder: the arbitrator, the advocate, and the protector.

The *arbitrator,* closest to Job's idea of an umpire, removes either party's use of power to overwhelm the other; the argument must proceed to discuss, and be judged upon, the merits of the case. The drawback to arbitration is that Authority must agree beforehand to be bound by its decision, and powers in the position of judgment do not usually want to turn that power over to another.

The *advocate*'s function is to marshal and present the arguments persuasively, using the rules of evidence or the psychology of the marketplace, but there is also a Joban role the advocate shares with the arbitrator: intimidation control.

The *protector,* in law, has emerged as court-appointed counsel or in the office of public defender; in the United States, we have decided to counter the accusing angel with a defending angel. In international law, the keening outcry of dissidents in newly spawned (and weak) nations has opened an exciting prospect: A new "right to intervene" is being spoken about. Up to now, nations that practiced genocide could reject intervention by outsiders as an intrusion on sovereignty, but the general revulsion against massive human-rights violations from Iraq to Tibet to the former Yugoslavia is challenging that. When a nation joins an association of nations that adopts a human-rights code, it surrenders a portion of its sovereignty; the time is now for that Joban dream of an anti-intimidation force with a "right to intervene" to be made a reality.

All three types of intervenor—the arbitrator, the advocate, and the protector—are answers to the human need for a go-between in dealings with Authority.

The great enemy of the little guy in a power challenge is a sense of helplessness in the face of Authority: "If the appeal is to force, see how strong he is; if to justice, who can compel him to give me a hearing?"[10] In the confirmation hearings on the nomination of Judge Clarence Thomas to the Supreme Court, we saw how the imbalance of power can be corrected by effective advocacy. I was among those who believed that the nominee accused of sexual harassment should be presumed innocent; for me, that tipped the scales against Professor Anita Hill, his accuser, who could offer no proof of her belated charges. But I had to admire the way she held her own in the crucible of sworn cross-examination under media lights. Beyond her own legal training, one big reason for her equanimity and resolution under fire, in my view, was her preparation and sustenance by some of the best, most committed legal and public-relations counsel that money could not buy.

In an essay that placed me, according to a valued op-ed colleague, among "the lunatic right", I denounced her advisers as high-powered legal eagles, media manipulators and Senate-staff ideologues driven by a desire to keep that black conservative off the Court at any price. I still think that was true, but I could not fault their client's coolly defiant presentation. Against the power of a white, male Senate club, under aggressive questioning in the panoply of pomp and impressiveness that is the hearing-room arena, Anita Hill did not wince or cry aloud. The citizen was able to counter Authority's force of intimidation with the help of strong intercession.

By twice raising the notion of an umpire, Job pointed out the need for a counterweight to the gravity of Authority. This did not undermine one of the great strengths of Judaism—its direct, personal connection between Man and God, with rabbinical instruction useful but with no priestly intermediation required—but it did introduce a note of political practicality into the contest between lord and voluntary vassal.

Job did not attract or find a way to retain that vindicating right arm, but Jobans today do not readily go unaided into the arena. If they must go it alone, they do; but they first try to align themselves with articulate, persuasive, well-connected allied interests.

### 3. Beware consensus.

In the heyday of the OPEC oil cartel, the ministers of the producing nations would meet at some posh resort to decide how high they would push the world's inflation rate. Sheik Yamani, the Saudi oil minister, would emerge from the secret deliberations and let the world know what the price of a barrel of sweet crude would be. Did the Saudis, always the largest producer, set the price? Why, of course not; that decision was reached, we were told, by an impenetrable process of decision called "consensus". (I grumbled about this in a piece entitled "Yamani or Ya Life"; he did not catch the allusion to a holdup.)

Consensus in handicapping horse races is found in the little box on the form sheet that indicates the horse that most experts think will finish first; I know from experience that the consensus choice rarely comes in.

Consensus in international relations is agreement by the lowest common denominator, the way too many undemocratic regional groups arrive at secret covenants. Perhaps because their culture distrusts the revelation of dissension, the consensualists resist an open vote and a clear decision. Instead, the minority is given not just a voice but a veto; nobody loses face, but the group must sail as if in convoy, with the speed of the group dictated by the slowest ship. Agreements by consensus are fuzzy and deniable, rarely subject to what President Woodrow Wilson, urging "open covenants openly arrived at", called "the white light of publicity".

Diplomats tend to embrace consensus as their goal, just as they see "the process" as a goal. But the process is not the goal; a "peace process" is not as important as the furtherance of freedom or the advancement of right, neither of which should be considered a "war process".

Consensus in American domestic politics was a term associated with Lyndon Johnson, who, as Senate majority leader before he became President, was a famed deal maker. His ideas competed in a cloakroom rather than a marketplace. Although that technique often gets things done, it does not get issues thrashed out, and the lack of a clear-cut and public victory by a majority makes such legislative deals easy to unmake.

Today, political consensus is most often synonymous with "conventional wisdom". John Kenneth Galbraith's coinage, updating religion's "received wisdom", denotes the average of the trendy and the voguish. This suspect mean calls to mind the humorist Garrison Keillor's report of the politician who promised to provide a school system in which every child was above average.

Consensus in religion can be just as respectable and just as mistaken. At a Waldorf dinner in New York, I was seated next to Dr. Norman Lamm, president of Yeshiva University. When I mentioned my interest in Job to this eminent Judaic scholar, he observed: "I read the Book of Job on Tishah b'Av. It's about the only part of the Bible you can read that day."

I well remembered Tishah b'Av. In Jerusalem the year before, as I was packing to go after a week's columniating, Mayor Teddy Kolleck called to say he wanted to see me before I left. I said fine, but it would have to be that night. The hardworking mayor hesitated—"It's Tishah b'Av, you know"—but rather than let me leave Israel uneducated, he named a popular restaurant. We met there and I wondered why we were the only people in the place; the mayor shrugged it off and went into his explanation of how Jews and Arabs could live peaceably and productively in the same city. A photographer materialized and took our picture, which appeared the next morning in a religious newspaper under an outraged headline: MAYOR DINES OUT ON TISHAH B'AV!

That religious holiday, I was soon instructed, observes the destruction of the Temple; it is almost as solemn an occasion as

Yom Kippur, the Day of Atonement, and for the mayor of the capital of Israel to be spotted entertaining somebody in a restaurant (which had opened at his request) on a day of mourning must have been a terrible embarrassment to him. That's how I know about Tishah b'Av, which means the ninth day of the month of Av in the Hebrew calendar.

But where is it written, I asked the Yeshiva president (usually a rhetorical question, but not in this case), that the study only of Job is permitted on that day? He informed me that the instruction was written in the part of the Talmud called the Baraita, meaning "outside"—legal edicts written about the same time as the Mishnah—in which rabbis of the second and third centuries agreed on interpretations of scriptural ordinances. Next day, he looked up the reference to Job and mailed me a photocopy of the page.

"Our Rabbis have taught:" the Baraita reads, "All the restrictions that apply to the mourner hold equally good on the Ninth of Av." The consensus of rabbinical thought then lists the restrictions: "Eating, drinking, bathing, anointing, the wearing of shoes and marital relations are forbidden thereon . . . *but he may read Job, Lamentations and the sad parts of Jeremiah.*"

The Talmudic point is that this is a day on which all pleasure should be denied. To the pious person, the greatest pleasure is to read the Bible; such study is not a chore, but a delight. So studying Scripture on Tishah b'Av is out, too—too much enjoyment—except for those few parts of the Bible that describe such pain that they cause anguish in the reader. Those really mournful passages are clearly specified: all of Job and Lamentations, and the sad parts of Jeremiah.

I am no expert on Lamentations or the sad parts, or even any happy parts, of Jeremiah. But I have spent enough time on Job in the twentieth century to take issue with the consensus of rabbis in the second century. As the reader surely knows by now, I find the Book of Job more intellectually challenging, emotionally satisfying, spiritually uplifting, and politically instructive than any other part of the Bible. I read Job to be discomforted, and I find something new and beautiful and provocative in it every time. Sitting through the reading of a list of begats or a soporific sermon in temple, I pick up the Bible in the slot of the bench ahead of me, riffle back to Job, and guiltlessly enjoy myself.

That enjoyment is evidently not what the consensus of sages who wrote the Baraita had in mind. The rabbinical consensus was that Job was concentrated agony; to identify with his suffering would be comfort for mourners, not food for thought on a day of fasting. That consensus, in my view, was mistaken, a part of an age-old attempt to conceal the Joban controversy. Therefore, to be observant on the Ninth of Av and diligently to mourn the destruction of the Temple, I would turn to the sad parts of Jeremiah but deny myself the pleasure of reading the Book of Job.

I would recall on that day, however, that the consensus position in that book was taken by Eliphaz, Bildad, and Zophar, backed up, if somewhat insultingly, by the interpolation of Elihu. Their consensus—holding that suffering was evidence of sin—was disputed by Job and in the end shattered by God.

The trouble with consensus decision-making today is that everyone has to agree to some watered-down version of any move. I dropped in at a meeting of the Planning Commission of the town of Frederick, Maryland, and was told I could not observe their discussion before a vote—that behind closed doors, "They're consensing." If this actionless verb describes the emerging voice of the people, we could look forward only to weak bleats of hesitant agreement in place of the healthy roar of controversy. Fortunately, Jobans refuse to consense.

### 4. Don't let disputes with Authority grow into challenges of its legitimacy.

Confronted by unfairness, oppressed people become sullen; free people get angry. The reason for the different reactions is that freedom encourages people to fume openly at those in charge, thereby preventing the festering of fury.

At his most outraged, Job never ceased to believe in God. Although at first his sudden turn of fortune made him feel forsaken, rejected, left out—"alienated", in the sixties' not-so-meaningful jargon—Job soon came to believe that the Supreme Being was scheming against him, organizing his abuse. What helped Job cling to his sanity was not just his focus on the injustice of his suffering but his anger at the way he was being held at a distance by his creator, of whose existence and power the abused man was only too well aware. Belief plus trust equals faith; belief minus trust equals a loss of faith. The second equation hurt Job more than any of his other losses.

Take his opening blast at the commencement of the poetic portion of the book; it has always sounded to me like the first four notes of Beethoven's Fifth Symphony. Job encapsulates his story in the lede: "Damn the day that I was born!"[11] Talmudic explicators forgave this blasphemy on the grounds that nobody can be held to account for actions taken under duress, a compassionate policy that our modern military has adopted regarding statements by prisoners of war under torture. Not only does he implicitly curse creation and its creator, but Job compounds that religious crime by parodying the story of Genesis and its "Let there be light" with his own "May that day turn to darkness".[12]

This is not mere blasphemy, defined as saying nasty things about God, which strikes reverent readers as bad enough; the case can be made that this day-damning is cursing God himself, a sin the ancient rabbis urged be punished through death by stoning. Scribes did not even dare to put the verb next to the proper noun. They replaced "curse" with the euphemism "bless", referring to the unspeakable crime as "blessing God", which has to be read as meaning the opposite.

A curse begins "God damn" for good reason: The idea is to call down the wrath and punishment of the highest power upon the object being cursed. But in cursing God, the meaning is "God damn God"—which is absurd, the product of muddled thinking, as Maimonides suggested—or a rational if outrageous demand by a believer that God discipline himself with the utmost severity. Job believed in God so resolutely—with all his heart and soul and might, as is prescribed—that he saw no contradiction in demanding that God force God to rectify God's faults. Even as he hoped for death, it never occurred to Job that the answer to the injustice inflicted so painfully on him was that no God existed. His belief in God's unfairness only buttressed his belief in God, who he was certain was up there being actively unfair to him.

In the same way, political man can lose faith in Authority's justice or its wisdom without necessarily losing belief in the legitimacy of that government. To make great changes, the lonely dissenter is unwise to talk prematurely about overthrowing the system. Not only does he risk his neck if he fails, but too-quick success in a coup would have its own price: He would lose the fertilizing force of disapproval needed to make a revolution permanent.

Job needs God's attention, God needs Job's worship, and a political dissenter needs public disapproval. Censure, contempt, and official repudiation are all expressions of attentive disapproval; the fertilizing force can be weakened by compromise, but more often results in a crackdown that radicalizes a larger public.

Dwight Eisenhower's strategy in 1953–54 to counter Senator Joe McCarthy was to ignore him, to "not bemean the Presidency", as he wrote a friend. The combative Wisconsin Republican had hoped the President would engage him when McCarthy stretched his most famous charge against five Democratic presidential terms to "twenty-*one* years of treason"—reaching into Eisenhower's first year. Civil libertarians thought Ike was being a weakling, what we would now call a wimp, when the only action the President took was to issue an order claiming executive privilege against Senate examination of thousands of documents. But his strategy—to deny McCarthy the presidential disapproval he needed for confrontational traction—worked; the ultimate censure took place on the senatorial level.

As the lamentations in the Book of Job offer a kind of cover for blasphemy elsewhere, a Bill of Rights or common law offers necessary cover for democratic protest. This is especially true when the protester gets the knack of appealing for popular support by currying official disfavor. That knack is based on protestations of limited goals: to change the policy or the regime rather than the system itself. In time, given a break or a mistake by Authority, the exploitation of disfavor can gain a momentum to change the system, as happened with the pulverization of communism in the disintegration of the Soviet empire.

It's foolish to treat every challenge to Authority's judgment as an expression of disbelief in its legitimacy. A central political point in Job is that protest is most effective when it is channeled through belief. Though it sounds as hopeless as Job calling on God to judge God severely, the effective dissident demands that government force government to redress the wrongs of government.

This is a practical approach to provoking major change or

accumulating power in a democratic system. Dissidents to despotism have little choice but to resist and suffer as publicly as possible, but even in overthrowing a despotic regime, a pretense of protecting legitimacy has its uses: Boris Yeltsin's Russian counterrevolution of 1991 succeeded under the umbrella of protecting Gorbachevian constitutional legitimacy, which had been threatened by a coup of Communist hacks allied with KGB and Red Army plotters.

Does this ostentatious embrace of belief in Authority's legitimacy—despite the context of loud, anguished howling at the unfairness being perpetrated in its name—suggest the possibility of upbeat nihilism? Not so oxymoronic: Murmuring the mantra "the system works" may take some of the stridency out of street theater and mass demonstrations, and will not trigger the skull-cracking repression that makes the pictures to put protest on the nightly news. But the system-works mantra is useful to dissidents seeking to provoke the stricture of the structure.

Dissidents in a democracy should not throw away the credentials that go with ardent professions of systemic belief; they are tickets to the forum. Even as Job berated God for not holding to Godlike standards of morality, he never doubted the divine power or legitimacy; he stayed inside religion's temple even as he shouted curses from the dungheap. Without turning anarchic, political dissidents can also find the liberty to abuse the democratic system for failing its highest ideals. In dealing with the inexplicable hostility of power in heaven or on earth, the best way is to keep the faith and wave the flag—to believe and focus and holler.

Take the political expression that gets patriotic people's dander up most: flag-burning. When this issue reached the Supreme Court in 1990, a coalition of the Court's liberals and libertarians rightly upheld the right to express symbolic protest. The repugnant act also stimulated demagogy to satisfy public disgust at the flag-burners by passing a law to counter the Court's decision.

Flag-burning, draftcard-burning, hanging the President in effigy—all are outrage provokers. *Desecrate* means to attack the sacred, to make un-sacred. As intended, these acts cause widespread offense, thereby attracting much attention. Libertarians know that a free society strengthens itself by protecting such distasteful but harmless insult, but most dissidents do not know how to get the asset of disapproving attention without getting the debit of outright disgust.

Drawing on the day-damning Joban analogy, here is a creed for the scruffiest flag burners who want to gain something more than momentary attention:

"I believe in the country, not the flag; the referent, not the symbol; the reality of allegiance, not the words in its Pledge. If I burn our country's flag, I may succeed in infuriating you (or may fail when you shrug off my act as tantrum politics). But even while wallowing in my provocative arrogance, and even indulging my lust for publicized punishment and mini-martyrdom, I affirm my belief in the legitimacy of the majority's wrongheaded rule.

"As a flag burner, I am, in my perverse way of thinking, more of a patriot than the most turned-off respectable observer, just as the irreverent Job was a truer believer than the pious pretenders who presumed to instruct and harass him. I am certain that the day will come when high authority will declare my protest to be right, and will condemn your incendiary flagwaving at me as the last refuge of scoundrels. I will have my reward in some stunning political epilogue yet to be revealed."

The secret to upbeat nihilism can be found in a shrewd Joban afterthought. Job has just told his visitors that he would not confess to sins he did not commit, and would not quaver "though he slay me". Then he shapes this very act of defiance as a perverse proof of his underlying piety: "This might even be my salvation, For no impious man would face him."[13]

### 5. Persuade yourself that no need is more urgent than the need to know.

Demanding to know the unknowable is right in the eyes of the ultimate Authority, even when "Top Secret, NoDis, Eyes of God Only" is engraven on the tablets.

William J. Casey was a lifelong friend of mine. We met in the Nixon-Kennedy campaign of 1960, when I worked as a volunteer hatchetman for Len Hall, the campaign manager, and Casey was Hall's junior law partner, setting up "front" committees and channeling bags of cash into their bank accounts to pay for the incendiary literature and deniable advertisements I was writing. He assured me years later it had not been illegal at the time.

After the defeat, he steered an old OSS associate, the oilman John Shaheen, to my firm as a client. Soon afterward, I handled Casey's campaign for Congress on Long Island, taking him to a speech teacher to get over the brilliant lawyer's terminal mumbles, but sometimes image-making asks too much; we lost. But we became the kind of comrades only war or politics produces. I threw the party welcoming him to Washington in 1970 to head the SEC and could count on his warm loyalty and devious personal counsel well into the time he became Ronald Reagan's director of Central Intelligence.

Our falling-out began over a minor incident. He made a speech arguing that reporters who print national-security secrets should be prosecuted for espionage, and I zinged him in print about such foolish zealotry. An FBI man at odds with the CIA called with a tip for me: "Your friend Casey, who is so worked up about leaks, has been seeing Bob Woodward of *The Washington Post* at night at Casey's house for months." I called Bill to check this out; he denied it, noting that Woodward was writing a book about intelligence and had cornered Casey at a party once or twice.

What Bill said was untrue, of course; Woodward's book, *Veil*, published just after Casey's death from a cancerous brain tumor, was based in part on extensive conversations with the spymaster. After that the friendship unraveled; he upbraided me at a public gathering for burning a CIA source; when a common friend, Leo Cherne, tried to heal the breach, Casey rebuffed him. But in the last month of Casey's reign at the CIA, as the use of Iranian arms sales profits to finance the Nicaraguan Contras came to light, a weakened Casey called me. "You froze me out," he said, as if our friendship's ending was my fault, and proceeded to try to sell what spooks call a cover story. It was a clumsy, un-Caseylike lie—I suspect that the golfball-sized tumor had affected the old patriot's thinking for months, perhaps years—and I didn't buy. When he couldn't understand that, I reminded him of the time he began to mislead me after his power-crazy speech about sending journalists to jail. He had a ready explanation for that and subsequent slammings of his door: "You had no need to know."

To Bill Casey, from the World War II days when he para-
chuted spies into Nazi Germany to the agony he suffered in the
1980s when his Beirut station chief was tortured to death by terrorists, secret information existed in compartments. If, for purposes of
a mission, you had a need to know a secret, you were let into the
compartment; if not, no matter how high your security clearance,
you were not told and were expected not to ask. Who decided who
had a "need to know"? Casey did, because only he could see the big
picture. (President Reagan also had a need to know, and Casey
would occasionally mumble it to him, but Reagan was too deaf to
hear and then too vain to wear a hearing aid.) Was Casey scrupulous about limiting that need-to-know decision to national secrets
and not merely to political embarrassments? No.

The "big picture" theory in theology is hard for citizens in a
free society to swallow in politics, because it is so often abused.
Besides, "it's not for you to know" is an insult to the questioner's
intelligence or loyalty.

Poet-Job deals with Man's need to know by raising the issue
of what theologians down the ages have called "the inscrutability of
God's ways". What seems to Man on earth to be morally unjust
may be part of God's grand design of the universe, goes the interpretation we examined in the chapter on lessons to believers; it all
may fit together, we are told, in some big picture known to God but
forever unknowable to Man.

The genius of poet-Job in offering the inscrutability possibility
is the way he puts the reader in God's shoes. Job is ignorant of the
celestial wager in the prologue, but the reader knows about it. Job
does not realize he is being put to the test, but the reader—looking
down from literary heaven—knows. The consolers do not know
that their condemnation of Job as a sinner by virtue of his suffering
is a mistake, but the reader knows.

Even if we knowing readers could whisper to Job out of a small
whirlwind, we could not reveal what we know for Job's edification,
because that would shatter the big picture, and abort the celestial
test. This shows us vividly what it is like to have God's problem: In
this case, because we have shared God's knowledge and not Job's
ignorance, we can identify with God in stressing universal order
over justice on earth. Having spent that dizzying moment in God's
shoes, we can go back to identifying with Job, understanding there

are some things that cannot be explained in a universe that is neither orderly-moral nor chaotic-evil.

Our knowledge of Job's ignorance is the classic example of dramatic irony, but it also serves to drive home the point that physicists have come to call "the Heisenberg effect". Werner Heisenberg, a quantum mechanicist, postulated his Uncertainty Principle: that the very act of observing a phenomenon changes it. Fixing the exact position of an atom affects its momentum, which limits the precision of all measurement. The metaphor of the Heisenberg effect runs through political polling and more: A central European banker told me that he closely watches the price of a certain commodity before making a decision on money supply, but that had to be kept secret. Why? Because if it became known that Commodity X was significant, its price changes would be affected by the very fact that it was being watched by the bank—and thereby ruin its value as an indicator to the bankers.

The "poet-Job effect", coined right here and now, is that injustice cannot be justified without subverting the moral experiment being conducted. Knowledge of the test affects the results of the test. Therefore, Job not only had no "need to know", God had a need for Job not to know.

With Job, unknowability applies for all time; his wealth was restored, his family replaced, but he will never have an answer to his "Why?" God held that it was not for him to know and he saw no reason to give any explanations. Job was given only the satisfaction of a quick glimpse at how hard it was to make order out of chaos, and a vague suggestion that maybe a little chaos adds some spice to the dreary business of universal management—showing Man just enough to reconcile him with his God and to give Man an incentive to inquire further.

When political authority says the public cannot know—usually on grounds of national security or pending investigation, occasionally on grounds of another person's privacy—it tries to apply the restriction for as long as it can. The Freedom of Information Act requires periodic review of security classifications and ends privacy restrictions at death. But bureaucrats find excuses to bury old secrets and embarrassments long past the law's legitimate delay.

Every modern biblical scholar seethes at the way access to the

Dead Sea Scrolls was limited to a tiny coterie of researchers, first by the Kingdom of Jordan, later by the government of Israel. Four decades went by as the select few academics at Harvard, Notre Dame, and Hebrew universities dribbled out pictures and translations, justifying their exclusivity on the arrogant notion that they were protecting the world from the shoddy research of others. But a wealthy and cunning old lady, Betty Bechtel, pointed out the threat of destruction in case of Mideast war, and persuaded the authorities that prudence required that a copy of the scrolls be kept on microfilm in a vault in the United States. The scholarly cartel agreed; she arranged for pictures to be taken of the entire cache and the strips of film secured in a center she built in Claremont, California.

Years later, the trustees of the center decided to kick out the persnickety founder, but the old lady kept what was called her "scroll in the hole"—a duplicate set of the precious negatives, which she slipped surreptitiously to the Huntington library, near Pasadena. After the philanthropist died, the academic monopoly got wind of the extra set and demanded that the Huntington hand it over. The library director, William Moffett, in the best tradition of academic freedom, promptly made the set available to any library in the world that wanted it.

I happened to be in Pasadena on that day, and interviewed Moffett; he told me some library officials were concerned about quoted threats of a lawsuit from the antiquities bureaucracy in Jerusalem. I got on the overseas phone to a few Israeli politicians and added my pundit's voice to those giving them the big political-academic picture. The Israeli Prime Minister's press advisers wisely sat on the antiquarian soreheads who thought that only an elite had the right to determine when the scrolls would be available to civilization.

A more personal experience to illustrate the need to challenge the abuse of "the need to know": In 1973, as a new columnist for *The New York Times,* I was still on the burning deck of the doomed ship *Nixon,* vainly but vigorously defending the President I had served as speechwriter. This reluctance to join in the gleeful general condemnation of the Watergate transgressions did not endear me to members of my resumed profession. One day, investigative reporter John Crewdson, one of my new colleagues at the *Times*, looked at me with new respect: He had learned, and at that point tipped me off, that I was one of seventeen administration aides and newsmen illegally wiretapped by the FBI, on White House orders, beginning in 1969. That evidence of unwitting but demonstrable outsidership took the onus off me at the newspaper, instantly transforming me in my colleagues' minds from one of "them" to one of "us".

But the surprise salvation really got to my sense of loyalty. Infuriated at having been considered a "leak" risk by Johnnies-come-lately to the Nixon entourage, I demanded to know why my phone had been tapped. Al Haig, who had induced the attorney general to sign off on the wiretap authorization, was then White House chief of staff. He assured me that the reason had nothing to do with my loyalty or discretion, but that if I pulled the string of inquiry, terrible things would unravel and good people—including longtime comrades in arms—would be hurt. No big deal, Al insisted; he suspected he had been tapped himself, and it gave him "no gas pains", a figure of speech that sticks in my mind.

I tugged on that loose end anyway, Job-style: why me? To no avail; first, national security was given as the reason for wiretap penetration of my privacy, and then I was told I could not know because that would invade the privacy of others, and finally the impossible obstacle was presented: The files had been shipped to storage in some midwestern depot as inaccessible as the Mindanao Deep.

Nearly two decades later, over a friendly lunch, John Mitchell—on the day before he died, as it happened—recollected the reason he, as attorney general, signed that authorization to eavesdrop on the home telephone of someone who had been a Nixon hand long before almost all the others: I had been overheard leaking some information about an upcoming Nixon speech to a journalist whose phone was already being tapped. The FBI routinely requested authority to extend the wiretap to my phone.

That reasoning staggered me. I told Mitchell I remembered that tap-triggering conversation: It was a call I made after the President told me to leak far and wide the contents of his forthcoming welfare reform message, which I had a hand in writing.

"Nixon's Good Deed" was what some liberals dubbed the reform; I had coined the term "workfare", or at least thought I had, to describe the transition from welfare to work, and the President wanted word out in advance to ensure him credit for sensible compassion in media not usually friendly to him.

But the damnable plumbing system was not set up to allow for such authorized leaking. The FBI was soon sending reports to the National Security Council staff recounting confidential conversations I had had with my doctor, my rabbi, and my wife, not to mention talks about speeches and policy with the President, who probably did not realize his remarks to me would be circulated among other aides. This warrantless phone tapping took place before the doom-laden Oval Office taping had begun.

My explanation of the original cause amused Mitchell. He liked the irony of Nixon issuing an order to eavesdrop that triggered another order, unknown to him, that eavesdropped on presidential conversations and wound up in J. Edgar Hoover's office safe. But it bugged me, in the other sense of the term; it also taught me that "you are not cleared for that" or "some things are better left alone" and other evasions should be invitations to relentless probing, even when the possibility exists that genuine national secrets are concerned. Ever since, when a door has been slammed shut because "you have no need to know," I have developed an abiding need to know. Authority always errs on the side of concealment, requiring subjects to strike a balance by erring on the side of revelation. The tension is good for the country.

This secrecy-privacy-publicity three-dimensional chess is played within the government at the highest levels. The President and the congressional leadership have an understanding about covert operations, which the Congress keeps trying to codify but the executive resists. The President must sign a "finding" authorizing our spooks to undertake a covert operation, and that document must be shown to a small group of senators within a few hours, or days, or weeks, or months—the time is always at issue. The Reagan administration was besmirched by the backdating and destruction of these findings. Why can't we know? the senators ask, and the President resists the urge to snap back with: "Who is this whose ignorant words cloud my design in darkness?"[14]

Authority loves mystery; the free hand it offers is the most delicious perk of power, and few thrills can equal the frisson that comes when a person in the lonely know can smile to himself, "if they only knew", followed by the kicker, "but they'll never know until I'm ready to tell them."

When truth must be concealed by what Churchill called "a bodyguard of lies" to mislead a wartime enemy or to protect lives, the piquancy of duplicity can be justified. As negotiations to end the war in Vietnam proceeded on a secret "back channel", President Nixon found himself having to disparage concessions called for by the peace movement at home even as his agent, Henry Kissinger, was making those concessions secretly. The taste of self-denial in the cause of secret diplomacy was delectable; Nixon savored every moment when he told me to write a speech spilling the beans at last, which I did from deep in a dungeon. (I was not imprisoned; it was on a visit to Ireland, and I was given a dank basement room in Dromoland Castle, where the presidential party was staying. General Brent Scowcroft, the White House military aide whose main job at the time was to make certain that Henry Kissinger's room was better than the one assigned to Secretary of State William Rogers, stuck the lowly speechwriter down in the castle dungeon. Even loyalists remember slights.) Was secrecy in the name of peace dealings justified? Yes, a delay in the release of the truth was justifiable, and no, because the delay bred other lies and the corrosive deception lasted too long.

This kind of experience propels many officials to flights of self-pity. "If they only knew" can lead to "If I could tell them all I know, my critics would shut up and get behind me, but I am condemned to concealment for their own good despite my falling ratings." On rare occasions, Hamlet's gushing line—"But break, my heart, for I must hold my tongue!"—rings true, and concealment is motivated by the need for privacy or security. More often, concealment is caused more by worry about embarrassment or by an interest in timing an announcement for the greatest benefit to the newsbreaker. And even when it is necessary to hide the truth, the hiding is almost always needlessly and harmfully extended.

As concealment is a weapon of the Ins, ignorance can be a device of the Outs. The political figure who refuses to take a stand because "I don't have the information the President has" is turning the "if you only knew" trick on its head. He professes not to be able to criticize because he is not privy to the big picture; rather than declaim a position, he declares a moratorium. But when all goes wrong, when the danger of decision is past and the lights of hindsight flood the landscape of the past, then he is free to claim "I would have told you so"—had he only known what those in Authority had been privileged to know.

Political opponents, nosy journalists, subgoverning moles, and the unruly ruled are required to try to lift Authority's veil even before they know what to look for. Their only justification is an assertion of the subject's sovereignty.

Sometimes an answer awaits only a probe. In the looseleaf "black books" prepared by staffers to brief their principals before media encounters, all the possible questions are anticipated, with answers outlined. I had the black-book detail in the White House one week in 1971 and tossed in the question "Who's your choice for running mate next year?" Vice President Agnew, among others, was dying to know, because the President was known to prefer his Treasury secretary, the Texas Democrat John Connally, hoping thereby to get the Democratic vote, too, and be elected by virtual acclamation. Nixon told me to put down a paragraph announcing his choice of Agnew (thereby denying Connally the presidential chair later occupied by Gerald Ford), but to keep it secret until the question was asked. For four months, through three press conferences, the question was not asked and the answer remained a mystery. Finally, Dan Rather tossed it in during a CBS year-end interview and out popped the news. All along, it had been there for the asking.

Rarely is information, much less the truth, so easily come by. The obstacle of "only the one at the top truly knows, and he can't say" has been growing in our system, but this deference to Authority is misplaced. Softball questions asked in stentorian tones substitute too often for the arrogant but necessary "Why can't we know?" And background rules are too readily accepted when the question should be: "Why can't we have this on the record?"

Knowledge is power, as the corrupt Lord Bacon held, and few in power want to share the knowledge that reduces that power.

Job's incessant demand for answers angered God, but brought the deity out of isolation into partial revelation. No wonder Authority gets irritated at our unwillingness to accept limits to knowledge: It knows that its inscrutability must ultimately yield to Man's need to know.


## 6. Play God for a day.

In the early days of television, a program called *Queen for a Day* appealed to an audience of vicarious hedonists. The contestant selected was ceremoniously crowned, bedecked with gifts, and given power to issue commands for goods and services, mimicking majesties everywhere. She was drenched in a shower of power; viewers placed themselves in her gleaming new shoes and loved it.

We all daydream about being in power, whether to do noble works or to lord it over the people who now push us around. But then we stop to ask ourselves: How would we really conduct ourselves if we had unlimited authority? What if we could play God for a day?

Okay, you vice overlords and drug kingpins, we're going to have a crackdown. No more red tape or legal niceties. Gluttony, sloth, and the rest of the seven sins are going to be punished; the wicked are going to pay; we're going to straighten out the universe. Chaos is finished; evil is out. This is the era of reform. "Action this day", as Churchill liked to record in his diary, and as Ross Perot took for his theme.

Is there any downside to this? Earlier in this book, we dealt with a pair of Joban opposites, chaos and order. Now let's take on a couple of related opposites, more directly in the business of governing: the atmosphere of freedom with all its inequities versus the aura of total control needed for perfect justice.

In the minus-first millennium, Job sought the equitable distribution of justice; that was the moral code he tried to impose on God. In the final stages of the second millennium, humanity sought a sense of fairness in life; that called for the redistribution of wealth and the rise of entitlements. In both cases, the requirement for central control turned out to be too great a price for a free society to pay, for the fairness gained. Sometimes morality asks too much.

At the start of his second tirade from the whirlwind, God—who has silenced Job but not convinced him—goes directly to the business of governing the universe, and to the difference between Job's moral order and the divine cosmic order. Job has already boasted of what he had done to administer justice, when he had been a power in his own world: "I broke the fangs of the miscreant and rescued the prey from his teeth."[15] By citing the way he snatched the booty from the criminal, Job proudly put his record forward as dispenser of equity, which was more than God could claim: "justice, like a cloak or a turban, wrapped me round."[16] God must have heard that and it must have bothered him. He raises the ante. Play God for a day, he suggests to the presumptuous human:

"Deck yourself out, if you can, in pride and dignity," says the voice from the whirlwind, "array yourself in pomp and splendour." With Job thus dressed in his imagination in the robes of royal power, God invites him to "unleash the fury of your wrath, look upon the proud man and humble him; look upon every proud man and bring him low, throw down the wicked where they stand." Go ahead, says God, bury the opposing dark forces of chaos—"hide them in the dust together, and shroud them in an unknown grave."[17]

Nobody can be certain what this passage means, but it seems to me that God is suggesting that Job, the fang-breaker of the wicked on earth, would have great difficulty, or would not be acting in the interests of the universe, in applying his sweeping retributive justice throughout creation. Would it be a good idea to throw down the wicked and defang the miscreant in some hellish final crackdown? There seems to be some doubt about the wisdom of that final crusade.

After Job abolished evil and all its practitioners, says God, "Then I in my turn will acknowledge that your own right hand can save you."[18] This can be read as a simple "Let's see you try to be as powerful as me," but a much more intriguing meaning is implicit: Poet-Job is suggesting that if Job were to have the power of God, he would abuse that power by killing Behemoth and Leviathan, defeating the forces of chaos, triumphing over darkness and evil—thereby knocking the whole balanced universe out of kilter. All ferment would be deadened, all moral choice denied. If Job were to apply his fierce sense of justice to the realm of God, he would have to act as a totalitarian, destroying all opposition until nothing but good was left standing and a great quiet settled in. Job has been thinking like a lawyer; God tells him to think like a governor.

The trick to cosmos management, the voice of God may be suggesting, is to control evil rather than destroy it. Chaos, inequity, and plain bad luck all figure in God's design, giving piquancy to choice and meaning to freedom. His method of management, as I read it, is more hands-off than hands-on. God does not take complete charge; he does not make the center the only source of decision; he resists having to enforce the immutable laws. Instead, his way of staying on top of things is to maintain just enough control to let liberty develop. The worldview of Attorney General Job is wholly different from the *Weltanschauung* of Chief Executive God. Poet-Job's concept of command is to control, not destroy, opposition—to set bounds to dissent but not to bury it. That fits with his willingness to put up with Job's annoying questions and curses.

In political terms, Behemoth may represent totalitarianism, Leviathan anarchy; God deals with them, even toys with them, but does not deny them the right to exist in his creation. That type of hands-off rule pervades the biblical wisdom literature: "Rule according to the wisdom principle," writes the Joban interpreter Norman C. Habel from his school in India, "leads to balance and freedom; rule according to the principle of retributive justice leads to imbalance and rigidity." The mocking you-play-God passage teaches that resistance to Authority has its place. Just as Job maintained his moral way before God, God—in his bombastic and dysresponsive voice from the whirlwind—maintains his cosmic way before Job.

We cannot derogate Man's attempt to achieve fairness, and especially equality of opportunity, on earth, but we can ask the price of its perfection. Realistic environmentalists want 99 percent purity; it's only the zealots who are willing to throw people out of work to squeeze out that last percentage point of pollution.

Communism, and to a lesser degree socialism, claimed the moral high ground in acting for the interests of the people. In Moscow late in 1991, after the fall of Gorbachev, I went into KGB

But he knoweth the way that I take
when he hath tried me I shall come forth like gold

Have pity upon me! Have pity upon me : O ye my friends
for the hand of God hath touched me

Though he slay me yet will I trust in him

# The Just Upright Man is laughed to scorn

Man that is born of a Woman is of few days & full of trouble
he cometh up like a flower & is cut down he fleeth also as a shadow
& continueth not And dost thou open thine eyes upon such a one
& bringest me into judgment with thee

London Published as the Act directs March 8: 1825 by William Blake N.3 Fountain Court Strand

W. Blake inven & Sculp

My bones are pierced in me in the
night season & my sinews
take no rest

My skin is black upon me
& my bones are burned
with heat

The triumphing of the wicked
is short, the joy of the hypocrite is
but for a moment
Satan himself is transformed into an Angel of Light & his Ministers into Ministers of Righteousness

With Dreams upon my bed thou scarest me & affrightest me
with Visions

Why do you persecute me as God & are not satisfied with my flesh. Oh that my words
were printed in a Book that they were graven with an iron pen & lead in the rock for ever
For I know that my Redeemer liveth & that he shall stand in the latter days upon
the Earth & after my skin destroy thou This body yet in my flesh shall I see God
whom I shall see for Myself and mine eyes shall behold & not Another tho consumed be

Who opposeth & exalteth himself above all that is called God or is Worshipped

W Blake invent & sculp
London Published as the Act directs March 8, 1825 by Will Blake N 3 Fountain Court Strand

God speaketh once yea twice
In a Dream in a Vision of the Night
in deep Slumberings upon the Bed
he openeth the ears of Men & sealeth to their instruction

That he may withdraw Man from his purpose
& hide Pride from Man
If there be with him an Interpreter One among a Thousand
then he is gracious unto him
& saith Deliver him from going down to the Pit
I have found a Ransom

For his eyes are upon
the ways of Man & he observeth
all his goings

I am Young & ye are very Old wherefore I was afraid

Lo all these things worketh God oftentimes with Man to bring

back his Soul from the pit to be enlightened

with the light of the living

Look upon the heavens & behold the clouds
which are higher
than thee

If thou sinnest what
doest thou against him or if thou be
righteous what givest thou unto him

WBlake invenit & sculpt.

London. Published as the Act directs March. 8:1825 by Will Blake No 3 Fountain Court Strand

Who is this that darkeneth counsel by words without knowledge

Then the Lord answered Job out of the Whirlwind

Who maketh the Clouds his Chariot & walketh on the Wings of the Wind    the Drops of the Dew

Hath the Rain        a Father & who hath begotten

W Blake invenit & sculp

London, Published as the Act directs March 8: 1825 by William Blake N 3 Fountain Court Strand

Hell is naked before him & Destruction has no covering

Canst thou find out the Almighty to perfection

Canst them by searching find out God

Canst him find out the Almighty to perfection

The Accuser of our Brethren is Cast down
which accused them before our God day & night

It is higher than Heaven what canst thou do

It is deeper than Hell what canst thou know

The Prince of this World shall be cast out

Even the Devils are Subject to Us thro thy Name. Jesus said unto them. I saw Satan as lightning fall from Heaven

Thou hast fulfilled the Judgment of the Wicked

God hath chosen the foolish things of the World to confound the wise
And God hath chosen the weak things of the World to confound the things that are mighty

WBlake inv & sculp

London, Published as the Act directs March 8: 1825 by William Blake N° 3 Fountain Court Strand.

He bringeth down to the Grave & bringeth up

We know that when he shall appear we shall be like him for we shall see him as He Is

When I behold the Heavens the work of thy hands the Moon & Stars which thou hast ordained. then I say. What is Man that thou art mindful of him, & the Son of Man that thou visitest him.

I have heard thee with the hearing of the Ear but now my Eye seeth thee

He that hath seen me

hath seen my Father also

I & my Father are One

If ye had known me ye would have known my Father also and from henceforth ye know him & have seen him

Believe me that I am in the Father & the Father in me He that loveth me shall be loved of my Father & I will manifest my self to him

At that day ye shall know that I am in my Father & you in me & I in you
If ye loved me ye would rejoice because I said I go unto the Father

He that loveth me shall be loved of my Father & I will manifest my self to him And the Father shall give ye another Comforter that he may abide with you for ever Even the Spirit of Truth whom the World cannot receive

W Blake

Inv & Sculp

London Published as the Act directs March 8 1825 by William Blake N 3 Fountain Court, Strand

How precious are thy thoughts
unto me O God
how great is the sum of them

re were not found Women fair as the Daughters of Job

in all the Land & their Father gave them Inheritance

among their Brethren

If I ascend up into Heaven thou art there
If I make my bed in Hell behold Thou
art there

WBlake invent & s

London  Published as the Act directs March 8 1825 by William Blake N 3 Fountain Court Strand

Great & Marvellous are thy Works Lord God Almighty

Just & True are thy Ways O thou King of Saints

So the Lord blessed the latter end of Job
more than the beginning

After this Job lived
an hundred & forty years
& saw his Sons & his
Sons Sons

even four Generations
So Job died
being old
& full of days

In burnt Offerings for Sin

thou hast had no Pleasure

W Blake inv & sculp

London Published as the Act directs March 8 1825 by William Blake Fountain Court Strand headquarters on Lubyanka Square. The huge statue of "Iron Felix" Dzerzhinsky, bloodstained founder of Lenin's secret police, had been toppled from its pedestal; in the square, the bare pedestal remained, supporting nothing, an Ozymandian memorial to the departure of what John Foster Dulles used to call "godless communism". Inside the secret-police headquarters, housed in an annex to the prison where countless dissidents had been tortured and murdered, the KGB director pretended he could find no answers to questions about Soviet complicity in Lee Harvey Oswald's assassination of President Kennedy. But his fellow apologists and aides insisted they could be sure of this: that had the philosophy of communism not been perverted into a new power autocracy by Lenin and Stalin, it might well have provided the most for the most—if not the most freedom, at least the most security and social welfare for the greatest number.

The KGB "reformers" still didn't get it. Communism was a throwback to Hobbes's Leviathan state. The problem was not in the Lenin-Stalin execution but in the idea itself. It contradicted the human spirit with its insistence on total control; on rule from the center; on its need for the Party to maintain a monopoly of power.

Authority's urge to control—for the best of purposes, of course—can come from victory in a democratic arena, too. In democracies, the danger of purge is most manifest after landslides. When FDR trounced the Republican opposition in 1936, he felt strong enough to attempt to pack the Supreme Court with up to six additional young, vigorous New Deal justices. He was dissuaded by public reaction, but the "nine old men" on the Court got the message and stopped overturning his legislation; the saying at the time was "a switch in time saved nine."

I saw that post-landslide bounce at firsthand, too, after the drubbing of George McGovern in the election of 1972. That's when the victorious Nixon rubbed his hands in anticipation of sweeping clean the Executive Branch, before the Watergate debacle led his opponents to the same vindictive feeling about sweeping the government clean of him. In the surge of confidence that comes with a great mandate, so much that seems like justice can be done; so many political and social scores can be settled, and so many dissidents both inside and on the other side rolled over.

"Throw down the wicked where they stand." Those sarcastic words from the whirlwind are not intended to be taken literally. Just the opposite: Poet-Job's God was saying that Authority should place boundaries around those called the wicked, but not throw them down. The Joban political message here is directed to victors and their triumphant supporters who become "sore winners": Do not stamp out opposition. Do not try to bury adversaries in the dust, no matter how wrong or deserving of political demolition you think they may be. Control the twisty serpent of chaos, but let it live.

### 7. The center should not hold.

"Things fall apart," wrote the poet Yeats, "the center cannot hold." That line from "The Second Coming" was the most quoted snippet of poetry in Washington as the decade of the nineties began and the truth about the economic implosion of the Soviet Union began to seep out. I was doing my Yeatsian bit at a Christmastime brunch when a Soviet diplomat slouched toward me.

"I read your novel about Lincoln," he began, and then talked about *Freedom* long enough to demonstrate that he had read at least the flap copy. Then he came to the point: "Our President is facing the same problem today that Lincoln faced in the last century. The voices of disunion are heard in the Baltic republics, in the Ukraine. Must not a great nation be held together at any cost?"

As he went on to develop that dubious message over the brunch's clatter, I was thinking about the Satan. The diplomat had bushy eyebrows that twisted to a point at both sides of his face that reminded me of Mr. Scratch, the role Walter Huston played in Stephen Benet's *The Devil and Daniel Webster*. I did not equate this hardworking professional envoy with the Devil, despite his representation of "the evil empire", but as he droned on earnestly about how the United States had found it necessary to strengthen the Articles of Confederation with a new document locking the states in a union, I could not keep my mind from wandering into the opening scene of the Book of Job.

The Satan (in my mind, with this diplomat's Walter Huston

eyebrows) is a born scene stealer. He has only moments on the stage but the Satan makes the most of them. The critic I. A. Richards found great literary skill in Job's prose prologue, usually dismissed as a mere folktale by admirers of the poetry. Of the Satan, Richards writes: "There is possibly no other character who establishes himself so solidly with so few words."

Poet-Job's judicious use of dialogue is partly the reason; the cultural character already fixed in the reader's mind is another part. In Milton's *Paradise Lost,* Satan is by far the most fascinating character; William Blake offered the stunning notion that the fallen angel in Milton's poem had the qualities of a redeemer: "In the book of Job, Milton's Messiah is call'd Satan."

As we've seen, translators precede the name with the definite article *the;* in the Hebrew, Satan is not a proper name, as it later came to be, but a title meaning "adversary, opponent" or, more specifically, "prosecutor, accuser, investigator"—one whose assignment is to doubt what seems to be, and to test that skepticism or suspicion at God's behest. Although he is rebuked by God in Chapter 3 of Zechariah for venting his spite on Jerusalem, nowhere in the Old Testament is the accusing angel taken to be the embodiment of evil. The Satan is an angel doing a provocative job, and sassily enjoying it, but he has not yet become the Devil, Lucifer, the Prince of Darkness standing against the Giver of Light. All that developed later.

The Satan in the Book of Job does makes things happen. "Stretch out your hand and touch all that he has," he suggests, deriding God's pride in the piety of Job, "and then he will curse you to your face."[19] The 1991 translation by Edwin Good interprets that to be an oath, translated as "If he doesn't curse you to your face—"with the result clause unstated but implied. As we saw with Job's dramatic oath of clearance—which brought *deus absconditus* out of hiding—an imprecation of this sort forces the deity's hand. An oath with a punishment attached pushes the train of events right out of the station. (If I'm misleading you on this, may you return this book to the bookseller, may I not get the royalty, may my publisher's children go without shoes, etc.)

As the prologue ends, the Satan drops out of the Book of Job; he's done his job of forcing God to put up a moral order or to get

Job to shut up about it. Along the way, he has put into question God's omniscience (why does an all-knowing God ask where the Satan has been?) as well as divine omnipotence (why should God doubt his own power to elicit disinterested obedience from Man?). Poet-Job does not bring the fascinating angel back for a curses-foiled-again turn in the epilogue because the book is not about the defeat of the Satan's design; on the contrary, the accusing angel turned out to be correct in predicting Job's damning reaction to injustice.

The modern reader can't help but admire the smooth, angelic skeptic; through the ages, artists and writers have made the Satan role the one that actors most like to play. (But Walter Huston, tucking souls in the form of butterflies into his wallet, will always be the Satan to me.) He has come to be the feared source of evil, as in Faustian bargaining, but also the respected source of defiance; moral philosophers need his temptation to vice to give meaning to the human being's choice of virtue, and artists need his sulfurous presence to bring the interest of conflict to high heaven. In Job, the Satan's cameo but pivotal appearance shows him at his needling best: not the anti-God, but the loyal opposition pushing the central Authority to do its best.

That, of course, is what strong central authorities want controlled political oppositions to do: to lose with honor; to make the authority look more authoritative; but not to pose the real possibility of taking power from the center. Only uncontrolled oppositions can shake up if not shake out the entrenched regime. Only the real risk of chaos can keep a political establishment from decay.

A phony professional basketball team called the Nationals was formed to play exhibitions against the razzle-dazzle Harlem Globetrotters. The Nationals always lost, as they were paid to do, because people did not come to see a real game but to see the Globetrotters perform funny stunts and acrobatic miracles. This is the sort of controlled opposition that persists in too many United States cities and congressional districts today. A one-party state can grimly maintain control for the better part of a century, as communism demonstrated, and a one-and-a-half-party state with a too-loyal opposition can poke along for generations, as Japan and Mexico have shown, but only a system offering the genuine possibility of a change in power can remain solid over the centuries. Too much stability is inherently unstable, but the slight instability of the actual possibility of change secures a state.

Authority without periodic discombobulation is tyranny. (Prose without aphorism is listless.) We like to think of a two-party system as a perfect balance, the equilibrium of power, but in fact it is the possibility of the Ins being ousted by the ideological Outs that introduces a note of chaos into the grandest designs. It can even introduce the idea, usually abhorrent to the party in power, of the devolution of central control to the states, republics, and provinces.

Poet-Job did not have in mind a satanic challenge to God's supremacy, or a lessening of God's central control of the universe. But the poet did move forward the process of using the Satan to measure God's powers, in this case through the testing of the motive of Man's worship. In the Book of Job we have the first example of God's dominion under challenge from a much lesser power—his human creation—which led to God's surprising revelation of his tribulations in taming the Leviathans of chaos. Dissidents, like skeptical angels, make unexpected things happen.

As absolute power can be seen as a form of civic death, regularly challenged power can be taken as the stirring of political life. That's a truism in the political order, but a question arises in challenging the heavenly order: If we use vice to define virtue, and if we depend on dark conspiracies to compel Authority to lighten up—aren't we making a case for the Devil? Aren't we equating dissent with evil and identifying the powers that be with good?

Dissenters challenging the established idea of truth, and disunionists tugging away from the center of a multicultural empire, have been condemned as agents of chaos and anarchy, and sometimes rightly so—but they are not necessarily bad. Authorities guaranteeing order and stability can contribute to the general serenity by keeping control in the center—but are not necessarily good. Political leaders have a habit of equating the status quo with good and dissent that leads to the roiling of the waters as evil. In the sixties and early seventies, Republicans never went as far as to hire antiwar demonstrators to come to rallies, but looked forward to their noisy attendance. The protesters' attempt at disruption served the cause of those of us who purveyed stability under the near-oxymoron "orderly change". (Watch out for that phrase; its users will err on the side of the adjective, rarely on the side of the noun.)

Which brings us back to the pitch being made by the Soviet diplomat with the dark satanic eyebrows for the Kremlin's central control of an empire spanning eleven time zones. "Must not a great nation be held together at all costs?" His analogy to our Civil War and the incipient breakup of the Soviet Union was false. A modern nation must rest on the consent of the majority of the governed, and that majority must not deny human rights to the minority. Lincoln was upholding majority rule after a free election; Gorbachev was upholding rule, period. The American Union was fighting slavery; the Soviet Union was resisting freedom.

The low point of President Bush's political thinking came on that Joban issue of absolute control versus the potential of chaos; in political terms it was expressed as the continued control from "Moscow center" versus the self-determination of the disparate republics. Mr. Bush did not see it in those stark terms, of course; he saw a struggle between orderly evolution and sudden upheaval, and thereby found his policy zigging as history zagged.

In the summer of 1991, after a summit conference in Moscow held in a vain attempt to prop up the central government headed by Mikhail Gorbachev, Mr. Bush went to Kiev, capital of the Ukraine. In an address that some of us came to derogate as his "Chicken Kiev speech", the President tossed a sopping-wet blanket over the aims of Ukrainian nationalists. He disheartened disunionist leaders from Kazakhstan to the Baltic States. Seizing on the rioting by extremist ethnics and nationalists in some areas to besmear all separatist movements, Mr. Bush told an audience of Ukrainians eager for freedom from Russian domination: "Americans will not aid those who promote a suicidal nationalism based on ethnic hatred."

That was artful, in that word's sense of "sly"; nobody wants "suicidal" nationalism, least of all a nationalism based on "ethnic hatred". But by not specifying the other kind of nationalism—vital rather than suicidal, based on cultural identity, common language, and historic bonds—Mr. Bush made common cause with Communist apparatchiks and Gorbachevites in Moscow resisting the pulling away of parts of the Soviet empire. Within a month, the KGB leaders and old Communists staged their abortive coup and the entire totalitarian structure—internal empire, rotted economic system, statuary, icons, and all—was swept aside by the Yeltsin countercoup. Reformers rode the despised nationalism of the unnatural union's constituent republics to a degree of freedom.

The United States President could have made a respectable strategic case for America's interest in a continuing Soviet Union, stressing the nuclear danger in any upheaval; some of us made the opposite geopolitical case for our interest in a broken-up, loosely confederated group of the former Soviet republics with no pretensions of superpower. But both arguments pale in the light of the moral imperative of national self-determination.

Mr. Bush, troubled by a politically potent outcry from Americans of Ukrainian descent living in New Jersey, soon reversed himself. But he never quite grasped the magnitude of his misreading of history: It was not the place of the leader of the world's foremost democracy, with its symbol a woman holding aloft the beacon of liberty, to be espousing stability and the status quo to people awakening to the new possibilities of national and cultural self-expression. But Mr. Bush persisted in labeling his dream "the New World Order", thus establishing his priority of countering the threat of anarchy, not the danger of reversion to totalitarianism.

Here is a paradox: What enables basic change to take place peacefully is not the inviolability of order but the possibility of conflict. We all hasten to articulate our preference for nonviolent change, but in the end it is the credible threat of an uprising (supported, or at least not wholly opposed, by elements of the army) that breaks the center's shackles. The outcome may be short of independence; on the Jordan River's west bank, for example, a shared sovereignty through a system of cantons federated with Jordan seems to me to be the peaceful route to Palestinian self-rule and Israeli security.

But for an American President to have actively discouraged self-determination by maligning its motive as "ethnic hatred" and characterizing its hopes as "suicidal" was an anathema. He could have expressed his concern about the central control of nuclear weaponry without seeming to align American foreign policy with that of George III or Ivan the Terrible.

Jobans want the center to hold only when its order is accompanied by justice. Whenever any free leader urges unfree people to be patient, or for the most compassionate of reasons discourages anguished patriots from seizing their moral moment, that leader is refuted by Job, as the man in despair searched for the succor in any glimmer of hope: "What strength have I to endure? What prospects to bolster my spirit?"[20] (I can hear words like those in the voice of Mulla Mustapha al-Barzani.) Job demonstrated that the strength to endure grows out of the will to insist on personal integrity; the prospect to bolster political Man's spirit is the vision of freedom and justice in a country of his own.

### 8. Make higher laws.

Two guys are lined up against a wall in front of a firing squad. One starts to protest and the other whispers to him, "Don't make trouble."

Those are diametrically different ways of looking at the universe. People can be divided into troublemakers and trouble averters, those who make waves and those who pour oil on wavy waters, the governed who will risk chaos to gain freedom and the governed who will risk totalitarianism to achieve stability. In an age that celebrates ambiguity—where some of us are of two minds about using a word like ambivalence—fear of being simplistic too often steers us away from the simple. But the simple truth is that all of us lean one way or the other—toward moral rebellion or submission.

When does a dissident put his conscience above the law? Poet-Job has a few answers: when the matter is not trivial, but about a bedrock principle; when nobody else seems to give a damn about innocent suffering; when disobedience noisily proclaimed will call attention to injustice; and when the objector is prepared to suffer the law's effect to dramatize the need to change the law.

The moral rebel knows that appealing to a "higher law" is rarely successful at the start. New York Governor William Seward's antislavery stance cost him the Republican nomination in 1860 to Abraham Lincoln, who stayed within the nation's written law when it came to abolition of slavery in the states where it already existed. Seward and the abolitionists were right to insist that a higher, or moral, or natural, law existed; the denial of that higher law led to what Seward impolitically called an "irrepressible conflict" with those slaveholders who refused to change the constitutional covenant that had formed the nation.

"And the war came," as Lincoln wrote in his most mournful sentence, in the cadence of Job's lament "Yet trouble came".[21] And the higher law of human rights prevailed; the Thirteenth Amendment adjusted the compact to conform lower law to higher.

If the Book of Job reaches across two and half millennia to teach anything to men and women who consider themselves normal, decent human beings, it is this: Human beings are sure to wander in ignorance and to fall into error, and it is better—more righteous in the eyes of God—for them to react by questioning rather than accepting. Confronted with inexplicable injustice, it is better to be irate than resigned. Job would not be intimidated or silenced until his God permitted him to see—to understand—how much he did not yet know. Only then did he submit, and it may have been too soon. Job teaches that it is for each person who assigns his portion of sovereignty to a higher authority, spiritual or temporal, to renegotiate the terms of submission so that we can see beyond our present ken.

The Joban interrogative—"why do the innocent suffer?"—was never a helpless plea of anguish. On the contrary, it generated the political dynamic that we have seen make changes in the here and now.

The tectonic shift in global politics leading to the collapse of communism was no accident of history, no gift from Gorbachev, or American triumph in an arms race. The first rumblings can be traced to the seemingly futile resistance of refuseniks who dramatized the effect of tyranny's injustice. These modern Jobans joined with political dissidents in other parts of the Gulag to bear witness to innocent suffering, which penetrated prison walls and pricked the conscience of people in their republics and the world.

The tiny caper plant was feared and banned in the old walled city of Dubrovnik because it grows in the crevices of rocks and has been known to break down the strongest wall. This generation's dissidents, with no power but their burning sense of injustice and yearning to be free, began the process of breaking apart the Communist monolith. When economic weakness forced the state to restructure some of its institutions, one condition of improvement was the increased freedom of the Soviet Jobans; they then seized the moment to strike their blow for freedom. As a result, despotism was not patched up by Communist reformers and allowed to regain its strength; instead, the whole rotten system was set aside, placed in what the old Bolsheviks called history's dustbin, and the captive nations of the empire were released. It all seems so inexorable in retrospect, but the internal Joban force struggling for freedom had to be in place, and in public view, to take advantage of despotic weakness.

The dissidents were superseded by pragmatic politicians, who will surely generate their own dissidents. But it was the sons and daughters of the man from Uz, winners of peace prizes or losers who lie in unknown graves—free spirits who braved isolation and pain for daring to curse the bad days—who carried Job's quest for morality and understanding into the third millennium.

# CONCLUSION:

# THE SPARKS
# FLY UPWARD

WRITING A BRIEF polemic, which is my calling and makes my living, helps the writer refine his thinking as he marshals his arguments and sets them marching off into print. But such political essays are more presentation than creation, a product of mind-set over matter; if it's a good piece, with some fresh information or a new slant, it helps the reader more than the writer.

A book, especially one that has been kicking around in the writer's head for a long time, is something else. The result of mental marination, of extended noodling around, it helps the writer at least as much as the reader. If the author is fortunate, he does not write the book he sets out to write. The work rips up its own outline and—though no book writes itself—affects a sea change, or at least a good half-sour pickling, in its author. The writer is not the prisoner of past positions in a format lockup. He has the time and room—that is to say, the freedom—to create a new arrangement in his head. He makes the marinade, the marinade remakes him.

I set out to write an angry book about an unfair God and a badly used man, presuming to write a wicked book so that I, like Melville, could feel as spotless as the lamb. To identify with Job—

more than that, to feel the surge of rage in a relatively innocent man that rattles the gates of heaven—was to align myself with the age of dissidence and, in a folk saying whose coiner has long eluded me, to strike a blow for freedom. To justify the expression of moral outrage, to elevate the underdog, to point a finger at the menacing hand, to dare, to dare, *toujours l'audace*—that was the romantic pose that attracted me, as it has so many others, to Job.

The timing seemed so right for such an enterprise. The rigid authority known as communism was in its death throes. The dissidents suffering in the world's Gulags were at last getting the recognition they deserved as the heroes of our time. Tyrants from Beijing to Havana sleep more uneasily than ever.

When the room fills with iconoclasts, however, I am overwhelmed by the urge to preach a new conformity. "Voguish iconoclasm" is an oxymoron, a jarring juxtaposition of opposites. But while so many of us discover the pleasure and profit in being contrarian, we have to ask ourselves: How can a crowd stand out from the crowd? Is our inclination to go against the grain driven by some profound purpose, or by a fashionable orneriness masquerading as a philosophy?

We know that the numbing misreading of the Book of Job as a paean to patience—"though he slay me, yet will I trust in him"— was a latter-day myth used to conceal the insurrection ignited by the clash of tradition with experience. Is the facile interpretation by artists and novelists today, of Job as patron saint of rebels, also a myth?

I have given this a book-writer's amount of thought and I think not. The dissidential mind pulls back at any trendy deification of defiance. Jobans do not go with any flow, even one that exalts dissent and condemns obedience. Just as thoughtless reverence is a mistake, so is its opposite—the avid identification with permissible heresy, topped with the residual popularity of the alienation of a generation ago.

The Job I found in working with him and his friends and interpreters for the past few years is neither the happy-ending patriarch of comfort-seeking religionists nor the archetypal sorehead of congenital rebels. He is a force for freedom within a stretchable framework of order. He is an autonomous power who strikes a balance with his chosen authority. Today's authentic Jobans as well as wannabe Jobans are complex, devious, hotheaded, original, stubborn, sentimental, appealing—in a word, human.

What of the summonable Almighty, the God of poet-Job's vision? He is troubled, overworked, more powerful than Leviathan but too shrewd to be all-powerful, willing to take a chance, in need of support from his creations—in a few words, not so superhuman as to be unapproachable.

In my political reading, the Book of Job sanctifies defiance of unjust authority. It enshrines dissent and demands moral self-reliance. Finally, this sore thumb sticking out of the Bible ennobles the admission of ignorance—and rewards that admission with a promise of ken to come. Poet-Job, in creating likenesses that are adversaries, has struck his imperishable balance. His work reaches across the ages to invite the rest of us to do the same for ourselves.

As it dawned on moralists that suffering is not evidence of sin, it later struck economists that prosperity is not proof of virtue, and now it must be impressed on leaders that political success is no verdict of wisdom. No wonder the individualist voice out of the muddle—Job's nagging, insistent challenge—is heard more clearly today. You can't keep a good idea down.

I started my journey into this book with doubt in my faith and have come out with faith in my doubt. (That's one of those turn-around sentences, an old speechwriter's trick to pull profundity out of a hat, but in this case it has the added advantage of compressing a mawkish personal chapter into a line.) To at least one of his modern followers, Job helps reaffirm faith in the engagement of God as well as the need for political allegiance—so long as God and the nation respect my right to damn the day that I was born.

Authority is fine until it starts getting authoritarian. As it loosens constraints, lightens up, and lets its sovereign vassals have the freedom to gain more knowledge, we questioners are less likely to darken counsel with words without wisdom.

The Book of Job stimulates irreverence but not disbelief. Poet-Job makes the case, in his favored legal metaphor, for the citizen's treatment of Authority as a covenantal equal: feeling free to dispute its judgment, not obligated to regret past or present doubts. And poet-Job makes the case for paradox, the creative contradiction that must have something to do with the way the universe stays in balance.

The counterpointing finger writes messages moral, spiritual, and political:

Job's moral message is that here on earth, in the distribution of justice and fairness, retribution and reward, humanity is on its own.

Job's spiritual message, contrariwise, offers the greatest form of solace and source of strength: No matter how solitary the confinement, the individual human being is not alone in the universe.

Job's political message is a paradigm of those paradoxes: Man's God leans toward order, God's Man leans toward chaos, and the tension in that eternal tug-of-war generates the energy of freedom.

# CREDITS

"OF THE MAKING of many books there is no end," declared an ancient sage, perhaps suffering from eyestrain. This is particularly true of the making of books about the Book of Job, which has generated an extensive library of literature explicating, praising, denouncing, and retranslating the controversial work.

The best modern introduction to Job for the general reader is *The Book of God and Man: A Study of Job* by Robert Gordis (University of Chicago Press, 1965; Phoenix Edition, paperback, 1978). Rabbi Gordis taught at the Jewish Theological Seminary in New York, which published his much more specialized commentary, translation, and special studies of Job in 1978. Also for the general reader, but now out of print, is *The Dimensions of Job,* a selection of readings edited by Nahum N. Glatzer (Schocken Books, New York, 1969).

The Anchor Bible's translation of the Book of Job by Marvin H. Pope was first published in 1965, and its lengthy introduction and notes have been revised twice to reflect recent discoveries of ancient texts. In 1985, J. Gerald Janzen wrote *Job (Interpretation: a Bible Commentary for Teaching and Preaching)* (John Knox

Press, Atlanta); in that year, Norman C. Habel wrote *The Book of Job* for The Old Testament Library (The Westminster Press, Philadelphia), a translation with an exegesis almost as detailed as that of Rabbi Gordis.

The liveliest and most iconoclastic analysis of the Book of Job as both a literary and religious work is Edwin M. Good's *In Turns of Tempest: A Reading of Job with Translation* (Stanford University Press, 1990). He takes the reader inside the translating process and is not ashamed of his deconstructionism. Professor Good's bibliography of books in many languages about the Book of Job, on pages 445–65, is the most recent and exhaustive survey of the commentary, absolving me from the need to go into greater detail here.

The most insightful short article on Job that I found was Matitiahu Tsevat's "The Meaning of the Book of Job" in Volume 37 of the *Hebrew Union College Annual* (Cincinnati, 1966). In *A Literary Guide to the Bible* (Alter, Kermode, eds., Belknap-Harvard, Cambridge, 1987), pp. 283–304, Moshe Greenberg provides an excellent review of the work as a literary masterpiece.

In my own work, thanks go to Nancy Evans, who first saw the potential in a book about the political lessons of Job when she was editor-in-chief at Doubleday. Professor Jacob Neusner, of the Institute for Advanced Study at Princeton and now at the University of South Florida, is the most prolific and far-ranging Talmudic scholar at work in Judaic studies today, but he found time to give me his active encouragement. At Random House, an orphan manuscript found its Rachel: Executive editor Kate Medina's conceptual, detailed, and inspired editing motivated the author to reshape a treatise into a book.

# INDEX OF
# BIBLICAL CITATIONS

# APPENDIX

# THE BOOK OF JOB, NEW ENGLISH BIBLE TRANSLATION

# THE BOOK OF JOB

### *Prologue*

THERE LIVED IN the land of Uz a man of blameless and upright life 1
named Job, who feared God and set his face against wrongdoing.
He had seven sons and three daughters; and he owned seven thou- 2–3
sand sheep and three thousand camels, five hundred yoke of oxen
and five hundred asses, with a large number of slaves. Thus Job was
the greatest man in all the East.

Now his sons used to foregather and give, each in turn, a feast 4
in his own house; and they used to send and invite their three sisters
to eat and drink with them. Then, when a round of feasts was 5
finished, Job sent for his children and sanctified them, rising early
in the morning and sacrificing a whole-offering for each of them; for
he thought that they might somehow have sinned against God and
committed blasphemy in their hearts. This he always did.

The day came when the members of the court of heaven took 6
their places in the presence of the LORD, and Satan*a* was there

---

*aOr* the adversary.

7 among them. The LORD asked him where he had been. 'Ranging
8 over the earth', he said, 'from end to end.' Then the LORD asked
Satan, 'Have you considered my servant Job? You will find no one
like him on earth, a man of blameless and upright life, who fears
9 God and sets his face against wrongdoing.' Satan answered the
10 LORD, 'Has not Job good reason to be God-fearing? Have you not
hedged him round on every side with your protection, him and his
family and all his possessions? Whatever he does you have blessed,
11 and his herds have increased beyond measure. But stretch out your
hand and touch all that he has, and then he will curse you to your
12 face.' Then the LORD said to Satan, 'So be it. All that he has is in
your hands; only Job himself you must not touch.' And Satan left
the LORD's presence.

13     When the day came that Job's sons and daughters were eating
14 and drinking in the eldest brother's house, a messenger came running to Job and said, 'The oxen were ploughing and the asses were
15 grazing near them, when the Sabaeans swooped down and carried
them off, after putting the herdsmen to the sword; and I am the only
16 one to escape and tell the tale.' While he was still speaking, another
messenger arrived and said, 'God's fire flashed from heaven. It
struck the sheep and the shepherds and burnt them up; and I am the
17 only one to escape and tell the tale.' While he was still speaking,
another arrived and said, 'The Chaldaeans, three bands of them,
have made a raid on the camels and carried them off, after putting
the drivers to the sword; and I am the only one to escape and tell
18 the tale.' While this man was speaking, yet another arrived and
said, 'Your sons and daughters were eating and drinking in the
19 eldest brother's house, when suddenly a whirlwind swept across
from the desert and struck the four corners of the house, and it fell
on the young people and killed them; and I am the only one to
20 escape and tell the tale.' At this Job stood up and rent his cloak;
21 then he shaved his head and fell prostrate on the ground, saying:

> *Naked I came from the womb,*
> *naked I shall return whence I came.*
> *The LORD gives and the LORD takes away;*
> *blessed be the name of the LORD.*

Throughout all this Job did not sin; he did not charge God with 22
unreason.

Once again the day came when the members of the court of 2
heaven took their places in the presence of the LORD, and Satan was
there among them. The LORD asked him where he had been. 'Rang- 2
ing over the earth', he said, 'from end to end.' Then the LORD asked 3
Satan, 'Have you considered my servant Job? You will find no one
like him on earth, a man of blameless and upright life, who fears
God and sets his face against wrongdoing. You incited me to ruin
him without a cause, but his integrity is still unshaken.' Satan 4
answered the LORD, 'Skin for skin! There is nothing the man will
grudge to save himself. But stretch out your hand and touch his 5
bone and his flesh, and see if he will not curse you to your face.'

Then the LORD said to Satan, 'So be it. He is in your hands; but 6
spare his life.' And Satan left the LORD's presence, and he smote Job 7
with running sores from head to foot, so that he took a piece of a 8
broken pot to scratch himself as he sat among the ashes. Then his 9
wife said to him, 'Are you still unshaken in your integrity? Curse
God and die!' But he answered, 'You talk as any wicked fool of a 10
woman might talk. If we accept good from God, shall we not accept
evil?' Throughout all this, Job did not utter one sinful word.

When Job's three friends, Eliphaz of Teman, Bildad of Shuah, 11
and Zophar of Naamah, heard of all these calamities which had
overtaken him, they left their homes and arranged to come and
condole with him and comfort him. But when they first saw him 12
from a distance, they did not recognize him; and they wept aloud,
rent their cloaks and tossed dust into the air over their heads. For 13
seven days and seven nights they sat beside him on the ground, and
none of them said a word to him; for they saw that his suffering was
very great.

### *Job's complaint to God*

After this Job broke silence and cursed the day of his birth: 3 1–2

Perish the day when I was born 3
and the night which said, 'A man is conceived'!
May that day turn to darkness; may God above not look for it, 4
nor light of dawn shine on it.

5   May blackness sully it, and murk and gloom,
    cloud smother that day, swift darkness eclipse its sun.
6   Blind darkness swallow up that night;
    count it not among the days of the year,
    reckon it not in the cycle of the months.
7   That night, may it be barren for ever,
    no cry of joy be heard in it.
8   Cursed be it by those whose magic binds even the monster of the deep,
    who are ready to tame Leviathan himself with spells.
9   May no star shine out in its twilight;
    may it wait for a dawn that never comes,
    nor ever see the eyelids of the morning,
10  because it did not shut the doors of the womb that bore me
    and keep trouble away from my sight.
11  Why was I not still-born,
    why did I not die when I came out of the womb?
12  Why was I ever laid on my mother's knees
    or put to suck at her breasts?
16  Why was I not hidden like an untimely birth,
    like an infant that has not lived to see the light?
13  For then I should be lying in the quiet grave,
    asleep in death, at rest,
14  with kings and their ministers
    who built themselves palaces,
15  with princes rich in gold
    who filled their houses with silver.
17[a] There the wicked man chafes no more,
    there the tired labourer rests;
18  the captive too finds peace there
    and hears no taskmaster's voice;
19  high and low are there,
    even the slave, free from his master.

20  Why should the sufferer be born to see the light?
    Why is life given to men who find it so bitter?
21  They wait for death but it does not come,
    they seek it more eagerly than[b] hidden treasure.
22  They are glad when they reach the tomb,
    and when they come to the grave they exult.
23  Why should a man be born to wander blindly,

---

[a] *Verse 16 transposed to follow verse 12.*
[b] *Or* seek it among . . .

hedged in by God on every side?
My sighing is all my food,                                          24
and groans pour from me in a torrent.
Every terror that haunted me has caught up with me,                 25
and all that I feared has come upon me.
There is no peace of mind nor quiet for me;                         26
I chafe in torment and have no rest.

## First cycle of speeches

Then Eliphaz the Temanite began:                                    4

If one ventures to speak with you, will you lose patience?          2
For who could hold his tongue any longer?
Think how once you encouraged those who faltered,                   3
how you braced feeble arms,
how a word from you upheld the stumblers                            4
and put strength into weak knees.
But now that adversity comes upon you, you lose patience;           5
it touches you, and you are unmanned.
Is your religion no comfort to you?                                 6
Does your blameless life give you no hope?
For consider, what innocent man has ever perished?                 7
Where have you seen the upright destroyed?
This I know, that those who plough mischief and sow trouble         8
reap as they have sown;
they perish at the blast of God                                    9
and are shrivelled by the breath of his nostrils.

The roar of the lion, the whimpering of his cubs, fall silent;     10
the teeth of the young lions are broken;
the lion perishes for lack of prey                                 11
and the whelps of the lioness are abandoned.

A word stole into my ears,                                         12
and they caught the whisper of it;
in the anxious visions of the night,                               13
when a man sinks into deepest sleep,
terror seized me and shuddering;                                   14
the trembling of my body frightened me.
A wind brushed my face                                             15
and made the hairs bristle on my flesh;

16    and a figure stood there whose shape I could not discern,
      an apparition loomed before me,
      and I heard the sound of a low voice:
17    'Can mortal man be more righteous than God,
      or the creature purer than his Maker?
18    If God mistrusts his own servants
      and finds his messengers at fault,
19    how much more those that dwell in houses whose walls are clay,
      whose foundations are dust,
      which can be crushed like a bird's nest
20    or torn down between dawn and dark,
      how much more shall such men perish outright and unheeded,
21    *a*die, without ever finding wisdom?'

5     Call if you will; is there any to answer you?
      To which of the holy ones will you turn?
2     The fool is destroyed by his own angry passions,
      and the end of childish resentment is death.
3     I have seen it for myself: a fool uprooted,
      his home in sudden ruin about him,*b*
4     his children past help,
      browbeaten in court with none to save them.
5     *c*Their rich possessions are snatched from them;
      what they have harvested others hungrily devour;
      the stronger man seizes it from the panniers,
      panting, thirsting for their wealth.
6     Mischief does not grow out of the soil
      nor trouble spring from the earth;
7     man is born to trouble,
      as surely as birds fly*d* upwards.

8     For my part, I would make my petition to God
      and lay my cause before him,
9     who does great and unsearchable things,
      marvels without number.
10    He gives rain to the earth
      and sends water on the fields;
11    he raises the lowly to the heights,
      the mourners are uplifted by victory;

*a*Prob. rdg.; transposing Their rich possessions are snatched from them *to follow 5. 4.*
*b*ruin about him: *prob. rdg.; Heb. obscure.*
*c*Line transposed from 4.21.
*d*Or as sparks shoot.

he frustrates the plots of the crafty,                                12
and they win no success,
he traps the cunning in their craftiness,                             13
and the schemers' plans are thrown into confusion.
In the daylight they run into darkness,                               14
and grope at midday as though it were night.
He saves the destitute from their greed,                              15
and the needy from the grip of the strong;
so the poor hope again,                                               16
and the unjust are sickened.

Happy the man whom God rebukes!                                       17
therefore do not reject the discipline of the Almighty.
For, though he wounds, he will bind up;                               18
the hands that smite will heal.
You may meet disaster six times, and he will save you;               19
seven times, and no harm shall touch you.
In time of famine he will save you from death,                       20
in battle from the sword.
You will be shielded from the lash of slander,*a*                    21
and when violence comes you need not fear.
You will laugh at violence and starvation                            22
and have no need to fear wild beasts;
for you have a covenant with the stones to spare your fields,        23
and the weeds have been constrained to leave you at peace.
You will know that all is well with your household,                  24
you will look round your home and find nothing amiss;
you will know, too, that your descendants will be many               25
and your offspring like grass, thick upon the earth.
You will come in sturdy old age to the grave                         26
as sheaves come in due season to the threshing-floor.

We have inquired into all this, and so it is;                        27
this we have heard, and you may know it for the truth.

Then Job answered:                                                   6

O that the grounds for my resentment might be weighed,               2
and my misfortunes set with them on the scales!
For they would outweigh the sands of the sea:                        3
what wonder if my words are wild?*b*

*a*from . . . slander: *or* when slander is rife.
*b*what . . . wild?: *or* therefore words fail me.

4 The arrows of the Almighty find their mark in me,
and their poison soaks into my spirit;
God's onslaughts wear me away.

5 Does the wild ass bray when he has grass
or the ox low when he has fodder?

6 Can a man eat tasteless food unseasoned with salt,
or find any flavour in the juice of mallows?

7 Food that should nourish me sticks in my throat,
and my bowels rumble with an echoing sound.

8 O that I might have my request,
that God would grant what I hope for:

9 that he would be pleased to crush me,
to snatch me away with his hand and cut me off!

10 For that would bring me relief,
and in the face of unsparing anguish I would leap for joy.[a]

11 Have I the strength to wait?
What end have I to expect, that I should be patient?

12 Is my strength the strength of stone,
or is my flesh bronze?

13 Oh how shall I find help within myself?
The power to aid myself is put out of my reach.

14 Devotion is due from his friends
to one who despairs and loses faith in the Almighty;

15 but my brothers have been treacherous as a mountain stream,
like the channels of streams that run dry,

16 which turn dark with ice
or are hidden with piled-up snow;

17 or they vanish the moment they are in spate,
dwindle in the heat and are gone.

18 Then the caravans, winding hither and thither,
go up into the wilderness and perish;[b]

19 the caravans of Tema look for their waters,
travelling merchants of Sheba hope for them;

20 but they are disappointed, for all their confidence,
they reach them only to be balked.

21 So treacherous have you now been to me:[c]
you felt dismay and were afraid.

22 Did I ever say, 'Give me this or that;

[a] *Prob. rdg.; Heb. adds* I have not denied the words of the Holy One.
[b] *Or* and are lost.
[c] *So . . . to me: prob. rdg.; Heb. obscure.*

open your purses to save my life;
rescue me from my enemy;                                          23
ransom me out of the hands of ruthless men'?

Tell me plainly, and I will listen in silence;                   24
show me where I have erred.
How harsh are the words of the upright man!                      25
What do the arguments of wise men*a* prove?
Do you mean to argue about words                                 26
or to sift the utterance of a man past hope?
Would you assail an orphan*b*?                                    27
Would you hurl yourselves on a friend?
So now, I beg you, turn and look at me:                           28
am I likely to lie to your faces?
Think again, let me have no more injustice;                      29
think again, for my integrity is in question.
Do I ever give voice to injustice?                               30
Does my sense not warn me when my words are wild?

Has not man hard service on earth,                                7
and are not his days like those of a hired labourer,
like those of a slave longing for the shade                       2
or a servant kept waiting for his wages?
So months of futility are my portion,                             3
troubled nights are my lot.
When I lie down, I think,                                          4
'When will it be day that I may rise?'
When the evening grows long and I lie down,
I do nothing but toss till morning twilight.
My body is infested with worms,                                   5
and scabs cover my skin.*c*
My days are swifter than a shuttle*d*
and come to an end as the thread runs out.*e*
Remember, my life is but a breath of wind;                        7
I shall never again see good days.
Thou wilt behold me no more with a seeing eye;                    8
under thy very eyes I shall disappear.
As clouds break up and disperse,                                  9
so he that goes down to Sheol never comes back;

*a*wise men: *prob. rdg.; Heb. unintelligible.*
*b*Or *a blameless man.*
*c*Prob. rdg.; Heb. adds *it is cracked and discharging.*
*d*Or *a fleeting odour.*
*e*as . . . out: *or without hope.*

10    he never returns home again,
and his place will know him no more.[a]

11    But I will not hold my peace;
I will speak out in the distress of my mind
and complain in the bitterness of my soul.

12    Am I the monster of the deep, am I the sea-serpent,
that thou settest a watch over me?

13    When I think that my bed will comfort me,
that sleep will relieve my complaining,

14    thou dost terrify me with dreams
and affright me with visions.

15    I would rather be choked outright;
I would prefer death to all my sufferings.

16    I am in despair, I would not go on living;
leave me alone, for my life is but a vapour.

17    What is man that thou makest much of him
and turnest thy thoughts towards him,

18    only to punish him morning by morning
or to test him every hour of the day?

19    Wilt thou not look away from me for an instant?
Wilt thou not let me be while I swallow my spittle?

20    If I have sinned, how do I injure thee,
thou watcher of the hearts of men?
Why hast thou made me thy butt,
and why have I become thy target?

21    Why dost thou not pardon my offence
and take away my guilt?
But now I shall lie down in the grave;
seek me, and I shall not be.

8    Then Bildad the Shuhite began:

2    How long will you say such things,
the long-winded ramblings of an old man?

3    Does God pervert judgement?
Does the Almighty pervert justice?

4    Your sons sinned against him,
so he left them to be victims of their own iniquity.

5    If only you will seek God betimes
and plead for the favour of the Almighty,

6    if you are innocent and upright,
then indeed will he watch over you

[a] *Or* and he will not be noticed any more in his place.

and see your just intent fulfilled.
Then, though your beginnings were humble,      7
your end will be great.

Inquire now of older generations      8
and consider the experience of their fathers;
for we ourselves are of yesterday and are transient;      9
our days on earth are a shadow.
Will not they speak to you and teach you      10
and pour out the wisdom of their hearts?
Can rushes grow where there is no marsh?      11
Can reeds flourish without water?
While they are still in flower and not ready to cut,*a*      12
they wither earlier than*b* any green plant.
Such is the fate of all who forget God;      13
the godless man's life-thread breaks off;
his confidence is gossamer,      14
and the ground of his trust a spider's web.
He leans against his house but it does not stand;      15
he clutches at it but it does not hold firm.
His is the lush growth of a plant in the sun,      16
pushing out shoots over the garden;
but its roots become entangled in a stony patch      17
and run against a bed of rock.
Then someone uproots it from its place,      18
which*c* disowns it and says, 'I have never known you.'
That is how its life withers away,      19
and other plants spring up from the earth.

Be sure, God will not spurn the blameless man,      20
nor will he grasp the hand of the wrongdoer.
He will yet fill your mouth with laughter,      21
and shouts of joy will be on your lips;
your enemies shall be wrapped in confusion,      22
and the tents of the wicked shall vanish away.

Then Job answered:      **9**

Indeed this I know for the truth,      2
that no man can win his case against God.
If a man chooses to argue with him,      3

*a*and . . . cut: *or* they are surely cut.
*bOr* wither like . . .
*cOr* and.

God will not answer one question in a thousand.*ᵃ*

4   He is wise, he is powerful;
    what man has stubbornly resisted him and survived?

5   It is God who moves mountains, giving them no rest,
    turning them over in his wrath;

6   who makes the earth start from its place
    so that its pillars are convulsed;

7   who commands the sun's orb not to rise
    and shuts up the stars under his seal;

8   who by himself spread out the heavens
    and trod on the sea-monster's back;*ᵇ*

9   who made Aldebaran and Orion,
    the Pleiades and the circle of the southern stars;

10  who does great and unsearchable things,
    marvels without number.

11  He passes by me, and I do not see him;
    he moves on his way undiscerned by me;

12  if he hurries on, who can bring him back?
    Who will ask him what he does?

13  God does not turn back his wrath;
    the partisans of Rahab lie prostrate at his feet.

14  How much less can I answer him
    or find words to dispute with him?

15  Though I am right, I get no answer,
    though I plead with my accuser for mercy.

16  If I summoned him to court and he responded,
    I do not believe that he would listen to my plea—

17  for he bears hard upon me for a trifle
    and rains blows on me without cause;

18  he leaves me no respite to recover my breath
    but fills me with bitter thoughts.

19  If the appeal is to force, see how strong he is;
    if to justice, who can compel him to give me a hearing?

20  Though I am right, he condemns me out of my own mouth;
    though I am blameless, he twists my words.

21  Blameless, I say; of myself
    I reck nothing, I hold my life cheap.

22  But it is all one; therefore I say,
    'He destroys blameless and wicked alike.'

*ᵃ*If a man ... thousand: *or* If God is pleased to argue with him, man cannot answer one quest
a thousand.
*ᵇOr* on the crests of the waves.

When a sudden flood brings death, 23
he mocks the plight of the innocent.
The land is given over to the power of the wicked, 24
and the eyes of its judges are blindfold.<sup>a</sup>

My days have been swifter than a runner, 25
they have slipped away and seen no prosperity;
they have raced by like reed-built skiffs, 26
swift as vultures swooping on carrion.
If I think, 'I will forget my griefs, 27
I will show a cheerful face and smile',
I tremble in every nerve;<sup>b</sup> 28
I know that thou wilt not hold me innocent.
If I am to be accounted guilty, 29
why do I labour in vain?
Though I wash myself with soap 30
or cleanse my hands with lye,
thou wilt thrust me into the mud 31
and my clothes will make me loathsome.

He is not a man as I am, that I can answer him 32
or that we can confront one another in court.
If only there were one to arbitrate between us 33
and impose his authority on us both,
so that God might take his rod from my back, 34
and terror of him might not come on me suddenly.
I would then speak without fear of him; 35
for I know I am not what I am thought to be.

I am sickened of life; **10**
I will give free rein to my griefs,
I will speak out in bitterness of soul.
I will say to God, 'Do not condemn me, 2
but tell me the ground of thy complaint against me.
Dost thou find any advantage in oppression, 3
in spurning the fruit of all thy labour
and smiling on the policy of wicked men?
Hast thou eyes of flesh 4
or dost thou see as mortal man sees?
Are thy days as those of a mortal 5
or thy years as the life of a man,

---

<sup>a</sup>*Prob. rdg.; Heb. adds* if not he, then who?
<sup>b</sup>*Or* I am afraid of all that I must suffer.

6   that thou lookest for guilt in me
     and dost seek in me for sin,

7   though thou knowest that I am guiltless
     and have none to save me from thee?

8   'Thy hands gave me shape and made me;
     and dost thou at once turn and destroy me?

9   Remember that thou didst knead me like clay;
     and wouldst thou turn me back into dust?

10  Didst thou not pour me out like milk
     and curdle me like cheese,

11  clothe me with skin and flesh
     and knit me together with bones and sinews?

12  Thou hast given me life and continuing favour,
     and thy providence has watched over my spirit.

13  Yet this was the secret purpose of thy heart,
     and I know that this was thy intent:

14  that, if I sinned, thou wouldst be watching me
     and wouldst not acquit me of my guilt.

15  If I indeed am wicked, the worse for me!
     If I am righteous, even so I may lift up my head;[a]

16  if I am proud as a lion, thou dost hunt me down
     and dost confront me again with marvellous power;

17  thou dost renew thy onslaught upon me,
     and with mounting anger against me
     bringest fresh forces to the attack.

18  Why didst thou bring me out of the womb?
     O that I had ended there and no eye had seen me,

19  that I had been carried from the womb to the grave
     and were as though I had not been born.

20  Is not my life short and fleeting?
     Let me be, that I may be happy for a moment,

21  before I depart to a land of gloom,
     a land of deep darkness, never to return,

22  a land of gathering shadows, of deepening darkness,
     lit by no ray of light,[b] dark[c] upon dark.'

11  Then Zophar the Naamathite began:

2   Should this spate of words not be answered?
     Must a man of ready tongue be always right?

3   Is your endless talk to reduce men to silence?

[a] *Prob. rdg.; Heb. adds* filled with shame and steeped in my affliction.
[b] lit . . . light: *or* a place of disorder.
[c] *Prob. rdg.; Heb. obscure.*

Are you to talk nonsense and no one rebuke you?
You claim that your opinions are sound;                              4
you say to God, 'I am spotless in thy sight.'
But if only he would speak                                          5
and open his lips to talk with you,
and expound to you the secrets of wisdom,                           6
for wonderful are its effects!
[Know then that God exacts from you less than your sin deserves.]
Can you fathom the mystery of God,                                  7
can you fathom the perfection of the Almighty?
It is higher than heaven; you can do nothing.                       8
It is deeper than Sheol; you can know nothing.
Its measure is longer than the earth                                9
and broader than the sea.
If he passes by, he may keep secret his passing;                   10
if he proclaims it, who can turn him back?
He surely knows which men are false,                               11
and when he sees iniquity, does he not take note of it?*a*
Can a fool grow wise?                                               12
can a wild ass's foal be born a man?
If only you had directed your heart rightly                        13
and spread out your hands to pray to him!
If you have wrongdoing in hand, thrust it away;                    14
let no iniquity make its home with you.
Then you could hold up your head without fault,                    15
a man of iron, knowing no fear.
Then you will forget your trouble;                                  16
you will remember it only as flood-waters that have passed;
life will be lasting, bright as noonday,                           17
and darkness will be turned to morning.
You will be confident, because there is hope;                      18
sure of protection, you will lie down in confidence;*b*
great men will seek your favour.                                   19
Blindness will fall on the wicked;                                 20
the ways of escape are closed to them,
and their hope is despair.


Then Job answered:                                                 12

No doubt you are perfect men*c*                                     2
and absolute wisdom is yours!
But I have sense as well as you;                                    3

---

*a*does . . . of it?: *or* he does not stand aloof.
*b Prob. rdg.; Heb. adds* and you will lie down unafraid.
*c Prob. rdg.; Heb.* No doubt you are people.

in nothing do I fall short of you;
what gifts indeed have you that others have not?

4 Yet I am a laughing-stock to my friend—
a laughing-stock, though I am innocent and blameless,
one that called upon God, and he answered.*ᵃ*

5 Prosperity and ease look down on misfortune,
on the blow that fells the man who is already reeling,

6 while the marauders' tents are left undisturbed
and those who provoke God live safe and sound.*ᵇ*

7 Go and ask the cattle,
ask the birds of the air to inform you,

8 or tell the creatures that crawl to teach you,
and the fishes of the sea to give you instruction.

9 Who cannot learn from all these
that the LORD's own hand has done this?

11*ᶜ* (Does not the ear test what is spoken
as the palate savours food?

12 There is wisdom, remember, in age,
and long life brings understanding.)

10 In God's hand are the souls of all that live,
the spirits of all human kind.

13 Wisdom and might are his,
with him are firmness and understanding.

14 If he pulls down, there is no rebuilding;
if he imprisons, there is no release.

15 If he holds up the waters, there is drought;
if he lets them go, they turn the land upside down.

16 Strength and success belong to him,
deceived and deceiver are his to use.

17 He makes counsellors behave like idiots
and drives judges mad;

18 he looses the bonds imposed by kings
and removes the girdle of office from their waists;

19 he makes priests behave like idiots
and overthrows men long in office;

20 those who are trusted he strikes dumb,
he takes away the judgment of old men;

21 he heaps scorn on princes
and abates the arrogance of nobles.

23*ᵈ* He leads peoples astray and destroys them,

*ᵃOr* and he afflicted me.
*ᵇProb. rdg.; Heb.* adds He brings it in full measure to whom he will *(cp. 21.17).*
*ᶜVerse 10 transposed to follow verse 12.*
*ᵈVerse 22 transposed to follow verse 25.*

he lays them low, and there they lie.
He takes away their wisdom from the rulers of the nations　24
and leaves them wandering in a pathless wilderness;
they grope in the darkness without light　25
and are left to wander like a drunkard.
He uncovers mysteries deep in obscurity　22
and into thick darkness he brings light.

All this I have seen with my own eyes,　13
with my own ears I have heard it, and understood it.
What you know, I also know;　2
in nothing do I fall short of you.
But for my part I would speak with the Almighty　3
and am ready to argue with God,
while you like fools are smearing truth with your falsehoods,　4
stitching a patchwork of lies, one and all.
Ah, if you would only be silent　5
and let silence be your wisdom!
Now listen to my arguments　6
and attend while I put my case.
Is it on God's behalf that you speak so wickedly,　7
or in his defence that you allege what is false?
Must you take God's part,　8
or put his case for him?
Will all be well when he examines you?　9
Will you quibble with him as you quibble with a man?
He will most surely expose you　10
if you take his part by falsely accusing me.
Will not God's majesty strike you with dread,　11
and terror of him overwhelm you?
Your pompous talk is dust and ashes,　12
your defences will crumble like clay.
Be silent, leave me to speak my mind,　13
and let what may come upon me!
I will put my neck in the noose　14
and take my life in my hands.
If he would slay me, I should not hesitate;　15
I should still argue my cause to his face.
This at least assures my success,　16
that no godless man may appear before him.
Listen then, listen to my words,　17
and give a hearing to my exposition.
Be sure of this: once I have stated my case　18
I know that I shall be acquitted.
Who is there that can argue so forcibly with me　19
that he could reduce me straightway to silence and death?

20 Grant me these two conditions only,
and then I will not hide myself out of thy sight:
21 take thy heavy hand clean away from me
and let not the fear of thee strike me with dread.
22 Then summon me, and I will answer;
or I will speak first, and do thou answer me.
23 How many iniquities and sins are laid to my charge?
let me know my offences and my sin.
24 Why dost thou hide thy face
and treat me as thy enemy?
25 Wilt thou chase a driven leaf,
wilt thou pursue dry chaff,
26 prescribing punishment for me
and making me heir to the iniquities of my youth,
27 putting my feet in the stocks*a*
and setting a slave-mark on the arches of my feet?*b*

14 Man born of woman is short-lived and full of disquiet.
2 He blossoms like a flower and then he withers;
he slips away like a shadow and does not stay;
*c*he is like a wine-skin that perishes
or a garment that moths have eaten.
3 Dost thou fix thine eyes on such a creature,
and wilt thou bring him into court to confront thee?*d*
5 The days of his life are determined,
and the number of his months is known to thee;
thou hast laid down a limit, which he cannot pass.
6 Look away from him therefore and leave him alone
counting the hours day by day like a hired labourer.

7 If a tree is cut down,
there is hope that it will sprout again
and fresh shoots will not fail.
8 Though its roots grow old in the earth,
and its stump is dying in the ground,
9 if it scents water it may break into bud
and make new growth like a young plant.
10 But a man dies, and he disappears;*e*
man comes to his end, and where is he?
11 As the waters of a lake dwindle,
or as a river shrinks and runs dry,

*aProb. rdg.; Heb. adds* keeping a close watch on all I do.
*bProb. rdg.; Heb. adds verse 28,* he is like . . . have eaten, *now transposed to follow 14.2.*
*c*he is like . . . have eaten: *13.28 transposed here.*
*dSo one Heb. MS.; others add* (4) Who can produce pure out of unclean? No one.
*eOr* and is powerless.

so mortal man lies down, never to rise,                         12
until the very sky splits open.
If a man dies, can he live again?<sup>*a*</sup>
He shall never be roused from his sleep.
If only thou wouldst hide me in Sheol                           13
and conceal me till thy anger turns aside,
if thou wouldst fix a limit for my time there, and then remember me!
<sup>*b*</sup>Then I would not lose hope, however long my service,   14
waiting for my relief to come.
Thou wouldst summon me, and I would answer thee;               15
thou wouldst long to see the creature thou hast made.
But now thou dost count every step I take,                      16
watching all my course.
Every offence of mine is stored in thy bag;                     17
thou dost keep my iniquity under seal.
Yet as a falling mountain-side is swept away,                   18
and a rock is dislodged from its place,
as water wears away stones,                                     19
and a rain-storm scours the soil from the land,
so thou hast wiped out the hope of frail man;
thou dost overpower him finally, and he is gone;                20
his face is changed, and he is banished from thy sight.
His flesh upon him becomes black,                             22<sup>*c*</sup>
and his life-blood dries up within him.<sup>*d*</sup>
His sons rise to honour, and he sees nothing of it;            21
they sink into obscurity, and he knows it not.


## Second cycle of speeches


Then Eliphaz the Temanite answered:                             15

Would a man of sense give vent to such foolish notions          2
and answer with a bellyful of wind?
Would he bandy useless words                                    3
and arguments so unprofitable?
Why! you even banish the fear of God from your mind,            4
usurping the sole right to speak in his presence;
your iniquity dictates what you say,                            5
and deceit is the language of your choice.

<sup>*a*</sup>*Line transposed from beginning of verse 14.*
<sup>*b*</sup>*See note on verse 12.*
<sup>*c*</sup>*Verses 21 and 22 transposed.*
<sup>*d*</sup>His flesh . . . within him: *or* His own kin, maybe, regret him, and his slaves mourn his loss.

6  You are condemned out of your own mouth, not by me;
   your own lips give evidence against you.

7  Were you born first of mankind?
   were you brought forth before the hills?
8  Do you listen in God's secret council
   or usurp all wisdom for yourself alone?
9  What do you know that we do not know?
   What insight have you that we do not share?
10 We have age and white hairs in our company,
   men older than your father.
11 Does not the consolation of God suffice you,
   a word whispered quietly in your ear?
12 What makes you so bold at heart,
   and why do your eyes flash,
13 that you vent your anger on God
   and pour out such a torrent of words?
14 What is frail man that he should be innocent,
   or any child of woman that he should be justified?
15 If God puts no trust in his holy ones,
   and the heavens are not innocent in his sight,
16 how much less so is man, who is loathsome and rotten
   and laps up evil like water!

17 I will tell you, if only you will listen,
   and I will describe what I have seen
18 [what has been handed down by wise men
   and was not concealed from them by their fathers;
19 to them alone the land was given,
   and no foreigner settled among them]:
20 the wicked are racked with anxiety all their days,
   the ruthless man for all the years in store for him.
21 The noise of the hunter's scare rings in his ears,
   and in time of peace the raider falls on him;
22 he cannot hope to escape from dark death;
   he is marked down for the sword;
23 he is flung out as food for vultures;
   such a man knows that his destruction is certain.
24 Suddenly a black day comes upon him,
   distress and anxiety overwhelm him
   [like a king ready for battle];
25 for he has lifted his hand against God
   and is pitting himself against the Almighty,
26 charging him head down,
   with the full weight of his bossed shield.

Heavy though his jowl is and gross,                                27
and though his sides bulge with fat,
the city where he lives will lie in ruins,                        28
his house will be deserted;
it will soon become a heap of rubble.
He will no longer be rich, his wealth will not last,              29
and he will strike no root in the earth;*a*
scorching heat will shrivel his shoots,                           30
and his blossom will be shaken off by the wind.
He deceives himself, trusting in his high rank,                   31
for all his dealings will come to nothing.
His palm-trees will wither unseasonably,                          32
and his branches will not spread;
he will be like a vine that sheds its unripe grapes,              33
like an olive-tree that drops its blossom.
For the godless, one and all, are barren,                         34
and their homes, enriched by bribery, are destroyed by fire;
they conceive mischief and give birth to trouble,                 35
and the child of their womb is deceit.

Then Job answered:                                                16

I have heard such things often before,                            2
you who make trouble, all of you, with every breath,
saying, 'Will this windbag never have done?                       3
What makes him so stubborn in argument?'
If you and I were to change places,                               4
I could talk like you;
how I could harangue you
and wag my head at you!
But no, I would speak words of encouragement,                     5
and then my condolences would flow in streams.
If I speak, my pain is not eased;                                 6
if I am silent, it does not leave me.
Meanwhile, my friend wearies me with false sympathy;             7
they tear me to pieces, he and his*b* fellows.                    8
He has come forward to give evidence against me;
the liar testifies against me to my face,
in his wrath he wears me down, his hatred is plain to see;       9
he grinds his teeth at me.

My enemies look daggers at me,
they bare their teeth to rend me,                                 10

*a*Prob. rdg.; Heb. adds he will not escape from darkness.
*b*Prob. rdg.; Heb. my.

they slash my cheeks with knives;
they are all in league against me.

11 God has left me at the mercy of malefactors
and cast me into the clutches of wicked men.

12 I was at ease, but he set upon me and mauled me,
seized me by the neck and worried me.
He set me up as his target;

13 his arrows rained upon me from every side;
pitiless, he cut deep into my vitals,
he spilt my gall on the ground.

14 He made breach after breach in my defences;
he fell upon me like a fighting man.

15 I stitched sackcloth together to cover my body
and I buried my forelock in the dust;

16 my cheeks were flushed with weeping
and dark shadows were round my eyes,

17 yet my hands were free from violence
and my prayer was sincere.

18 O earth, cover not my blood
and let my cry for justice find no rest!

19 For look! my witness is in heaven;
there is one on high ready to answer for me.

20 My appeal will come before God,
while my eyes turn again and again to him.

21 If only there were one to arbitrate between man and God,
as between a man and his neighbour!

22 For there are but few years to come
before I take the road from which I shall not return.

17 My mind is distraught, my days are numbered,
and the grave is waiting for me.

2 Wherever I turn, men taunt me,
and my day is darkened by their sneers.

3 Be thou my surety with thyself,
for who else can pledge himself for me?

4 Thou wilt not let those men triumph,
whose minds thou hast sunk in ignorance;

5 if such a man denounces his friends to their ruin,
his sons' eyes shall grow dim.

6 I am held up as a byword in every land,
a portent for all to see;

my eyes are dim with grief,                                        7
my limbs wasted to a shadow.
Honest men are bewildered at this,                                 8
and the innocent are indignant at my plight.
In spite of all, the righteous man maintains his course,           9
and he whose hands are clean grows strong again.

But come on, one and all, try again!                              10
I shall not find a wise man among you.

My days die away like an echo;                                    11
my heart-strings*a* are snapped.
Day is turned into night,                                         12
and morning*b* light is darkened before me.
If I measure Sheol for my house,                                  13
if I spread my couch in the darkness,
if I call the grave my father                                     14
and the worm my mother or my sister,
where, then, will my hope be,                                     15
and who will take account of my piety?
I cannot take them down to Sheol with me,                         16
nor can they descend with me into the earth.

Then Bildad the Shuhite answered:                                 18

How soon will you bridle*c* your tongue?                            2
Do but think, and then we will talk.
What do you mean by treating us as cattle?                         3
Are we nothing but brute beasts to you?*d*
Is the earth to be deserted to prove you right,                    4
or the rocks to be moved from their place?

No, it is the wicked whose light is extinguished,                  5
from whose fire no flame will rekindle;
the light fades in his tent,                                       6
and his lamp dies down and fails him.
In his iniquity his steps totter,                                  7
and his disobedience trips him up;
he rushes headlong into a net                                      8
and steps through the hurdle that covers a pit;

*a Prob. rdg.; Heb.* the desires of my heart.
*b* morning: *prob. rdg.; Heb.* near.
*c* bridle: *prob. rdg.; Heb. unintelligible.* in his anger.
*d Prob. rdg.; Heb. adds* rending himself

9   his heel is caught in a snare,
    the noose grips him tight;
10  a cord lies hidden in the ground for him
    and a trap in the path.
11  The terrors of death suddenly beset him
    and make him piss over his feet.
12  For all his vigour he is paralysed with fear;
    strong as he is, disaster awaits him.
13  Disease eats away his skin,
    Death's eldest child devours his limbs.
14  He is torn from the safety of his home,
    and Death's terrors escort him to their king.[a]
15  Magic herbs lie strewn about his tent,
    and his home is sprinkled with sulphur to protect it.
16  His roots beneath dry up,
    and above, his branches wither.
17  His memory vanishes from the face of the earth
    and he leaves no name in the world.
18  He is driven from light into darkness
    and banished from the land of the living.
19  He leaves no issue or offspring among his people,
    no survivor in his earthly home;
20  in the west men hear of his doom and are appalled;
    in the east they shudder with horror.
21  Such is the fate of the dwellings of evildoers,
    and of the homes of those who care nothing for God.

19  Then Job answered:

2   How long will you exhaust me
    and pulverize me with words?
3   Time and time again you have insulted me
    and shamelessly done me wrong.
4   If in fact I had erred,
    the error would still be mine.
5   But if indeed you lord it over me
    and try to justify the reproaches levelled at me,
6   I tell you, God himself has put me in the wrong,
    he has drawn the net round me.
7   If I cry 'Murder!' no one answers;
    if I appeal for help, I get no justice.
8   He has walled in my path so that I cannot break away,
    and he has hedged in the road before me.

[a]*Or* and you conduct him to the king of terrors.

He has stripped me of all honour                                    9
and has taken the crown from my head.
On every side he beats me down and I am gone;                       10
he has pulled up my tent-rope<sup>a</sup> like a tree.
His anger is hot against me                                         11
and he counts me his enemy.
His raiders gather in force<sup>b</sup>                              12
and encamp about my tent.

My brothers hold aloof from me,                                     13
my friends are utterly estranged from me;
my kinsmen and intimates fall away,                                 14–15
my retainers have forgotten me;
my slave-girls treat me as a stranger,
I have become an alien in their eyes.
I summon my slave, but he does not answer,                          16
though I entreat him as a favour.
My breath is noisome to my wife,                                    17
and I stink in the nostrils of my own family.
Mere children despise me                                            18
and, when I rise, turn their backs on me;
my intimate companions loathe me,                                   19
and those whom I love have turned against me.
My bones stick out through my skin,<sup>c</sup>                     20
and I gnaw my under-lip with my teeth.

Pity me, pity me, you that are my friends;                          21
for the hand of God has touched me.
Why do you pursue me as God pursues me?                             22
Have you not had your teeth in me long enough?
O that my words might be inscribed,                                 23
O that they might be engraved in an inscription,
cut with an iron tool and filled with lead                          24
to be a witness<sup>d</sup> in hard rock!
But in my heart I know that my vindicator lives                     25
and that he will rise last to speak in court;
and I shall discern my witness standing at my side<sup>e</sup>      26
and see my defending counsel, even God himself,
whom I shall see with my own eyes,                                  27
I myself and no other.

<sup>a</sup>*Or* he has uprooted my hope.
<sup>b</sup>*Prob. rdg.; Heb. adds* they raise an earthwork against me.
<sup>c</sup>*Prob. rdg.; Heb. adds* and my flesh.
<sup>d</sup>to . . . witness: *or* for ever.
<sup>e</sup>my witness . . . side: *prob. rdg.; Heb. unintelligible.*

28    My heart failed me when you said,
      'What a train of disaster he has brought on himself!
      The root of the trouble lies in him.'
29    Beware of the sword that points at you,
      the sword that sweeps away all iniquity;
      then you will know that there is a judge.*a*

20    Then Zophar the Naamathite answered:

2     My distress of mind forces me to reply,
      and this is why*b* I hasten to speak:
3     I have heard arguments that are a reproach to me,
      a spirit beyond my understanding gives me the answers.
4     Surely you know that this has been so since time began,
      since man was first set on the earth:
5     the triumph of the wicked is short-lived,
      the glee of the godless lasts but a moment?
6     Though he stands high as heaven,
      and his head touches the clouds,
7     he will be swept utterly away like his own dung,
      and all that saw him will say, 'Where is he?'
8     He will fly away like a dream and be lost,
      driven off like a vision of the night;
9     the eye which glimpsed him shall do so no more
      and shall never again see him in his place.
11*c*  The youth and strength which filled his bones
      shall lie with him in the dust.
10    His sons will pay court to the poor,
      and their*d* hands will give back his wealth.
12    Though evil tastes sweet in his mouth,
      and he savours it, rolling it round his tongue,
13    though he lingers over it and will not let it go,
      and holds it back on his palate,
14    yet his food turns in his stomach,
      changing to asps' venom within him.
15    He gulps down wealth, then vomits it up,
      or God makes him discharge it.
16    He sucks the poison of asps,
      and the tongue of the viper kills him.

*a Or* judgement.
*b*this is why: *prob. rdg.; Heb. obscure.*
*c Verses 10 and 11 transposed.*
*d Prob. rdg.; Heb.* his.

Not for him to swill down rivers of cream*a*                 17
or torrents of honey and curds;
he must give back his gains without swallowing them,          18
and spew up his profit undigested;
for he has hounded and harassed the poor,                     19
he has seized houses which he did not build.
Because his appetite gave him no rest,                        20
and he cannot escape his own desires,
nothing is left for him to eat,                               21
and so his well-being does not last;
with every need satisfied his troubles begin,                22
and the full force of hardship strikes him.
God vents his anger upon him                                  23
and rains on him cruel blows.
He is wounded by weapons of iron                              24
and pierced by a bronze-tipped arrow;
out at his back the point comes,                              25
the gleaming tip from his gall-bladder.
Darkness unrelieved awaits him,                               26
a fire that needs no fanning will consume him.
[Woe betide any survivor in his tent!]
The heavens will lay bare his guilt,                          27
and earth will rise up to condemn him.
A flood will sweep away his house,                            28
rushing waters on the day of wrath.
Such is God's reward for the wicked man                       29
and the lot appointed for the rebel*b* by God.

Then Job answered:                                            21

Listen to me, do but listen,                                  2
and let that be the comfort you offer me.
Bear with me while I have my say;                             3
when I have finished, you may mock.
May not I too voice*c* my thoughts?                           4
Have not I as good cause to be impatient?
Look at my plight, and be aghast;                             5
clap your hand to your mouth.
When I stop to think, I am filled with horror,                6
and my whole body is convulsed.

*a*rivers of cream: *prob. rdg.; Heb. obscure.*
*b*the rebel: *prob. rdg.; Heb.* his word.
*c*May . . . voice: *prob. rdg.; Heb. obscure.*

7    Why do the wicked enjoy long life,
     hale in old age, and great and powerful?

8    They live to see their children settled,
     their kinsfolk and descendants flourishing;

9    their families are secure and safe;
     the rod of God's justice does not reach them.

10    Their bull mounts and fails not of its purpose;
     their cow calves and does not miscarry.

11    Their children like lambs run out to play,
     and their little ones skip and dance;

12    they rejoice with tambourine and harp
     and make merry to the sound of the flute.

13    Their lives close in prosperity,
     and they go down to Sheol in peace.

14    To God they say, 'Leave us alone;
     we do not want to know your ways.

15    What is the Almighty that we should worship him,
     or what should we gain by seeking his favour?'

16    Is not the prosperity of the wicked in their own hands?
     Are not their purposes very different from God's[a]?

17    How often is the lamp of the wicked snuffed out,
     and how often does their ruin come upon them?
     How often does God in his anger deal out suffering,
     bringing it in full measure to whom he will?[b]

18    How often is that man like a wisp of straw before the wind,
     like chaff which the storm-wind whirls away?

19    You say, 'The trouble he has earned, God will keep for his sons';
     no, let him be paid for it in full and be punished.

20    Let his own eyes see damnation come upon him,
     and the wrath of the Almighty be the cup he drinks.

21    What joy shall he have in his children after him,
     if his very months and days are numbered?

22    Can any man teach God,
     God who judges even those in heaven above?

23    One man, I tell you, dies crowned with success,
     lapped in security and comfort,

24    his loins full of vigour
     and the marrow juicy in his bones;

25    another dies in bitterness of soul

[a]God's: *prob. rdg.; Heb.* mine.
[b]*Line transposed from 12.6.*

and never tastes propserity;
side by side they are laid in earth,                                          26
and worms are the shroud of both.

I know well what you are thinking                                            27
and the arguments you are marshalling against me;
I know you will ask, 'Where is the great man's home now,                     28
what has become of the home of the wicked?'
Have you never questioned travellers?                                        29
Can you not learn from the signs they offer,
that the wicked is spared when disaster comes                                30
and conveyed to safety before the day of wrath?
No one denounces his conduct to his face,                                    31
no one requites him for what he has done.
When he is carried to the grave,                                             32–33
all the world escorts him, before and behind;
the dust of earth is sweet to him,
and thousands keep watch at his tomb.
How futile, then, is the comfort you offer me!                               34
How false your answers ring!

## Third cycle of speeches

Then Eliphaz the Temanite answered:                                          22

Can man be any benefit to God?                                               2
Can even a wise man benefit him?
Is it an asset to the Almighty if you are righteous?                         3
Does he gain if your conduct is perfect?
Do not think that he reproves you because you are pious,                     4
that on this count he brings you to trial.
No: it is because you are a very wicked man,                                 5
and your depravity passes all bounds.
Without due cause you take a brother in pledge,                              6
you strip men of their clothes and leave them naked.
When a man is weary, you give him no water to drink                         7
and you refuse bread to the hungry.
Is the earth, then, the preserve of the strong                             8
and a domain for the favoured few?
Widows you have sent away empty-handed,                                     9
orphans you have struck defenceless.
No wonder that there are pitfalls in your path,                            10
that scares are set to fill you with sudden fear.

11  The light is turned into darkness, and you cannot see;
    the flood-waters cover you.
12  Surely God is at the zenith of the heavens
    and looks down on all the stars, high as they are.
13  But you say, 'What does God know?
    Can he see through thick darkness to judge?
14  His eyes cannot pierce the curtain of the clouds
    as he walks to and fro on the vault of heaven.'
15  Consider the course of the wicked man,
    the path the miscreant treads:
16  see how they are carried off before their time,
    their very foundation flowing away like a river;
17  these men said to God, 'Leave us alone;
    what can the Almighty do to us?'
18  Yet it was he that filled their houses with good things,
    although their purposes and his were very different.
19  The righteous see their fate and exult,
    the innocent make game of them;
20  for their riches are swept away,
    and the profusion of their wealth is destroyed by fire.


21  Come to terms with God and you will prosper;
    that is the way to mend your fortune.
22  Take instruction from his mouth
    and store his words in your heart.
23  If you come back to the Almighty in true sincerity,
    if you banish wrongdoing from your home,
24  if you treat your precious metal as dust*a*
    and the gold of Ophir as stones from the river-bed,
25  then the Almighty himself will be your precious metal;
    he will be your silver in double measure.
26  Then, with sure trust in *b* the Almighty,
    you will raise your face to God;
27  you will pray to him, and he will hear you,
    and you will have cause to fulfil your vows.
28  In all your designs you will succeed,
    and light will shine on your path;
29  but God brings down the pride of the haughty*c*

*a Prob. rdg.; Heb.* if you put your precious metal on dust.
*b* with . . . in: *or* delighting in.
*c* but . . . haughty: *prob. rdg.; Heb. obscure.*

and keeps safe the man of modest looks.
He will deliver the innocent,*a*                                                                          30
and you will be delivered, because your hands are clean.

Then Job answered:                                                                              23

My thoughts today are resentful,                                                                    2
for God's hand is heavy on me in my trouble.
If only I knew how to find him,                                                                        3
how to enter his court,
I would state my case before him                                                                     4
and set out my arguments in full;
then I should learn what answer he would give                                              5
and find out what he had to say.
Would he exert his great power to browbeat me?                                         6
No; God himself would never bring a charge against me.
There the upright are vindicated before him,                                               7
and I shall win from my judge an absolute discharge.
If I go forward,*b* he is not there;                                                                    8
if backward,*c* I cannot find him;
when I turn*d* left,*e* I do not descry him;                                                         9
I face right,*f* but I see him not.
But he knows me in action or at rest;                                                             10
when he tests me, I prove to be gold.
My feet have kept to the path he has set me,                                               11
I have followed his way and not turned from it.
I do not ignore the commands that come from his lips,                                 12
I have stored in my heart what he says.
He decides,*g* and who can turn him from his purpose?
He does what his own heart desires.
What he determines, that he carries out;                                                       14
his mind is full of plans like these.
Therefore I am fearful of meeting him;                                                          15
when I think about him,*h* I am afraid;
it is God who makes me faint-hearted                                                            16
and the Almighty who fills me with fear,

*a*Prob. rdg.; *Heb.* the not innocent.
*b*Or east.
*c*Or west.
*d*Prob. rdg.; *Heb.* he turns.
*e*Or north.
*f*Or south.
*g*He decides: *prob. rdg.; Heb.* He in one.
*h*when . . . him: *or* I stand aloof.

17   yet I am not reduced to silence by the darkness
   nor*a* by the mystery which hides him.

24   *b*The day of reckoning is no secret to the Almighty,
   though those who know him have no hint of its date.
2   Wicked men move boundary-stones
   and carry away flocks and their shepherds.
6*c*   In the field they reap what is not theirs,
   and filch the late grapes from the rich*d* man's vineyard.
3   They drive off the orphan's ass
   and lead away the widow's ox with a rope.
9   They snatch the fatherless infant from the breast
   and take the poor man's child in pledge.
4   They jostle the poor out of the way;
   the destitute huddle together, hiding from them.
5   The poor rise early like the wild ass,
   when it scours the wilderness for food;
   but though they work till nightfall,*e*
   their children go hungry.*f*
7   Naked and bare they pass the night;
   in the cold they have nothing to cover them.
8   They are drenched by rain-storms from the hills
   and hug the rock, their only shelter.
10   Naked and bare they go about their work,
   and hungry they carry the sheaves;
11   they press the oil in the shade where two walls meet,
   they tread the winepress but themselves go thirsty.
12   Far from the city, they groan like dying men,
   and like wounded men they cry out;
   but God pays no heed to their prayer.
13   Some there are who rebel against the light of day,
   who know nothing of its ways
   and do not linger in the paths of light.
14   The murderer rises before daylight
   to kill some miserable wretch.*g*
15   The seducer watches eagerly for twilight,
   thinking, 'No eye will catch sight of me.'

*a*yet I am not . . . nor: *or* indeed I am . . . and . . .
*b*Prob. rdg.; Heb. prefixes* Why.
*cVerses 3–9 re-arranged to restore the natural order.*
*dOr* wicked.
*eProb. rdg.; Heb.* Arabah.
*f*go hungry: *prob. rdg.; Heb.* to it food.
*gSee note on verse 15.*

The thief prowls[a] by night,[b]
his face covered with a mask,
and in the darkness breaks into houses                                16
which he has marked down in the day.
One and all,[c] they are strangers to the daylight,
but dark night is morning to them;                                   17
and in the welter of night they are at home.
Such men are scum on the surface of the water;                       18
their fields have a bad name throughout the land,
and no labourer will go near their vineyards.
As drought and heat make away with snow,                             19
so the waters of Sheol[d] make away with the sinner.
The womb forgets him, the worm sucks him dry;                        20
he will not be remembered ever after.[e]
He may have wronged the barren childless woman                       21
and been no help to the widow;
yet God in his strength carries off even the mighty;                 22
they may rise, but they have no firm hope of life.
He lulls them into security and confidence;                          23
but his eyes are fixed on their ways.
For a moment they rise to the heights, but are soon gone;            24
iniquity is snapped like a stick.[f]
They are laid low and wilt like a mallow-flower;
they droop like an ear of corn on the stalk.
If this is not so, who will prove me wrong                           25
and make nonsense of my argument?

Then Bildad the Shuhite answered:                                    25

Authority and awe rest with him                                      2
who has established peace in his realm on high.
His squadrons are without number;                                    3
at whom will they not spring from ambush?
How then can a man be justified in God's sight,                      4
or one born of woman be innocent?
If the circling moon is found wanting,                               5
and the stars are not innocent in his eyes,

---

[a]The thief prowls: *prob. rdg.; Heb.* Let him be like a thief.
[b]*Line transposed from end of verse 14.*
[c]One and all: *transposed from after* but *in next verse.*
[d]snow . . . Sheol: *prob. rdg.: Heb.* snow-water, Sheol.
[e]*Prob. rdg.; Heb. here adds* iniquity is snapped like a stick *(see note on verse 24).*
[f]*Line transposed from end of verse 20.*

6    much more so man who is but a maggot,
     mortal man who is only a worm.

26   Then Job answered:

2    What help you have given to the man without resource,
     what deliverance you have brought to the powerless!
3    What counsel you offer to a man at his wit's end,
     what sound advice to the foolish!
4    Who has prompted you to say such things,
     and whose spirit is expressed in your speech?

5    In the underworld the shades writhe in fear,
     the waters and all that live in them are struck with terror.*a*
6    Sheol is laid bare,
     and Abaddon uncovered before him.
7    God spreads the canopy of the sky over chaos
     and suspends earth in the void.
8    He keeps the waters penned in dense cloud-masses,
     and the clouds do not burst open under their weight.
9    He covers the face of the full moon,*b*
     unrolling his clouds across it.
10   He has fixed the horizon on the surface of the waters
     at the farthest limit of light and darkness.
11   The pillars of heaven quake
     and are aghast at his rebuke.
12   With his strong arm he cleft the sea-monster,
     and struck down the Rahab by his skill.
13   At his breath the skies are clear,
     and his hand breaks the twisting*c* sea-serpent.
14   These are but the fringe of his power;
     and how faint the whisper that we hear of him!
     [Who could fathom the thunder of his might?]

27   Then Job resumed his discourse:

2    I swear by God, who has denied me justice,
     and by the Almighty, who has filled me with bitterness:
3    so long as there is any life left in me
     and God's breath is in my nostrils,
4    no untrue word shall pass my lips

*a*are struck with terror: *prob. rdg.; Heb. om.*
*b*Or He overlays the surface of his throne.
*c*Or primeval.

and my tongue shall utter no falsehood.
God forbid that I should allow you to be right;          5
till death, I will not abandon my claim to innocence.
I will maintain the rightness of my cause, I will never give up;    6
so long as I live, I will not change.

May my enemy meet the fate of the wicked,               7
and my antagonist the doom of the wrongdoer!
What hope has a godless man, when he is cut off,*a*      8
when God takes away his life?
Will God listen to his cry                              9
when trouble overtakes him?
Will he trust himself to the Almighty                   10
and call upon God at all times?

I will teach you what is in God's power,                11
I will not conceal the purpose of the Almighty.
If all of you have seen these things,                   12
why then do you talk such empty nonsense?

This is the lot prescribed by God for the wicked,       13
and the ruthless man's reward from the Almighty.
He may have many sons, but they will fall by the sword,    14
and his offspring will go hungry;
the survivors will be brought to the grave by pestilence,    15
and no widows will weep for them.
He may heap up silver like dirt                         16
and get himself piles of clothes;
he may get them, but the righteous will wear them,      17
and his silver will be shared among the innocent.
The house he builds is flimsy as a bird's nest          18
or a shelter put up by a watchman.
He may lie down rich one day, but never again;          19
he opens his eyes and all is gone.
Disaster overtakes him like a flood,                    20
and a storm snatches him away in the night;
the east wind lifts him up and he is gone;              21
it whirls him far from home;
it flings itself on him without mercy,                  22
and he is battered and buffeted by its force;
it snaps its fingers at him                             23
and whistles over him wherever he may be.

*a Or* What is a godless man's thread of life when it is cut . . .

## *God's unfathomable wisdom*

28  There are mines for silver
     and places where men refine gold;
2    where iron is won from the earth
     and copper smelted from the ore;
3    the end of the seam lies in darkness,
     and it is followed to its farthest limit.[a]
4    Strangers cut the galleries;[b]
     they are forgotten as they drive forward far from men.[c]
5    While corn is springing from the earth above,
     what lies beneath is raked over like a fire,
6    and out of its rocks comes lapis lazuli,
     dusted with flecks of gold.
7    No bird of prey knows the way there,
     and the falcon's keen eye cannot descry it;
8    proud beasts do not set foot on it,
     and no serpent comes that way.
9    Man sets his hand to the granite rock
     and lays bare the roots of the mountains;
10   he cuts galleries in the rocks,
     and gems of every kind meet his eye;
11   he dams up the sources of the streams
     and brings the hidden riches of the earth to light.
12   But where can wisdom be found?
     And where is the source of understanding?
13   No man knows the way to it;
     it is not found in the land of living men.
14   The depths of ocean say, 'It is not in us',
     and the sea says, 'It is not with me.'
15   Red gold cannot buy it,
     nor can its price be weighed out in silver;
16   it cannot be set in the scales against gold of Ophir,
     against precious cornelian or lapis lazuli;
17   gold and crystal are not to be matched with it,
     no work in fine gold can be bartered for it;
18   black coral and alabaster are not worth mention,
     and a parcel of wisdom fetches more than red coral;
19   topaz[d] from Ethiopia is not to be matched with it,

[a]*Prob. rdg.; Heb. adds* stones of darkness and deep darkness.
[b]Strangers . . . galleries: *prob. rdg.; Heb. obscure.*
[c]*Prob. rdg.; Heb. adds* languishing without foothold.
[d]*Or* chrysolite.

it cannot be set in the scales against pure gold.
Where then does wisdom come from,                           20
and where is the source of understanding?
No creature on earth can see it,                            21
and it is hidden from the birds of the air.
Destruction and death say,                                  22
'We know of it only by report.'
But God understands the way to it,                          23
he alone knows its source;
for he can see to the ends of the earth                     24
and he surveys everything under heaven.
When he made a counterpoise for the wind                    25
and measured out the waters in proportion,
when he laid down a limit for the rain                      26
and a path for the thunderstorm,
even then he saw wisdom and took stock of it,               27
he considered it and fathomed its very depths.
And he said to man:                                         28
    The fear of the Lord is wisdom,
    and to turn from evil is understanding.


## *Job's final survey of his case*

Then Job resumed his discourse:                             29

If I could only go back to the old days,                    2
to the time when God was watching over me,
when his lamp shone above my head,                          3
and by its light I walked through the darkness!
If I could be as in the days of my prime,                   4
when God protected my home,
while the Almighty was still there at my side,              5
and my servants stood round me,
while my path flowed with milk,                             6
and the rocks streamed oil!
If I went through the gate out of the town                  7
to take my seat in the public square,
young men saw me and kept out of sight;                     8
old men rose to their feet,
men in authority broke off their talk                       9
and put their hands to their lips;
the voices of the nobles died away,                         10
and every man held his tongue.

21[a]    They listened to me expectantly
         and waited in silence for my opinion.
22       When I had spoken, no one spoke again;
         my words fell gently on them;
23       they waited for them as for rain
         and drank them in like showers in spring.
24       When I smiled on them, they took heart;
         when my face lit up, they lost their gloomy looks.
25       I presided over them, planning their course,
         like a king encamped with his troops.[b]

11       Whoever heard of me spoke in my favour,
         and those who saw me bore witness to my merit,
12       how I saved the poor man when he called for help
         and the orphan who had no protector.
13       The man threatened with ruin blessed me,
         and I made the widow's heart sing for joy.
14       I put on righteousness as a garment and it clothed me;
         justice, like a cloak or a turban, wrapped me round.
15       I was eyes to the blind
         and feet to the lame;
16       I was a father to the needy,
         and I took up the stranger's cause.
17       I broke the fangs of the miscreant
         and rescued the prey from his teeth.
18       I thought, 'I shall die with my powers unimpaired
         and my days uncounted as the grains of sand,[c]
19       with my roots spreading out to the water
         and the dew lying on my branches,
20       with the bow always new in my grasp
         and the arrow ever ready to my hand.'[d]

30       But now I am laughed to scorn
         by men of a younger generation,
         men whose fathers I would have disdained
         to put with the dogs who kept my flock.
2        What use were their strong arms to me,
         since their sturdy vigour had wasted away?

[a]*Verses 21–25 transposed to this point.*
[b]*Prob. rdg.; Heb. adds* as when one comforts mourners.
[c]*Or* as those of the phoenix.
[d]*Verses 21–25 transposed to follow verse 10.*

They gnawed roots*ᵃ* in the desert,                                              3
gaunt with want and hunger,*ᵇ*
they plucked saltwort and wormwood                                          4
and root of broom*ᶜ* for their food.
Driven out from the society of men,*ᵈ*                                            5
pursued like thieves with hue and cry,
they lived in gullies and ravines,                                                    6
holes in the earth and rocky clefts;
they howled like beasts among the bushes,                                    7
huddled together beneath the scrub,
vile base-born wretches,                                                               8
hounded from the haunts of men.
Now I have become the target of their taunts,                             9
my name is a byword among them.
They loathe me, they shrink from me,                                          10
they dare to spit in my face.
They run wild and savage*ᵉ* me;                                                   11
at sight of me they throw off all restraint.
On my right flank they attack in a mob;*ᶠ*                                    12
they raise their siege-ramps against me,
they tear down my crumbling defences to my undoing,             13
and scramble up against me unhindered;
they burst in through the gaping breach;                                      14
at the moment of the crash they come rolling in.
Terror upon terror overwhelms me,                                            15
it sweeps away my resolution like the wind,
and my hope of victory vanishes like a cloud.
So now my soul is in turmoil within me,                                      16
and misery has me daily in its grip.
By night pain pierces my very bones,                                          17
and there is ceaseless throbbing in my veins;
my garments are all bespattered with my phlegm,                       18
which chokes me like the collar of a shirt.
God himself*ᵍ* has flung me down in the mud,                             19
no better than dust or ashes.

I call for thy help, but thou dost not answer;                              20

---

*ᵃ*roots: *prob. rdg.; Heb. om.*
*ᵇProb. rdg.; Heb. adds* yesterday waste and derelict land.
*ᶜ*root of broom: *probably* fungus on broom root.
*ᵈ*the society of men: *prob. rdg.; Heb. obscure.*
*ᵉ*They run . . . savage: *prob. rdg.; Heb.* He runs . . . savages.
*ᶠProb. rdg.; Heb. adds* they let loose my feet.
*ᵍ*God himself: *prob. rdg.; Heb. om.*

I stand up to plead, but thou sittest aloof;
21   thou hast turned cruelly against me
and with they strong hand pursuest me in hatred;
22   thou dost snatch me up and set me astride the wind,
and the tempest<sup>a</sup> tosses me up and down.
23   I know that thou wilt hand me over to death,
to the place appointed for all mortal men.

24   Yet no beggar held out his hand
but was relieved<sup>b</sup> by me in his distress.
25   Did I not weep for the man whose life was hard?
Did not my heart grieve for the poor?
26   Evil has come though I expected good;
I looked for light but there came darkness.
27   My bowels are in ferment and know no peace;
days of misery stretch out before me.
28   I go about dejected and friendless;
I rise in the assembly, only to appeal for help.
29   The wolf is now my brother,
the owls of the desert have become my companions.
30   My blackened skin peels off,
and my body is scorched by the heat.
31   My harp has been tuned for a dirge,
my flute to the voice of those who weep.

31 2<sup>c</sup>   What is the lot prescribed by God above,
the reward from the Almighty on high?
3   Is not ruin prescribed for the miscreant
and calamity for the wrongdoer?
4   Yet does not God himself see my ways
and count my every step?

5   I swear I have had no dealings with falsehood
and have not embarked on a course of deceit.
1   I have come to terms with my eyes,
never to take notice of a girl.
6   Let God weigh me in the scales of justice,
and he will know that I am innocent!
7   If my steps have wandered from the way,
if my heart has followed my eyes,
or any dirt stuck to my hands,

<sup>a</sup>the tempest: *prob. rdg.; Heb. unintelligible.*
<sup>b</sup>was relieved: *prob. rdg.; Heb. unintelligible.*
<sup>c</sup>*Verse I transposed to follow verse 5.*

may another eat what I sow, 8
and may my crops be pulled up by the roots!
If my heart has been enticed by a woman 9
or I have lain in wait at my neighbour's door,
may my wife be another man's slave, 10
and may other men enjoy her.
[But that is a wicked act, an offence before the law; 11
it would be a consuming and destructive fire, 12
raging*ᵃ* among my crops.]
If I have ever rejected the plea of my slave 13
or of my slave-girl, when they brought their complaint to me,
what shall I do if God appears? 14
What shall I answer if he intervenes?
Did not he who made me in the womb make them? 15
Did not the same God create us in the belly?
If I have withheld their needs from the poor 16
or let the widow's eye grow dim with tears,
if I have eaten my crust alone, 17
and the orphan has not shared it with me—
the orphan who from boyhood honoured me like a father, 18
whom I guided from the day of his*ᵇ* birth—
if I have seen anyone perish for lack of clothing, 19
or a poor man with nothing to cover him,
if his body had no cause to bless me, 20
because he was not kept warm with a fleece from my flock,
if I have raised*ᶜ* my hand against the innocent,*ᵈ* 21
knowing that men would side with me in court,
then may my shoulder-blade be torn from my shoulder, 22
my arm be wrenched out of its socket!
But the terror of God was heavy upon me,*ᵉ* 23
and for fear of his majesty I could do none of these things.
If I have put my faith in gold 24
and my trust in the gold of Nubia,
if I have rejoiced in my great wealth 25
and in the increase of riches;
if I ever looked on the sun in splendour 26
or the moon moving in her glory,
and was led astray in my secret heart 27
and raised my hand in homage;

---

*ᵃProb. rdg.; Heb.* uprooting.
*ᵇProb. rdg.; Heb.* my.
*ᶜOr* waved.
*ᵈOr* orphan.
*ᵉProb. rdg.; Heb.* A fear towards me is a disaster from God.

28    this would have been an offence before the law,
      for I should have been unfaithful to God on high.

38*ª*   If my land has cried out in reproach at me,
      and its furrows have joined in weeping,

39    if I have eaten its produce without payment
      and have disappointed my creditors,

40    may thistles spring up instead of wheat,
      and weeds instead of barley!


29    Have I rejoiced at the ruin of the man that hated me
      or been filled with malice when trouble overtook him,

30    even though I did not allow my tongue to sin
      by demanding his life with a curse?

31    Have the men of my household never said,
      'Let none of us speak ill of him!

32    No stranger has spent the night in the street'?
      For I have kept open house for the traveller.

33    Have I ever concealed my misdeeds as men do,
      keeping my guilt to myself,

34    because I feared the gossip of the town
      or dreaded the scorn of my fellow-citizens?

35    Let me but call a witness in my defence!
      Let the Almighty state his case against me!
      If my accuser had written out his indictment,
      I would not keep silence and remain indoors.*b*

36    No! I would flaunt it on my shoulder
      and wear it like a crown on my head;

37    I would plead the whole record of my life
      and present that in court as my defence.*c*


                    Job's speeches are finished.*d*




## Speeches of Elihu


32    So these three men gave up answering Job; for he continued to think him
2     self righteous. Then Elihu son of Barakel the Buzite, of the family of Ram,

---

*ªVerses 38–40 transposed (but see note d, below).*
*bLine transposed from verse 34.*
*cVerses 38–40 transposed to follow verse 28 (but see note d).*
*dThe last line of verse 40 retained here.*

grew angry; angry because Job had made himself out more righteous than
God,[a] and angry with the three friends because they had found no answer      3
to Job and had let God appear wrong.[b] Now Elihu had hung back while          4
they were talking with Job because they were older than he; but, when he       5
saw that the three had no answer, he could no longer contain his anger.
So Elihu son of Barakel the Buzite began to speak:                             6

I am young in years,
and you are old;
that is why I held back and shrank
from displaying my knowledge in front of you.
I said to myself, 'Let age speak,                                              7
and length of years expound wisdom.'
But the spirit of God himself is in man,                                       8
and the breath of the Almighty gives him understanding;
it is not only the old who are wise                                            9
or the aged who understand what is right.
Therefore I say: Listen to me;                                                10
I too will display my knowledge.
Look, I have been waiting upon your words,                                    11
listening for the conclusions of your thoughts,
while you sought for phrases;
I have been giving thought to your conclusions,                              12
but not one of you refutes Job or answers his arguments.
Take care then not to claim that you have found wisdom;                      13
God will rebut him, not man.
I will not string[c] words together like you[d]                              14
or answer him as you have done.

If these men are confounded and no longer answer,                            15
if words fail them,
am I to wait because they do not speak,                                       16
because they stand there and no longer answer?
I, too, have a furrow to plough;                                              17
I will express my opinion;
for I am bursting with words,                                                 18
a bellyful of wind gripes me.
My stomach is distended as if with wine,                                     19
bulging like a blacksmith's bellows;
I must speak to find relief,                                                  20
I must open my mouth and answer;

[a]*Or* had justified himself with God.
[b]*Prob. original rdg., altered in Heb. to* and had not proved Job wrong.
[c]*Prob. rdg.; Heb.* He has not strung.
[d]*Prob. rdg.; Heb.* towards me.

21   I will show no favour to anyone,
     I will flatter no one, God or man;[a]
22   for I cannot use flattering titles,
     or my Maker would soon do away with me.

33   Come now, Job, listen to my words
     and attend carefully to everything I say.
2    Look, I am ready to answer;
     the words are on the tip of my tongue.
3    My heart assures me that I speak with knowledge,
     and that my lips speak with sincerity.
4    For the spirit of God made me,
     and the breath of the Almighty gave me life.
5    Answer me if you can,
     marshal your arguments and confront me.
6    In God's sight[b] I am just what you are;
     I too am only a handful of clay.
7    Fear of me need not abash you,
     nor any pressure from me overawe you.
8    You have said your say and I heard you;
     I have listened to the sound of your words:
9    'I am innocent', you said, 'and free from offence,
     blameless and without guilt.
10   Yet God finds occasions to put me in the wrong
     and counts me his enemy;
11   he puts my feet in the stocks
     and keeps a close watch on all I do.'

12   Well, this is my answer: You are wrong.
     God is greater than man;
13   why then plead your case with him?
     for no one can answer his arguments.
14   Indeed, once God has spoken
     he does not speak a second time to confirm it.
15   In dreams, in visions of the night,
     when deepest sleep falls upon men,
16   while they sleep on their beds, God makes them listen,
     and his correction strikes them with terror.
17   To turn a man from reckless conduct,
     to check the pride[c] of mortal man,

[a] *Prob. rdg.; Heb.* I will not flatter man.
[b] In God's sight: *or* In strength.
[c] the pride: *prob. rdg.; Heb. obscure.*

at the edge of the pit he holds him back alive                              18
and stops him from crossing the river of death.
Or again, man learns his lesson on a bed of pain,                          19
tormented by a ceaseless ague in his bones;
he turns from his food with loathing                                       20
and has no relish for the choicest meats;
his flesh hangs loose upon him,                                            21
his bones are loosened and out of joint,
his soul draws near to the pit,                                            22
his life to the ministers of death.
Yet if an angel, one of thousands, stands by him,                          23
a mediator between him and God,
to expound what he has done right
and to secure mortal man his due;*a*
if he speaks in the man's favour and says, 'Reprieve him,                  24
let him not go down to the pit, I have the price of his release';
then that man will grow sturdier*b* than he was in youth,                  25
he will return to the days of his prime.
If he entreats God to show him favour,                                     26
to let him see his face and shout for joy;*c*
if he declares before all men, 'I have sinned,                             27
turned right into wrong and thought nothing of it';
then he saves himself from going down to the pit,                          28
he lives and sees the light.
All these things God may do to a man,                                      29
again and yet again,
bringing him back from the pit                                             30
to enjoy the full light of life.

Listen, Job, and attend to me;                                             31
be silent, and I myself will speak.
If you have any arguments, answer me;                                      32
speak, and I would gladly find you proved right;
but if you have none, listen to me:                                        33
keep silence, and I will teach you wisdom.

Then Elihu went on to say:                                                 **34**

Mark my words, you wise men;                                               2
you men of long experience, listen to me;
for the ear tests what is spoken                                           3

---

*a*Line transposed from verse 26.
*b*will grow sturdier: *prob. rdg.; Heb. unintelligible.*
*c*See note on verse 23.

as the palate savours food.
4   Let us then examine for ourselves what is right;
    let us together establish the true good.
5   Job has said, 'I am innocent,
    but God has deprived me of justice,
6   he has falsified my case;
    my state is desperate, yet I have done no wrong.'
7   Was there ever a man like Job
    with his thirst for irreverent talk,
8   choosing bad company to share his journeys,
    a fellow-traveller with wicked men?
9   For he says that it brings a man no profit
    to find favour with God.
10  But listen to me, you men of good sense.
        Far be it from God to do evil
        or the Almighty to play false!
11  For he pays a man according to his work
    and sees that he gets what his conduct deserves.
12  The truth is, God does no wrong,
    the Almighty does not pervert justice.
13  Who committed the earth to his keeping?
    Who but he established the whole world?
14  If he were to turn his thoughts inwards
    and recall his life-giving spirit,
15  all that lives would perish on the instant,
    and man return again to dust.

16  Now, Job, if you have the wit, consider this;
    listen to the words I speak.
17  Can it be that a hater of justice holds the reins?
    Do you disparage a sovereign whose rule is so fair,
18  who will say to a prince, 'You scoundrel',
    and call his magnates blackguards to their faces;
19  who does not show special favour to those in office
    and thinks no more of rich than of poor?
    All alike are God's creatures,
20  who may die in a moment, in the middle of the night;
    at his touch the rich are no more,
    and the mighty vanish though no hand is laid on them.
21  His eyes are on the ways of men,
    and he sees every step they take;
22  there is nowhere so dark, so deep in shadow,
    that wrongdoers may hide from him.
25  Therefore he repudiates all that they do;

he turns on them in the night, and they are crushed.
There are no appointed days for men                                   23
to appear before God for judgement.
He holds no inquiry, but breaks the powerful                          24
and sets up others in their place.
For their crimes he strikes them down*b*                              26*a*
and makes them disgorge their bloated wealth,*c*
because they have ceased to obey him                                  27
and pay no heed to his ways.
Then the cry of the poor reaches his ears,                            28
and he hears the cry of the distressed.
[Even if he is silent, who can condemn him?                           29-30
If he looks away, who can find fault?
What though he makes a godless man king
over a stubborn nation and all its people?]

But suppose you were to say to God,                                   31
'I have overstepped the mark; I will do no more*d* mischief.
Vile wretch that I am, be thou my guide;                              32
whatever wrong I have done, I will do wrong no more.'
Will he, at these words, condone your rejection of him?               33
It is for you to decide, not me:
but what can you answer?
Men of good sense will say,                                           34
any intelligent hearer will tell me,
'Job talks with no knowledge,                                         35
and there is no sense in what he says.
If only Job could be put to the test once and for all                 36
for answers that are meant to make mischief!
He is a sinner and a rebel as well*e*                                 37
with his endless ranting against God.'

Then Elihu went on to say:                                            35

Do you think that this is a sound plea                                2
or maintain that you are in the right against God?—
if you say, 'What would be the advantage to me?                       3
how much should I gain from sinning?'
I will bring arguments myself against you,                            4

---

*a*Verse 25 transposed to follow verse 22.
*b*he strikes them down: *prob. rdg.; Heb. om.*
*c*Or and chastises them where people see.
*d*more: *prob. rdg.; Heb. obscure.*
*e*Prob. rdg.; Heb. adds between us it is enough.

you and your three friends.

5    Look up at the sky and then consider,
     observe the rain-clouds towering above you.

6    How does it touch him if you have sinned?
     However many your misdeeds, what does it mean to him?

7    If you do right, what good do you bring him,
     or what does he gain from you?

8    Your wickedness touches only men, such as you are;
     the right that you do affects none but mortal man.

9    Men will cry out beneath the burdens of oppression
     and call for help against the power of the great;

10   but none of them asks, 'Where is God my Maker
     who gives protection by night,

11   who grants us more knowledge than the beasts of the earth
     and makes us wiser than the birds of the air?'

12   So, when they cry out, he does not answer,
     because they are self-willed and proud.

13   All to no purpose! God does not listen,
     the Almighty does not see.

14   The worse for you when you say, 'He does not see me'!
     Humble yourself*a* in his presence and wait for his word.

15   But now, because God does not grow angry and punish
     and because he lets folly pass unheeded,

16   Job gives vent to windy nonsense
     and makes a parade of empty words.

36   Then Elihu went on to say:

2    Be patient a little longer, and let me enlighten you;
     there is still something more to be said on God's side.

3    I will search far and wide to support my conclusions,
     as I defend the justice of my Maker.

4    There are no flaws in my reasoning;
     before you stands one whose conclusions are sound.

5    God,*b* I say, repudiates the high and*c* mighty
6    and does not let the wicked prosper,
     but allows the just claims of the poor and suffering;

---

*a*Humble yourself: *prob. rdg.; Heb.* Judge.
*b*Prob. rdg.; Heb. adds* a mighty one and not.
*c*and: *prob. rdg.; Heb. om.*

he does not deprive the sufferer of his due.*a*　　　　　　7
Look at kings on their thrones:
when God gives them sovereign power, they grow arrogant.
Next you may see them loaded with fetters,　　　　　　8
held fast in captives' chains:
he denounces their conduct to them,　　　　　　9
showing how insolence and tyranny was their offence;
his warnings sound in their ears　　　　　　10
and summon them to turn back from their evil courses.
If they listen to him, they spend*b* their days in prosperity　　　11
and their years in comfort.
But, if they do not listen, they die, their lesson unlearnt,　　　12
and cross the river of death.
Proud men rage against him　　　　　　13
and do not cry to him for help when caught in his toils;
so they die in their prime,　　　　　　14
like male prostitutes,*c* worn out.*d*

Those who suffer he rescues through suffering　　　　　15
and teaches them by the discipline of affliction.

Beware, if you are tempted to exchange hardship for comfort,*e*　　16
for unlimited plenty spread before you, and a generous table;
if you eat your fill of a rich man's fare　　　　　17
when you are occupied with the business of the law,
do not be led astray by lavish gifts of wine　　　　18
and do not let bribery warp your judgement.
Will that wealth of yours, however great, avail you,　　　19
or all the resources of your high position?
Take care not to turn to mischief;　　　　　21*f*
for that is why you are tried by affliction.

Have no fear if in the breathless terrors of the night　　　20
you see nations vanish where they stand.
God towers in majesty above us;　　　　　22
who wields such sovereign power as he?
Who has prescribed his course for him?　　　　　23
Who has said to him, 'Thou hast done wrong'?
Remember then to sing the praises of his work,　　　　24

*a*deprive . . . due: *or* withdraw his gaze from the righteous.
*b*Prob. rdg.; Heb. adds they end.
*c*Cp. Deut. 23. 17.
*d*worn out: *prob. rdg.; Heb. unintelligible.*
*e*for comfort: *prob. rdg.; Heb. om.*
*f*Verses 20 and 21 transposed.

as men have always sung them.

25  All men stand back from<sup>a</sup> him;
    the race of mortals look on from afar.

26  Consider; God is so great that we cannot know him;
    the number of his years is beyond reckoning.

27  He draws up drops of water from the sea<sup>b</sup>
    and distils rain from the mist he has made;

28  the rain-clouds pour down in torrents,<sup>c</sup>
    they descend in showers on mankind;

31  thus he sustains the nations
    and gives them food in plenty.

29  Can any man read the secret of the sailing clouds,
    spread like a carpet under<sup>d</sup> his pavilion?

30  See how he unrolls the mist across the waters,
    and its streamers<sup>e</sup> cover the sea.

32<sup>f</sup>  He charges the thunderbolts with flame
    and launches them straight<sup>g</sup> at the mark;

33  in his anger he calls up the tempest,
    and the thunder is the herald of its coming.<sup>h</sup>

37  This too makes my heart beat wildly
    and start from its place.

2   Listen, listen to the thunder of God's voice
    and the rumbling of his utterance.

3   Under the vault of heaven he lets it roll,
    and his lightning reaches the ends of the earth;

4   there follows a sound of roaring
    as he thunders with the voice of majesty.<sup>i</sup>

5   God's voice is marvellous in its working;<sup>j</sup>
    he does great deeds that pass our knowledge.

6   For he says to the snow, 'Fall to earth',
    and to the rainstorms, 'Be fierce.'
    And when his voice is heard,

<sup>a</sup>*Or* gaze at.
<sup>b</sup>from the sea: *prob. rdg.; Heb. om.*
<sup>c</sup>in torrents: *prob. rdg.; Heb.* which.
<sup>d</sup>spread . . . under: *prob. rdg.; Heb.* crashing noises.
<sup>e</sup>its streamers: *prob. rdg.; Heb.* the roots of.
<sup>f</sup>*Verse 31 transposed to follow verse 28.*
<sup>g</sup>and . . . straight: *prob. rdg.; Heb.* and gives orders concerning it.
<sup>h</sup>in his anger . . . coming: *Prob. rdg.; Heb.* obscure.
<sup>i</sup>*See note on verse 6.*
<sup>j</sup>*Prob. rdg.; Heb.* thundering.

the floods of rain pour down unchecked.*a*

He shuts every man fast indoors,*b*                              7
and all men whom he has made must stand idle;
the beasts withdraw into their lairs                            8
and take refuge in their dens.
The hurricane bursts from its prison,                           9
and the rain-winds bring bitter cold;
at the breath of God the ice-sheet is formed,                  10
and the wide waters are frozen hard as iron.
He gives the dense clouds their load of moisture,              11
and the clouds spread his mist abroad,
as they travel round in their courses,                         12
steered by his guiding hand
to do his bidding
all over the habitable world.*c*
Listen, Job, to this argument;                                 14
stand still, and consider God's wonderful works.
Do you know how God assigns them their tasks,                  15
how he sends light flashing from his clouds?
Do you know why the clouds hang poised overhead,               16
a wonderful work of his consummate skill,
sweating there in your stifling clothes,                       17
when the earth lies sultry under the south wind?
Can you beat out the vault of the skies, as he does,           18
hard as a mirror of cast metal?
Teach us then what to say to him;                              19
for all is dark, and we cannot marshal our thoughts.
Can any man dictate to God when he is*d* to speak?             20
or command him to make proclamation?
At one moment the light is not seen,                           21
it is overcast with clouds and rain;
then the wind passes by and clears them away,
and a golden glow comes from the north.*e*                     22
But the Almighty we cannot find; his power is beyond our ken,  23
and his righteousness not slow to do justice.
Therefore mortal men pay him reverence,                        24
and all who are wise look to him.

---

*a*And when . . . unchecked: *prob. rdg.; some words in these lines transposed from verse 4.*
*b*indoors: *prob. rdg.; Heb. obscure.*
*cProb. rdg.; Heb. adds* (13) whether he makes him attain the rod, or his earth, or constant love.
*dProb. rdg.; Heb.* I am.
*eProb. rdg.; Heb. adds* this refers to God, terrible in majesty.

## God's answer and Job's submission

38   Then the LORD answered Job out of the tempest:

2      Who is this whose ignorant words
         cloud my design in darkness?
3      Brace yourself and stand up like a man;
         I will ask questions, and you shall answer.
4      Where were you when I laid the earth's foundations?
         Tell me, if you know and understand.
5      Who settled its dimensions? Surely you should know.
         Who stretched his measuring-line over it?
6      On what do its supporting pillars rest?
         Who set its corner-stone in place,
7      when the morning stars sang together
         and all the sons of God shouted aloud?
8      Who watched over the birth of the sea,*a*
         when it burst in flood from the womb?—
9      when I wrapped it in a blanket of cloud
         and cradled it in fog,
10     when I established its bounds,
         fixing its doors and bars in place,
11     and said, 'Thus far shall you come and no farther,
         and here your surging waves shall halt.'*b*
12     In all your life have you ever called up the dawn
         or shown the morning its place?
13     Have you taught it to grasp the fringes of the earth
         and shake the Dog-star from its place;
14     to bring up the horizon in relief as clay under a seal,
         until all things stand out like the folds of a cloak,
15     when the light of the Dog-star is dimmed
         and the stars of the Navigator's Line go out one by one?
16     Have you descended to the springs of the sea
         or walked in the unfathomable deep?
17     Have the gates of death been revealed to you?
         Have you ever seen the door-keepers of the place of darkness?
18     Have you comprehended the vast expanse of the world?
         Come, tell me all this, if you know.
19     Which is the way to the home of light
         and where does darkness dwell?
20     And can you then take each to its appointed bound

---

*a*Who . . . sea: *prob. rdg.; Heb.* And he held back the sea with two doors.
*b*Prob. rdg.; Heb.* here one shall set on your surging waves.

and escort it on its homeward path?
Doubtless you know all this; for you were born already,                21
so long is the span of your life!

Have you visited the storehouse of the snow                            22
or seen the arsenal where hail is stored,
which I have kept ready for the day of calamity,                       23
for war and for the hour of battle?
By what paths is the heat spread abroad                                24
or the east wind carried far and wide over the earth?
Who has cut channels for the downpour                                  25
and cleared a passage for the thunderstorm,
for rain to fall on land where no man lives                            26
and on the deserted wilderness,
clothing lands waste and derelict with green                          27
and making grass grow on thirsty ground*a*?
Has the rain a father?                                                 28
Who sired the drops of dew?
Whose womb gave birth to the ice,                                      29
and who was the mother of the frost from heaven,
which lays a stony cover over the waters                               30
and freezes the expanse of ocean?
Can you bind the cluster of the Pleiades                               31
or loose Orion's belt?
Can you bring out the signs of the zodiac in their season             32
or guide Aldebaran and its train?
Did you proclaim the rules that govern the heavens,                   33
or determine the laws of nature on earth?
Can you command the dense clouds                                       34
to cover you with their weight of waters?
If you bid lightning speed on its way,                                 35
will it say to you, 'I am ready'?
Who put wisdom in depths of darkness                                   36
and veiled understanding in secrecy*b*?
Who is wise enough to marshal the rain-clouds                          37
and empty the cisterns of heaven,
when the dusty soil sets hard as iron,                                 38
and the clods of earth cling together?
Do you hunt her prey for the lioness                                   39
and satisfy the hunger of young lions,
as they crouch in the lair                                             40

*a*thirsty ground: *prob. rdg.; Heb.* source.
*b*secrecy: *prob. rdg.; Heb. word unknown.*

or lie in wait in the covert?
41 Who provides the raven with its quarry
and when its fledglings croak*a* for lack of food?


39 Do you know when the mountain-goats are born
or attend the wild doe when she is in labour?
2 Do you count the months that they carry their young
or know the time of their delivery,
3 when they crouch down to open their wombs
and bring their offspring to the birth,
4 when the fawns grow and thrive in the open forest,
and go forth and do not return?
5 Who has let the wild ass of Syria range at will
and given the wild ass of Arabia its freedom?—
6 whose home I have made in the wilderness
and its lair in the saltings;
7 it disdains the noise of the city
and is deaf to the driver's shouting;
8 it roams the hills as its pasture
and searches for anything green.
9 Does the wild ox consent to serve you,
does it spend the night in your stall?
10 Can you harness its strength*b* with ropes,
or will it harrow the furrows*b* after you?
11 Can you depend on it, strong as it is,
or leave your labour to it?
12 Do you trust it to come back
and bring home your grain to the threshing-floor?


13 The wings of the ostrich are stunted;*c*
*d*her pinions and plumage are so scanty*e*
14 that she abandons her eggs to the ground,
letting them be kept warm by the sand.
15 She forgets that a foot may crush them,
or a wild beast trample on them;
16 she treats her chicks heartlessly as if they were not hers,
not caring if her labour is wasted
17 (for God has denied her wisdom
and left her without sense),

*a Prob. rdg.; Heb. adds* they cry to God.
*b Prob. rdg.; Heb. transposes* strength *and* furrows.
*c are stunted: prob. rdg.; Heb. unintelligible.*
*d Prob. rdg.; Heb. prefixes* if.
*e Prob. rdg.; Heb.* godly *or* stork.

while like a cock she struts over the uplands,     18
scorning both horse and rider.

Did you give the horse his strength?     19
Did you clothe his neck with a mane?
Do you make him quiver like a locust's wings,     20
when his shrill neighing strikes terror?
He shows his mettle as he paws and prances;     21
he charges the armoured line with all his might.
He scorns alarms and knows no dismay;     22
he does not flinch before the sword.
The quiver rattles at his side,     23
the spear and sabre flash.
Trembling with eagerness, he devours the ground     24
and cannot be held in when he hears the horn;
at the blast of the horn he cries 'Aha!'     25
and from afar he scents the battle.*a*
Does your skill teach the hawk to use its pinions     26
and spread its wings towards the south?
Do you instruct the vulture to fly high     27
and build its nest aloft?
It dwells among the rocks and there it lodges;     28
its station is a crevice in the rock;
from there it searches for food;     29
keenly scanning the distance,
that its brood may be gorged with blood;     30
and where the slain are, there the vulture is.
Can you pull out the whale*b* with a gaff     41 1*c*
or can you slip a noose round its tongue?
Can you pass a cord through its nose     2
or put a hook through its jaw?
Will it plead with you for mercy     3
or beg its life with soft words?
Will it enter into an agreement with you     4
to become your slave for life?
Will you toy with it as with a bird     5
or keep it on a string like a song-bird for your maidens?
Do trading-partners haggle over it     6
or merchants share it out?

*a Prob. rdg.; Heb. adds* the thunder of the captains and the shouting.
*b Or* Leviathan.
*c 41. 1–6 (in Heb. 40. 25–30) transposed to this point.*

40   Then the LORD said to Job:

2    Is it for a man who disputes with the Almighty to be stubborn?
     Should he that argues with God answer back?

3    And Job answered the LORD:

4    What reply can I give thee, I who carry no weight?
     I put my finger to my lips.
5    I have spoken once and now will not answer again;
     twice have I spoken, and I will do so no more.

6    Then the LORD answered Job out of the tempest:

7    Brace yourself and stand up like a man;
     I will ask questions, and you shall answer.
8    Dare you deny that I am just
     or put me in the wrong that you may be right?
9    Have you an arm like God's arm,
     can you thunder with a voice like his?
10   Deck yourself out, if you can, in pride and dignity,
     array yourself in pomp and splendour;
11   unleash the fury of your wrath,
     look upon the proud man and humble him;
12   look upon every proud man and bring him low,
     throw down the wicked where they stand;
13   hide them in the dust together,
     and shroud them in an unknown grave.
14   Then I in my turn will acknowledge
     that your own right hand can save you.

15   Consider the chief of the beasts, the crocodile,*a*
     who devours cattle as if they were grass:*b*
16   what strength is in his loins!
     what power in the muscles of his belly!
17   His tail is rigid as*c* a cedar,
     the sinews of his flanks are closely knit,
18   his bones are tubes of bronze,
     and his limbs like bars of iron.
19   He is the chief of God's works,
     made to be a tyrant over his peers;*d*

*a*chief . . . crocodile: *prob. rdg.; Heb.* beasts (behemoth) which I have made with you.
*b*cattle . . . grass: *prob. rdg.; Heb.* grass like cattle.
*cOr* He bends his tail like . . .
*d*Prob. rdg.; Heb.* his sword.

for he takes*ᵃ* the cattle of the hills for his prey      20
and in his jaws he crunches all wild beasts.
There under the thorny lotus he lies,      21
hidden in the reeds and the marsh;
the lotus conceals him in its shadow,      22
the poplars of the stream surround him.
If the river is in spate, he is not scared,      23
he sprawls at his ease though the stream is in flood.
Can a man blind*ᵇ* his eyes and take him      24
or pierce his nose with the teeth of a trap?
Can you fill his skin with harpoons      41 7*ᶜ*
or his head with fish-hooks?
If ever you lift your hand against him,      8
think of the struggle that awaits you, and let be.

No, such a man is in desperate case,      9
hurled headlong at the very sight of him.
How fierce he is when he is roused!      10
Who is there to stand up to him?
Who has ever attacked him*ᵈ* unscathed?      11
Not a man*ᵉ* under the wide heaven.
I will not pass over in silence his limbs,      12
his prowess and the grace of his proportions.
Who has ever undone his outer garment      13
or penetrated his doublet of hide?
Who has ever opened the portals of his face?      14
for there is terror in his arching teeth.
His back*ᶠ* is row upon row of shields,      15
enclosed in a wall*ᵍ* of flints;
one presses so close on the other      16
that air cannot pass between them,
each so firmly clamped to its neighbour      17
that they hold and cannot spring apart.
His sneezing sends out sprays of light,      18
and his eyes gleam like the shimmer of dawn.
Firebrands shoot from his mouth,      19
and sparks come streaming out;

*ᵃProb. rdg.; Heb.* they take.
*ᵇ*Can a man blind: *prob. rdg.; Heb. obscure.*
*ᶜVerses 1–6 transposed to follow 39.30.*
*ᵈProb. rdg.; Heb.* me.
*ᵉProb. rdg.; Heb.* He is mine.
*ᶠProb. rdg.; Heb.* pride.
*ᵍProb. rdg.; Heb.* seal.

20  his nostrils pour forth smoke
    like a cauldron on a fire blown to full heat.
21  His breath sets burning coals ablaze,
    and flames flash from his mouth.
22  Strength is lodged in his neck,
    and untiring energy dances ahead of him.
23  Close knit is his underbelly,
    no pressure will make it yield.
24  His heart is firm as a rock,
    firm as the nether millstone.
25  When he raises himself, strong men*a* take fright,
    bewildered at the lashings of his tail.
26  Sword or spear, dagger or javelin,
    if they touch him, they have no effect.
27  Iron he counts as straw,
    and bronze as rotting wood.
28  No arrow can pierce him,
    and for him sling-stones are turned into chaff;
29  to him a club is a mere reed,
    and he laughs at the swish of the sabre.
30  Armoured beneath with jagged sherds,
    he sprawls on the mud like a threshing-sledge.
31  He makes the deep water boil like a cauldron,
    he whips up the lake like ointment in a mixing-bowl.
32  He leaves a shining trail behind him,
    and the great river is like white hair in his wake.
33  He has no equal on earth;
    for he is made quite without fear.
34  He looks down on all creatures, even the highest;
    he is king over all proud beasts.

42  Then Job answered the LORD:

2   I know that thou canst do all things
    and that no purpose is beyond thee.
3   But I have spoken of great things which I have not understood,
    things too wonderful for me to know.*b*
5   I knew of thee then only by report,
    but now I see thee with my own eyes.
6   Therefore I melt away;*c*
    I repent in dust and ashes.

*a*strong men: *or* leaders *or* gods.
*b*Prob. rdg.; Heb. adds* (4) O listen, and let me speak; I will ask questions, and you shall answ‹
*c*Or* despise myself.

## *Epilogue*

WHEN THE LORD had finished speaking to Job, he said to Eliphaz the 7
Temanite, 'I am angry with you and your two friends, because you
have not spoken as you ought about me, as my servant Job has
done. So now take seven bulls and seven rams, go to my servant Job 8
and offer a whole-offering for yourselves, and he will intercede for
you; I will surely show him favour by not being harsh with you
because you have not spoken as you ought about me, as he has
done.' Then Eliphaz the Temanite and Bildad the Shuhite and 9
Zophar the Naamathite went and carried out the LORD's command,
and the LORD showed favour to Job when he had interceded for his
friends. So the LORD restored Job's fortunes and doubled all his 10
possessions.

Then all Job's brothers and sisters and his former acquaint- 11
ance came and feasted with him in his home, and they consoled and
comforted him for all the misfortunes which the LORD had brought
on him; and each of them gave him a sheep*a* and a gold ring.
Furthermore, the LORD blessed the end of Job's life more than the 12
beginning; and he had fourteen thousand head of small cattle and
six thousand camels, a thousand yoke of oxen and as many she-
asses. He had seven*b* sons and three daughters; and he named his 13-14
eldest daughter Jemimah, the second Keziah and the third Keren-
happuch. There were no women in all the world so beautiful as 15
Job's daughters; and their father gave them an inheritance with
their brothers.

Thereafter Job lived another hundred and forty years, he saw 16
his sons and his grandsons to four generations, and died at a very 17
great age.

*a Or* piece of money.
*b Or* fourteen.

# INDEX

## ABOUT THE AUTHOR

WILLIAM SAFIRE is a writer of many incarnations: reporter, publicist, White House speechwriter, historian, novelist, lexicographer, essayist, and now—to coin a term—theopolitician.

His primary occupation since 1972 has been political columnist for *The New York Times,* usually taking the point of view of a libertarian conservative; in 1978, he was awarded the Pulitzer Prize for distinguished commentary. His column "On Language" in *The New York Times Magazine* is syndicated around the world and has made him the most widely read and argued-with writer on the subject of the English language.

Mr. Safire is married, has a son and daughter, and lives in a suburb of Washington, D.C.

ABOUT THE TYPE

This book was set in Times Roman, designed by Stanley Morison specifically for *The Times* of London. The typeface was introduced in the newspaper in 1932. Times Roman has had its greatest success in the United States as a book and commercial typeface, rather than one used in newspapers.